GRAPHIC
T·O·O·L·S
& TECHNIQUES

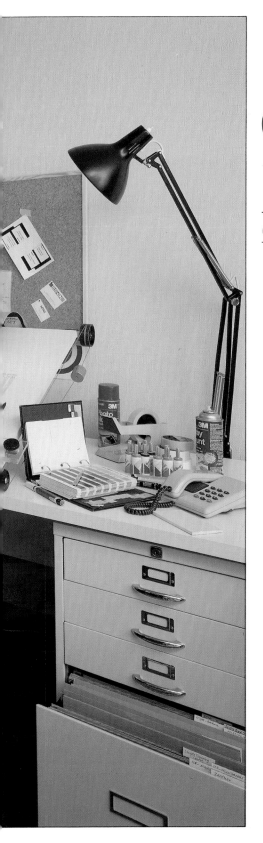

GRAPHIC
T·O·O·L·S
& TECHNIQUES

JOHN LAING
RHIANNON SAUNDERS-DAVIES

NORTH
LIGHT

Cincinnati, Ohio

CONTENTS

First published in North America by North Light. An imprint of Writer's Digest Books, 9933 Alliance Road, Cincinnati, Ohio 45242

First printing 1986

Conceived and produced by
Swallow Publishing Limited
32 Hermes Street, London N1.

Art director   David Allen
Editor   Anne Yelland
Editorial consultant   Bart Drury
Editorial assistant   Nigel Odell
Photography   Tim Imrie
Studio   Barry Walsh
Artwork   Aziz Khan

Swallow Publishing Limited wish to thank CJ Graphic Supplies Limited, 35-39 Old Street, London EC1, for the loan of the graphic equipment used in the photographs throughout this book.

Typeset by Dorchester Typesetting, Dorchester, Dorset
Printed through PBD in Singapore

PREFACE

Among the many innovations of our century the explosion in the use of mass communications is particularly outstanding. This expansion of activity has, increasingly, not been confined to a small and knowledgeable elite. Access to and participation in media activity has become astonishingly open. Any person can now publish or advertise; and the industries surrounding the media are huge and diverse. The jobs market offered by these concerns is rich and varied. Many people are finding the prospect of working as a designer increasingly possible, as well as attractive in terms of lifestyle.

This book attempts to give an introduction to the vast range of materials and equipment that is available. Obviously, not every item on the market has been mentioned but the product lists give a brief description of the most familiar and popular ones to help both the beginner and the confirmed user in making a more informed choice about the right tool for each job. We also offer some basic 'how-to-do-it' sections, outlining some of the simpler procedures that designers perform every day of their working lives. It is only a start and those who are interested can then move on to more advanced study. . .

A note on measurement: draftsmen, architects and designers are at present faced with a confusion of different measuring systems. Type, for instance, is not only specified in pica and inches but now millimetres are also jostling for position as computer typesetting becomes more dominant. The metric system has all but taken over in Britain and Europe and manufacturers of every kind are having to produce goods which conform to international metric specifications. Use of the metric system is also increasing in the USA and the pace of change is likely to speed up over the next few years. Similarly, the 'A' system of sizing papers is the most common in Britain and Europe, and is starting to become more widespread in the United States. In this book we have given imperial measurements wherever possible but metric ones take precedence as these are becoming the internationally recognized standard.

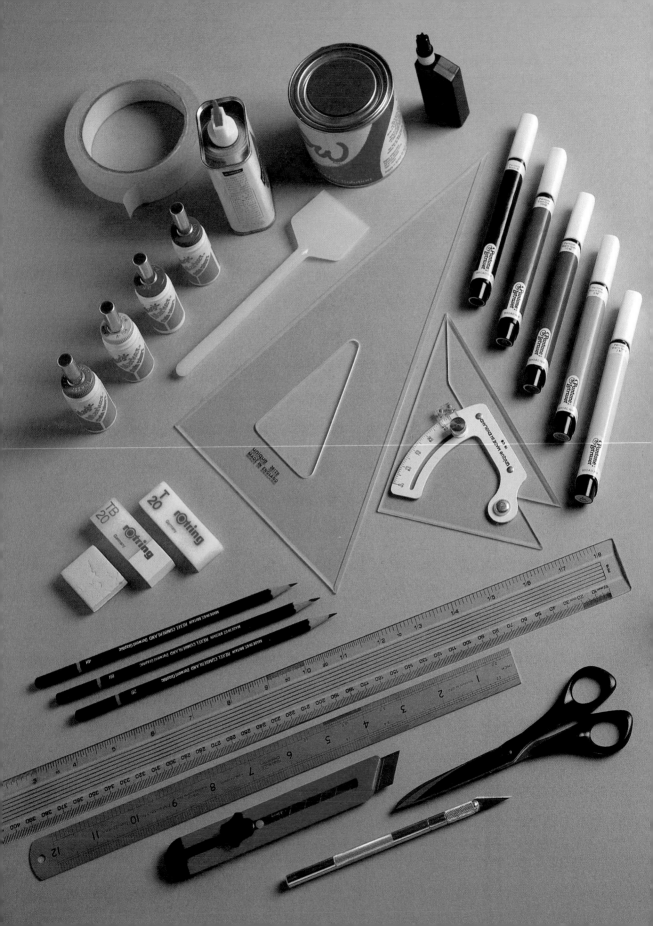

SETTING UP A STUDIO

In this section, we start with the most basic, and obvious, requirement of a designer – a room – and look at which rooms are suitable, and why. Once you have your room, there is a wide variety of equipment which you can purchase. We look here at what you will need to start with, and the larger purchases which are useful in the longer term.

Setting up a studio can so often be approached in the way some amateur photographers start out. They buy lots of very expensive equipment which far exceeds their immediate needs and their technical competence. An expensive camera does not necessarily make you a better photographer – a simple camera in the hands of a skilled photographer can produce very high-quality work.

The message we want to convey here must be obvious: it is not necessary to spend vast sums of money on setting yourself up with perfectly decent studio facilities that will enable you to produce excellent work. Very highly sophisticated and specialized techniques are best bought from people who make it their business to produce just that very narrow part of the market's needs. Computer graphics is an obvious example of this. It would not be difficult to spend some hundreds of thousands of dollars buying the equipment required.

So, what are the priorities? The first requirement, and not necessarily the most

obvious one, is a room – preferably a room you use for no other purpose. Choose a room, if you can, that has good natural light. A large window facing north (in the northern hemisphere) is considered to be the best. Why facing north? That way you avoid direct sunlight which changes in intensity and direction throughout the day. It is very difficult for the eyes to adjust to a situation where, one minute, you have piercingly strong and intense sunlight falling on your work and, the next minute, a cloud passes across the sun and you can hardly see what is in front of you. North light offers a filtered, reflected and fairly constant level of illumination. A room at the top of the house can be best of all, especially if it also has a roof light.

Of course, you will need artificial light some of the time. For general studio lighting, strip fluorescent lights give the most even illumination over larger areas. One of the problems with all interior lighting is that the values of colours change from what they are in daylight. Strip lighting can be obtained with light

Your studio need not be a large room, but it should be light, airy, and well-organized, with the items you use most frequently to hand.

values balanced very closely to those of daylight.

You will certainly need a good drawing board. It is worth spending as much as you can afford on this item. To do really accurate mechanicals you have to have the guarantee of absolute squareness at all parts of the working surface. If you cannot afford one with an attached drafting machine system, it should have a well set straight-edge down the left-hand side, offering a good 'run' for a T-square.

Your board can either be a free-standing unit or one placed on a table-top. If it is free-standing, choose one that has a sturdy base. The height and the angle of the board must be adjustable. If you are using a table as a mount for your board make sure that the table too is solid and strong. In either situation you cannot do accurate work on a rickety base.

For lighting close to the working surface you can buy good light fittings which clamp on to your board. This is particularly useful on free-standing units. Good fittings are also available mounted on a heavy base, or they can be fixed to a wall just where you want them. Whichever means you prefer, make sure that you have the floating arm type of light so that you can direct the beam to the part of your work that requires it most. Some adjustable lamps come with fluorescent light sources, others with a combination of fluorescent and incandescent. These are better for colour work than the purely incandescent type.

A swivel chair is the most convenient, although not essential. It is helpful if the height of the chair is adjustable so that you can arrange the best position for different kinds of work. Generally speaking, your height should be such that you are looking down on your work rather than along a shallow angle of view. Some designers use stools but this is not always either comfortable or good for your posture. Typists' chairs support the base of the back and enable you to work over long periods in comfort.

A light box or table is very helpful for visualizing purposes. It saves time in tracing down material from illustrations, type or photographs, and it gives you greater control of accuracy over small details. It is also very useful for viewing colour slides and transparencies. Table-top models of various sizes are available.

You will need also space for cutting, trimming and mounting work, so allow room for a cutting mat.

BASIC STUDIO TOOLKIT

Three blacklead pencils: 4H, HB and 2B	Ellipse guide
Blue pencil for mechanicals (the camera does not pick up blue)	French curves
Two drafting pens: 0.25mm and 0.50mm	Springbow compass
Ink for the drafting pens	A pair of sharp scissors
Compass attachment for the drafting pens	A scalpel (X-Acto knife) and a craft (mat) knife
Selection of fibre-tipped markers	Plastic eraser
Selection of felt-tipped markers	Kneadable (kneaded) eraser
Clear plastic 300 or 450mm (12 or 18in.) ruler	Rubber-based adhesive (cement) and spreader (container for brush)
Steel straight-edge	Lighter fuel (fluid) for removing rubber adhesive
Type scale	Masking tape
T-square	A tube of process white
60° 300mm (12in.) set square (triangle)	A selection of gouache paints
45° adjustable set square (triangle)	A broad wash brush and a fine sable brush
	Last, but not least, a telephone!

A pinboard on the wall helps you to see what your work looks like when it is vertical and also what it looks like from a greater distance. It is also useful for day to day reminders.

You now have your basic furniture.

Take a similar approach to purchasing tools. The list above gives a good idea of the minimum requirements. When you want to update, then the next items to consider might include a projector/viewer. These are fairly large, usually free-standing, pieces of equipment which illuminate the images you wish to use in your design, but they will also enlarge or reduce them to just the size your design needs. The image is cast on to a sheet of glass enabling you to trace it off. This is an expensive but very useful piece of studio equipment.

A flat file is very useful for storing and preserving work. Without one, you run the risk of pieces becoming dusty, crumpled, spilt on or otherwise damaged. It also adds to the general tidiness of your working room and the flat top of the file provides another useful surface – maybe for a cutting mat.

An airbrush and compressor allow you to do more sophisticated artwork but, of course, a lot of practice is necessary if you are to become proficient.

A waxing machine facilitates paste-up work, and a dry-mounting press for fixing photographs and other suitable pieces of artwork on to board can also be useful.

EQUIPMENT AND SURFACES

The last chapter offered an overview of the basic equipment the graphic designer will need for his studio. Here we consider in detail some of the larger, more expensive, pieces – drawing boards and their accessories, light boxes and tables, and precision drawing aids – as well as the smaller, but still essential, items such as sharpeners, erasers and cutting tools.

DRAWING BOARDS AND ACCESSORIES

Drawing boards and their associated equipment and accessories probably offer the most complex range of choices and the widest range of financial outlay. A simple drawing board of squared-up wood will cost very little. Next in price, and slightly more versatile, is a board covered in melamine or some such similar smooth finish which is moisture-proof and solvent-resistant and allows for the easy use of a T-square. Such a board, however, still does not offer the degree of precision required by some work. If great accuracy is required, without going in for a complete assemblage of related hardware, then a board constructed from several separate pieces of wood dovetailed into each other and fixed rigidly to each other by screw-fixed cross-members, will prove more effective. This composite construction eliminates any warping or other distortion of the board. Such a board will also have an inserted strip of hardwood, traditionally ebony, or metal down one edge. This provides for the reliable use of a good T-square, guaranteeing a high level of accuracy.

Such boards can be, and are, used quite free from other equipment, either leaned or propped up on a table. But they can, with advantage, be attached to a stand. This offers either a fixed position or the opportunity of tilting the angle of use to suit the needs of any specific situation. It also increases the range of useful attachments available. Variations between manufacturers are not great; the major ones are Belmont, Bieffe, Blundell Harling, Designer Plus, Plandale and Stacor. The list that follows gives a selection representing the various types available.

Once the board is on a stand, the most useful facility, after being able to control the angle of the working surface, is to have the T-square actually attached to the board. This device, called a parallel motion unit (parallel straight-edge/rule), duplicates the purpose of the detached T-square, namely the ability to draw lines parallel to each other without having to make time-consuming measurements.

Simple parallel motion units (parallel straight-edges/rules) are available in two basic patterns: one is a cross-wire system, the other uses a counterweight system. Of the two, the counterweight system is preferable, as cross-wires can become warped or tangled, resulting in inaccuracy. More sophisticated devices employ tooth and gear mechanisms to carry the drawing edge. Best of all are precision machined steel or aluminium tracking systems in which the reference edge is carried on steel bearings. Various highly accurate drafting devices and lighting fixtures can be attached to this reference edge.

A beginner or student, should choose a board of light- to mediumweight construction with a simple height and angle adjustment system. A good size for a graphic designer is approximately 915 × 660mm (36 × 26 in.). This will provide a large enough working area for most jobs without taking up too much space. Larger boards are used mostly by architects and technical draftsmen.

Note: In the product listings which follow, height always precedes width.

The Bieffe BF8 drawing table.

BIEFFE

BF8

This drawing table has a tubular steel base of great stability. It comes in board sizes from A1 (594 × 841mm/23½ × 33 in.) up to A0 (841 × 1189mm/33 × 47 in.). The height is adjustable from 740mm up to 1100mm (29 in. to 43 in.) and the board tilt range is 30°. Chrome finished adjustment bars raise and lower the assembly very easily through the aid of a simple system of locking knobs.

BF5

Suitable for use at home or in the professional studio. The height can be adjusted for either sitting or standing use and the board will tilt through a full 90°. The sprung counter-balance allows the board to float into any position and be locked by a single lever, and the stand takes boards from A1 (594 × 841mm/23½ × 33 in.) to A0 (841 × 1189mm/33 × 47 in.).

ANGOLO

A four-post drawing base that can also be used as a general work table. It has a spring-balanced, white laminate board 940 × 1500mm (37 × 59in.) to which a parallel motion unit (parallel straight-edge) can be attached.

ARCHITETTO

Made of square tubular steel with independent front and rear adjustments with a range from 790mm to 1150mm (31 in. to 45 in.), the Architetto's maximum angle of elevation is 25°. The sliding adjustment members are locked within the square, tubular legs by four handwheels.

It takes boards from 800 × 1200mm (31½ × 47 in.) up to 1200 × 2300mm (47 × 90 in.) and is easily foldable for storage or shipment.

GLOBUS

This drawing stand comes in two versions – low, 760mm (30 in.) high, and high, 965mm (38 in.). On the low version, height adjustment is controlled by a hand screw on the central column. On the high version, height is controlled by depressing a lever at the base of the stand. When the lever is released again, the whole mechanism locks. These units will take drawing boards from A1 (594 × 841mm/23½ × 33 in.) up to 920 × 1500mm (36 × 59 in.).

Whichever board is chosen, it can be rotated through 360° to gain the fullest advantage of changing natural light. The tilt of the board is variable through 90° by releasing a lever on the underside of the board. The weight of the board is counter-balanced by a torsion spring so that very little effort is required to change its angle.

BFIT

A twin 'T'-shaped stand which takes boards from 920 × 1270mm (36 × 50 in.) up to 1200 × 2000mm (47 × 78 in.). This construction gives an exceptionally stable base. The height and angle adjustments are made through a parallelogram system counter-balanced by mechanical springs and a pneumatic piston. A full-length foot pedal releases the system for simultaneous height and angle adjustment. The BF2T stand (for boards up to 1000 × 1700mm/39 × 67 in.) and the BF3T stand (for boards up to 920 × 1500mm/36 × 50 in.) are similar in most respects, but have only the mechanical spring for height and angle adjustment, with no pneumatic aid.

STABILUS

A very robust board combining the advantages of the parallelogram principle for sturdiness and ease of operation with a pedestal construction offering the maximum usefulness in a minimum of space. The minimum horizontal height of the board is 1000mm (39 in.) and this height can be increased a further 300mm (12 in.). A counter-balanced spring system aids easy height adjustment by operating a central foot pedal. The angle of the board can be changed by operating a hand lever underneath the board.

This stand accepts boards of other makes up to 1200 × 2300mm (47 × 90 in.).

The Bieffe Angolo drawing base.

The Blundell Harling Sherborne table-top drawing stand.

OPUS

The Opus incorporates an oleo-pneumatic balancing system through the use of a single foot pedal which makes height adjustment particularly easy. The angle of the board is controlled by a hand lever on the underside of the board which is easily released and relocked by very strong clutch-type brakes. The drawing board is counter-balanced by two tension springs which are housed elegantly behind chrome-plated covers.

This stand takes boards from other manufacturers from 1000 × 1500mm (39 × 59 in.) up to 1200 × 2300mm (47 × 90 in.).

BLUNDELL HARLING

Not available in the USA

ACADEMY

Sizes: A1, A2
These are white, extra-thick, melamine-faced drawing boards.

SUPERBOARD

Sizes: A0 ext, A0a, A0, A1 ext. large, A1 ext, A1
This is a high-density particle board free from voids, thereby ensuring stability and freedom from warping or twisting. Both faces are covered with an extra-thick layer of white melamine. All edges are trimmed with the same material, making them suitable for the easy and accurate use of a T-square.

SHERBORNE

A table-top inclined stand with four settings allowing the board, when attached, to be set at 15, 30, 45 or 60°. This stand will accept boards up to size A1.

ADAPTABLE

A floor stand made from 25mm sq. (1 in. sq.) section welded steel tube finished in white epoxy resin. It offers full angle adjustment from vertical to horizontal and also a 130mm (5 in.) height adjustment. It will take drawing boards up to A1 size.

RIDGEWAY

An inexpensive, folding drawing stand ideal for the student and for home use. It is made from 25mm sq. (1 in. sq.) section steel tube and finished to a high standard in white epoxy resin. The open metal parts are stainless steel and nickel-plated throughout. It is fully adjustable for angle and the telescopic legs give a total of 250mm (10 in.) variation – a generous control of height. This stand is suitable for boards up to A0 size.

STRATTON

This floor stand is designed to take both A0 and A1 drawing boards. The main uprights give telescopic vertical adjustment and a handwheel operates the angle which is variable from horizontal to almost vertical. The stand is manufactured from welded, heavyweight, round, steel tube with steel cross-braces for extra rigidity. It is finished in white epoxy resin with the bright parts either stainless steel or nickel-plated.

BLANDFORD

A strong and rigid stand at a moderate price. The height adjustment is provided by a spring-loaded parallelogram linkage and the angle of the board is made through a simple fulcrum bar. Both of these variables are controlled by a single lever to the side of the stand.

The stand is constructed from square and rectangular section, steel tube finished in white epoxy resin. Bright parts are stainless steel or nickel-plated. Adjustable feet compensate for uneven floors. This unit will accept boards up to A0 size.

FOSTER

Not available in the UK

BELMONT DRAWING TABLES

A pedestal type of hydraulic stand which can carry three sizes of board – 23 × 31 in., 24 × 36 in. and 31 × 42 in. The central supporting column which carries the hydraulic system enables the board to be turned freely around the vertical axis, adjusted to any height from 27½ in. to 40½ in., or locked into any position with a simple one-handed movement.

PLAN HOLD

DESIGNER PLUS DRAWING TABLES

A well-designed lightweight and manoeuvrable drawing table made from square-section tubular steel with a white laminate board attached. Height can be simply adjusted from 30 in. to 40 in. and the board positioned at any angle between vertical and horizontal. Available in three board sizes – 24 × 36 in., 30 × 42 in. and 36 × 48 in.

STACOR

Not available in the UK

TYROTEC DRAFTING TABLE

A simple but sturdy desk-height drafting table with an adjustable tilt option. A bracket at the rear of the board fits into one of four slots on the sides, offering a choice of angles from 0° to 60°. A full-width shelf underneath gives useful storage space. Available with 30 × 40 in. or 36 × 48 in. board area.

VARITEC DRAFTING TABLE

A slightly more sophisticated drafting table incorporating both height and tilt adjustment options. Height is raised and lowered from 30 in. to 46 in. by large screw knobs and the board can be tilted from 0° to 40°. Available with 30 × 42 in. or 36 × 48 in. board areas.

SUPRETEC DRAFTING TABLE

A high-quality professional drafting table available in larger board sizes – 36 × 60 in. and 36 × 72 in. Tilt can be adjusted from 0° to 35° and height from 30 in. to 44½ in. by means of screw knobs. A full-width shelf underneath the board provides convenient storage space for tools or reference material.

Both this and the VariTec have rubber encased foot-rests for comfortable working posture.

FOLD AWAY DRAWING TABLE

A useful collapsible table for maximum use of studio space. It folds away flat to a width of 4 in. When erected, it offers both stability and versatility, being adjustable in height from 29 in. to 45 in. and tilt from 0° to 40°. The table has a square steel tube base and the board itself is made from easy-to-clean laminate which can be reversed to provide either a white or black working surface. Available with 24 × 36 in. or 30 × 42 in. board areas.

PARALLEL MOTION/ STRAIGHT-EDGE AND DRAFTING UNITS

BLUNDELL HARLING

Not available in the USA

TRUELINE PARALLEL MOTION

This portable parallel motion system uses a cross-wire assembly controlled by nylon-covered, stranded steel cable running on acetyl corner pulleys with ball bearings. The corners of the board are protected by moulded blocks which also attach the pulleys to the board. A cam brake is attached to the straight-edge allowing it to be clamped into position when desired. The unit comes with a double-bevelled transparent, tinted straight-edge which can be easily removed and exchanged with either of the optional cutting or centring straight-edges. All of these can be tilted or raised to allow artwork or cutting mats, and so on, to be positioned at will underneath.

STUDLAND PARALLEL MOTION

An extremely accurate, smooth-running unit based on the toothed belt system. The belt is made from non-stretch polyurethane which is reinforced with steel wire. Matched pulleys ensure the accuracy and repeatability of any movement. The unit is mounted on its chosen board by four moulded corner bearings which are smooth running and maintenance free.

A locking device is built in to the blocks at the end of the straight-edge which can be exchanged for the optional cutting or centring edges. Whichever straight-edge is used, the board can be tilted or raised to allow work to be positioned underneath it.

WEYMOUTH PARALLEL MOTION

This unit comes in kit form in four sizes suited to fit most standard drawing boards. The straight-edge is controlled by a spring-loaded braided cable and counter-balance is provided by weights which maintain constant tension on the wires, enabling the whole action to move smoothly. Ball-bearing races are used on the pulleys and these require no maintenance. The double-bevelled transparent acrylic straight-edge, which is slotted at the ends to reduce end float, runs on nylon rollers to reduce both friction and static.

SWANAGE PARALLEL MOTION

This unit uses a toothed belt which makes it most suitable for work where accuracy and repeatability are of the greatest importance, for example, with multiple overlays.

The top axle runs in sealed precision ball races housed in square section steel tube. The lower axle also turns in a steel tube but on long-life nylon bearings.

The non-stretch, steel-reinforced, polyurethane belt drives accurately matched pulleys which eliminate backlash. The double-bevelled, transparent acrylic straight-edge is slotted at both ends so that it can be adjusted to reduce end float and runs on nylon rollers to reduce both friction and static.

TRUELINE DRAFTING HEAD

A simple 90° drafting head which runs on the straight-edge of the Trueline or Studland parallel motion units. It can be locked in position and carries a pair of interchangeable scale rules.

CARDINELL

Not available in UK

PROFESSIONAL PARALLEL STRAIGHT-EDGE

A straight-edge which lies flat on the board. The blade of this model is made of maple and mahogany, and the bevelled edge is transparent. The tunnel rides on a keyway to counteract expansion and contraction.

PARA-STEEL PARALLEL STRAIGHT-EDGE

This was designed for those who need the accuracy of a stainless steel blade for precision cutting and technical drawing. Both edges are bevelled, and the model is guaranteed not to warp.

KEUFFEL & ESSER

AUTO FLOW III DRAFTING MACHINE

This unit is counter-balanced to handle any board angle without the need for adjustment. Features include aluminium tracks, adjustable roller bracket, C-clamp mounting, and two-point permanent and portable support.

PORTABLE DRAWING SYSTEMS

A few companies have, enterprisingly enough, sought to extend the availability of drawing office technology to occasional users working at home, in offices otherwise not equipped for studio work and, if required, any other non-permanent working environment.

These products are, understandably, not to be confused with the precision engineered, specialist equipment described earlier in this chapter but they are practical, convenient, useful and reasonably inexpensive and, therefore, also of use to students and others whose budget circumstances restrict the financial outlay available.

FABER-CASTELL

TZ-STANDARD DRAWING BOARD

Sizes: A4 (210 × 297mm/8¼ × 11¾ in.), A3 (297 × 420mm/11¾ × 16½ in.)
This board is made from dimensionally stable, warp-free, high impact plastic. The non-reflecting surface is very durable and is resistant to many instrument marks. It has guide grooves, enabling the attachment of parallel drafting arms on to any of the four sides. The drafting arm glides smoothly along these grooves and features a gradated edge for the use of supplementary triangles and set squares.

Both board sizes have a recessed paper clamp bar which will hold several sheets if required. This clamp has a lock-release key which will stay open to allow for the desired alignment of the paper. The drafting arm is clamped at two points on the left and, in the A3 version, is also clamped at the right.

TZ-PLUS DRAWING BOARD

Sizes: A4 (210 × 297mm/8¼ × 11¾ in.), A3 (297 × 420mm/11¾ × 16½ in.)
In addition to the features offered by the Standard version, the Plus also has magnetic sliding scales with zero-point axis for symmetrical drawing. There are special gradations for circular contours, polygons and angle designs. Both sizes will accept the TZ Swivel action, Special Drawing Head instead of the standard parallel ruler. This allows the user to turn the ruler through a range of 150°.

CONTURA

Size: A3 (297 × 420mm/11¾ × 16½ in.)

An economical student drawing board with the paper clamping device of the Standard and Plus versions. It comes with a fixed angle combination square and protractor.

KOH-I-NOOR

Not available in the UK

PORTABLE DRAWING BOARD

Size: 19½ × 14¾ in.

A light plastic board, durable enough to withstand continuous use, this includes paper clamps, an automatic locking straight-edge, and guide rails for holding the straight-edge on all four edges. The board is white, and the straight-edge amber.

The optional drafting head features a brake mechanism to facilitate repeated cross-hatching and the drawing of parallel lines, and the protractor head locks to any angle in 15° increments.

ROTRING

RAPID DRAWING BOARDS

Sizes: A4 (210 × 297mm/8¼ × 11¾ in.), A3 (297 × 420mm/11¾ × 16½ in.)

Both sizes have two paper clamp strips with a central lever to ensure that the drawing surface is lying absolutely in the position required. These anchoring clamps have a wide opening making it easy to insert the paper, card or film being used. The guide rails for the straight-edge are open at every corner, enabling full use to be made of the drawing surface. Signal humps indicate when the straight-edge is getting close to the end of the drawing board. The gradations are in millimetres and one is also provided for picking off compass radii.

PROFIL DRAWING BOARD

Sizes: A4 (210 × 297mm/8¼ × 11¾ in.), A3 (297 × 420mm/11¾ × 16½ in.)

The Profil is made of light, scratch- and shock-resistant plastic which is washable and resistant to compass point indentation. There is a magnetic clamp along the side with an additional clip for the accurate fitting and alignment of the drawing surface. Signal humps indicate to the user when the straight-edge is approaching the end of the board.

The scales are gradated in millimetres, including one for picking off compass radii. As with the Rapid drawing boards, the straight-edge is smooth running with a 'stop' and 'go' mechanism for fixing and releasing the drawing edge.

ROTRING A2 DRAUGHTING MACHINE UNIT

The draughting machine unit consists of a white plastic-coated A2 (420 × 594mm/16½ × 23½ in.) board which can, if required, be fixed to a table using a universal ball and socket drawing-board clamp. The board comes with a transparent yellow straight-edge which does not obscure the drawing underneath it and is gradated in millimetres along both edges. The straight-edge runs on ball-bearing rollers along a precision aluminium guide track. The unit comes complete with the Rapid Drawing Head (which is available separately). With automatic setting in increments of 15°, it can also be set to any desired angle with a free-swing setting. The 0-90° scale is registered in contra-rotating figures and the head is provided with its own braking mechanism.

ROTRING UNIVERSAL

Size: A4 (210 × 297mm/8¼ × 11¾ in.).

A handy-sized board ideal for school or college use. It has a magnetic clamp for securing the paper, straight-edge guide slots along all four sides, a straight-edge with holes for line drawing and a locking and releasing facility.

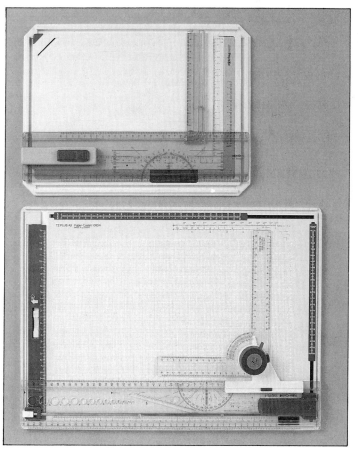

The Rotring Rapid (top) and Faber-Castell TZ-Plus portable drawing boards.

DRAWING INSTRUMENTS AND DRAWING AIDS

The graphic designer's job does not necessarily end with the presentation of roughs and visuals to explain his design ideas. Often he is also required to produce highly accurate drawings and artwork in order that the design may be taken through to the printing stage. For this he has to acquire certain hand skills, learn to be neat and clean in working method and presentation, and pick up a few useful tricks of the trade which will make the production of beautifully finished artwork at some speed a pleasure rather than a chore!

Many pieces of specialist drawing equipment are now available which both save valuable time and make a high degree of accuracy attainable even to the non-specialist draftsman. A certain number of precision-engineered instruments are essential elements of any graphic designer's toolkit. However, these items are expensive and so, for the beginner, it is best to start off with a few basics and gradually build up the range

by acquiring particular tools as they are needed. With a bit of experience and a little judicious borrowing you will soon discover which pieces of equipment are really useful. The basic checklist given on p. 9 provides an outline of what you should buy at the outset. Here we note a few important points to remember when choosing various additional items of drawing equipment.

Of course, the most expensive ranges of equipment give the highly accurate standard of performance required by professional technical draftsmen but this is probably not necessary for the student or even professional graphic designer. A mid-priced tool is often quite sufficient and will give long-lasting, reliable use if looked after with a little care. It is really more important to learn to use the equipment properly and treat it with respect. Precision instruments do not take kindly to being dropped, used roughly or allowed to collect dirt and grime. They should be kept in their cushioned boxes

1 Adjustable set square (triangle); 2 300mm (12in.) plastic set square (triangle); 3 steel ruler; 4 compositor's typescale; 5 typographer's depth scale; 6 450mm (18in.) plastic ruler; and 7 T-square.

when not in use and all equipment should be cleaned regularly with lighter fuel (fluid) or a similar grease-dissolving agent.

Many companies, especially those who produce drafting pens like Faber-Castell, Rotring and Staedtler, now manufacture starter sets of drawing instruments which are ideally suited to and economical for the beginner. A good set should contain a springbow compass (one where the two arms are separated by a screw-threaded bar) with appropriate leads, a small radius compass for drawing extra small circles, an extension bar for drawing large circles, dividers and a ruling pen attachment for drawing with other media such as paint. Make a note to choose a compass which will accept a standard drafting pen attachment, extending its capabilities considerably. Sometimes these are supplied in a starter set of drafting pens but should be obtainable singly if not. Always check that the screw of the springbow is not too loose or the two arms will gradually separate when the compass is in use. A traditional school compass which holds a pencil is really not accurate or solid enough for professional standard work.

A ruler is an indispensable basic tool. If possible it is best to have two. A clear plastic one marked in both centimetres and inches is good for measuring as it can be aligned more accurately. It should be at least 300mm (12 in.) long (450mm/18 in. is a particularly useful length) and have bevelled edges for easy ink drawing without smudging. A steel ruler should always be used for cutting against although this could be a steel straight-edge and does not necessarily need to be provided with scale measurements. A compositor's typescale and depth or typographer's scale should also be acquired for measuring type and marking off line widths and column depths in text matter. These are vital for calculating space in any typographic design.

Perspex set squares (plastic triangles) are another essential, used for constructing angles and parallel lines in conjunction with a parallel motion (parallel straight-edge), ruler or T-square. They are produced in a variety of sizes and degrees, 45° and 60° being the most common and, like rulers, should have bevelled edges. One or two manufacturers now produce special set squares (triangles) with steel edges for cutting against. These are particularly useful for

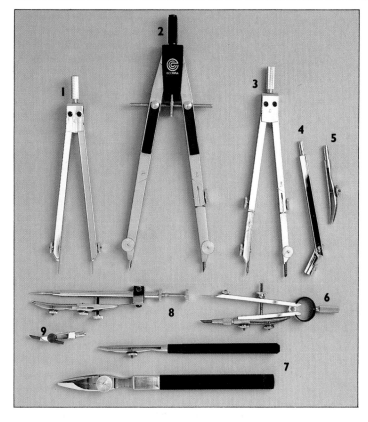

anyone doing quantities of paste-up work but can be regarded as an expensive luxury by the general graphic designer. Again it is advisable to acquire two set squares (triangles): a large 60° (at least 300mm/12 in. on the longest side) is convenient for larger work while a smaller, more manoeuvrable adjustable set square (triangle) which can be set at a variety of angles is a very versatile and useful instrument for detailed drawings. For measuring angles to an accuracy of within a quarter degree a clear plastic protractor (either 180° or 360°) is valuable although not essential – an adjustable set square (triangle) will fulfil most measuring requirements up to an accuracy of one degree.

If you have a drawing board without a parallel motion (parallel straight-edge), or are using an ordinary board propped up on a table, a T-square is a useful acquisition for constructing parallel lines. If the head of the 'T' is placed over the side of the board, accurate lines can be drawn by sliding the T-square up and down. An alternative to this would be a parallel ruler, which looks like two rulers joined together with angled hinges.

Various other drawing instruments

1 Dividers; 2 large adjustable compass; 3 adjustable compass; 4 extension arm for adjustable compass; 5 ruling attachment for extension arm; 6 springbow compass; 7 ruling pens; 8 compass for drawing small circles, in ink (attached) and in pencil (9).

which could be classified as non-essential for the beginner may, however, come into their own in a larger studio set-up. A speedliner allows a series of parallel lines to be drawn horizontally or vertically without lifting the ruler from the page. A pantograph can be used for enlarging and reducing maps, drawings and plans and is especially applicable to layout, cartography, drafting and engineering work. The original drawing is traced over with a point and these movements are transmitted, by a series of hinged arms, to a lead which then draws a copy on a larger or smaller scale. These are not all that easy to use and a little practice is necessary to achieve a reasonably accurate result. A proportional scale for calculating the sizes and percentages of enlargements and reductions for artwork is also a useful time-saving tool. Ellipsographs and circleometers are used for constructing ellipses and circles of specific dimensions but these functions are more generally catered for by the use of ordinary stencils and templates.

There is now an enormous variety of stencils and templates available to make drawing particular shapes a great deal easier and faster. These range from those produced for specific subjects, such as engineering, computer or electronic symbols, to the more general circle and ellipse templates most frequently used by graphic designers. Ellipse guides are supplied by most manufacturers in a range of angles of projection between 15° and 60°, usually in increments of 5°.

Obviously this large selection is only required by the technical draftsman. A good choice to have to hand for general drawing and designing would be an isometric projection (35°16′) and a 45° projection. Note particularly whether the templates you choose have axis guidelines as these are helpful in positioning the shape correctly. All templates should, if possible, have bevelled edges or ink bosses to raise them from the paper surface, to prevent smudges occurring when used with a drafting pen. If not, try placing a small lump of rolled up sticky masking tape under each end of the template. The same proviso should apply to the choice of lettering stencils and sets of French curves, useful plastic guides providing a variety of differently shaped and angled curves. A flexible curve, having a metal core encased in a vinyl covering, performs the same task but in many ways is even more versatile as it can be moulded into any desired configuration. Lettering stencils provide a quick and easy method of rendering type on to such things as plans and technical drawings.

When using a drafting pen with any type of stencil it is important to keep the nib of the pen at a constant 90° angle to the paper to ensure perfect accuracy and line width. If this proves difficult, a lettering joint is a simple but effective attachment to a drafting pen (see Drafting Pens, pp. 72-6) which helps to maintain the correct angle for the pen while allowing a more comfortable hand and wrist position to be used.

1 Lettering templates;
2 ellipse guide; *3* technical template; *4* lettering joint; *5* protractor; *6* circle guide; *7* pantograph; *8* French curves; *9* flexicurve.

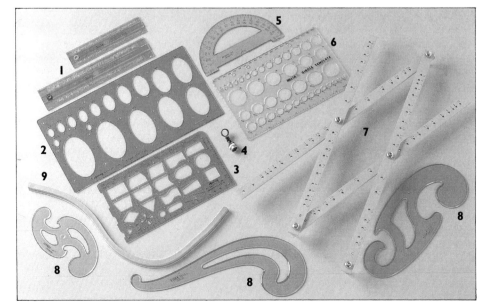

A ruling pen is a useful instrument for drawing accurate straight lines with a full range of ink and paint media. It consists of a handle with two blades – one curved and one straight – held together by an adjustable screw. This is used to alter the distance between the blades and so change the width of the line produced. Some makes have a scale on the screw which helps in resetting the pen accurately should the blades have to be opened during use. A ruling pen is more versatile than an individual drafting pen and more economical than buying a whole set of pens. It is more difficult to use accurately, being prone to flooding, but with a little practice can become a precision tool. Always open up and clean the blades thoroughly after use to prevent damage to the smooth finish at the tips.

The choice of a compass depends largely on the size of the circle to be drawn. A springbow compass is the most generally useful and versatile instrument but for drawing very small or very large circles a drop compass (small radius compass) and beam compass respectively are the best instruments to choose. A drop compass has a delicate, inward-pointing, curved drawing tip which will not track off during tight rotations, while a beam compass has movable needle and drawing heads suspended along a rigid metal beam. Whichever type you are using, the same basic techniques apply for accurate use. Always adjust the arms to the required width on a separate scrap of paper and not on the finished artwork. Position the needle accurately while keeping the drawing tip raised away from the paper surface. Placing a piece of masking tape over the centre of the circle will help to reduce the size of the hole created by the needle. Hold the top of the compass lightly but firmly between your thumb and index finger and practise rotating it smoothly in a clockwise direction. Now lower the drawing tip and construct the circle in one, smooth, continuous movement, extending the line beyond the starting point to avoid creating an uneven join.

LIGHT BOXES

A light box or light table consists of a translucent glass or perspex (plastic) screen held in a rigid frame and illuminated from below by several strip lights. The slight opacity of the screen helps to diffuse the light evenly over the area – an important consideration for effective colour evaluation and the control of colour in reprographic and printing work.

It is in these areas that a light box is used most frequently. Transmitted light is very useful for work on film surfaces and any piece requiring 'registration' with other related drawings. However, a designer may often also employ the light box as an aid to accurate tracing and retouching where a high degree of 'show through' from the original is required in order to see small details. Small portable models, about the size of an attaché case, are ideal to have at home for personal use or for taking to client presentations where it is necessary to view slides. These are available from such manufacturers as Halco and DW Viewboxes in the UK and Stacor, Mayline and Idealite in the USA.

In the studio, a larger model with a big working area is generally more useful, especially for film make-up work. Here, clips to hold slippery photographic materials are an asset, as is an integral steel parallel rule unit which allows the light table to be used like an illuminated drawing board for accurate trimming and cutting. An adjustable dimmer switch is an optional extra on some models and can be useful for viewing or tracing with different light intensities. Any light box or table should have cooling vents to prevent the screen getting too hot. Apart from the obvious safety reasons, excess heat can also cause paper and photographic materials to warp badly.

For viewing wet films in the photographic studio or darkroom, choose a specialist light box which can be wall mounted and has a drip tray to collect and drain excess liquids. Special care should always be taken over the electrical wiring and switches on any model which is to come into contact with water.

CUTTING EQUIPMENT

Cutting knives:
manufactured by
Mecanorma (left) and
Edding.

KNIVES

A knife of some sort is an essential in the designer's toolkit and can, in many practical ways, be as creative a tool as a pencil or precision drawing instrument. At least two different types of knife will be required for the many different cutting and trimming tasks which are likely to take place in the studio.

Firstly, a knife carrying a fine extended blade with a very sharp point is necessary for the accurate and detailed cutting of items during paste-up. This should be both light and manoeuvrable enough to be used with the necessary delicacy and precision. It is most important for clean, neat artwork that a knife remain sharp at all times so change the blade as soon as it loses its first keenness. Surgical scalpel blades are cheap and easy to obtain, making them an economical choice for sustained use. The Swann-Morton range, made from high-quality Sheffield carbon steel, has proved very popular with designers in the UK. Although a long, pointed blade is generally the most useful, other shapes can be more convenient for certain jobs. A rounded blade, for instance, copes far better with cutting curves while one with a narrow end is good for particularly small shapes.

Specialist graphics manufacturers now produce 'designers' knives' such as the X-Acto range in the USA, or the Letraset range, with a similar choice of variously shaped blades. These usually have slightly longer, rounded, aluminium handles, about the thickness of a ballpoint pen, with a screw clutch head which grips the blade. These are comfortable and convenient to use, especially with the easy blade change procedure, and make a good alternative to surgical scalpels. For carrying about in a pocket, fountain pen style versions of these knives are sometimes available with a safety-conscious protective cap over the blade. Another alternative offers a small swivel-headed blade which makes cutting curves and intricate shapes even easier to accomplish.

The second essential type of knife is a general utility or craft (mat) knife with a squarer, broader blade. This is used for cutting heavier paper, board and tough craft materials. A fairly recent development in Europe has been the advent of semi- or completely disposable craft (mat) knives, consisting of a plastic body and screw mechanism which carries a retractable, segmented, snap-off blade. The shorter and stumpier the body of the knife, the more pressure can be applied upon it, but for really heavy-duty use a good quality, solid metal-bodied knife with a screw-in blade is probably a better choice. These are much more suitable for work on very difficult surfaces since they offer a higher degree of safety.

CUTTING MATS

For accurate, safe cutting always remember to use a steel rule or straight-edge (see Drawing Instruments, pp. 18-19) and a cutting mat. Never press too firmly into the surface to be cut in an attempt to get right through straight away as the blade may well slip or track off. Several light cuts in the same groove are better than one hard one.

Non-slip cutting mats provide a firm base for cutting upon and protect work surfaces around the studio from score marks. They are made from a remarkable self-sealing plastic which closes up behind the knife as it passes through, leaving a smooth cutting surface which cannot deflect the blade in the direction of a previous cut. Excessive pressure with heavy-duty craft (mat) knives should, however, be avoided as this may result in permanent damage to the mat. They should also not be exposed to sunlight for extended periods of time if this can possibly be avoided.

Translucent mats are particularly useful for film and transparency work on a light box or table, providing a perfect cutting surface while, at the same time, giving good visibility of the work to be cut.

SCISSORS

Scissors are more convenient than knives for some cutting operations. They obviously cannot be relied upon for perfect accuracy but are quick and simple to use for much rough trimming, layout and paste-up work. The most appropriate to choose are those with extended stainless steel blades which taper to a fine point, and comfortable moulded plastic handles to give greater control. Good quality, very sharp scissors are often quite expensive items but are worth the extra outlay as they perform more precisely, last longer and can be resharpened when necessary. The Dahle, Fiskars, and Kaicut ranges all offer an excellent choice. A small pair – between 100 and 130mm (4 and 5 in.) in overall length – is ideal for delicate cutting tasks while a 200-250mm (8-10 in.) pair is a good size for larger work. Always reserve your scissors for cutting papers, films and similar thin surfaces only. Thick boards, plastics and other modelling materials should be trimmed with a heavy craft (mat) knife as they can easily blunt or even bend scissor blades.

GUILLOTINES/ PAPER CUTTERS AND ROTARY/ ROLLING TRIMMERS

Guillotines (paper cutters) and rotary (rolling) trimmers are used for cutting larger items more quickly and safely and in multiple quantities. They can usually cope with a variety of different materials such as paper, tissue, film, thick card, heavy art board and even some wood and metal. A stop along the bottom edge, placed at 90° to the blade, allows sheets to be trimmed accurately at right angles without first having to be marked up with a set square (triangle). There is often also a calibrated scale along this stop which makes trimming to specific measurements a great deal faster.

Guillotines (paper cutters) have a long hinged knife blade which moves vertically up and down. For safety, all guillotines (paper cutters) must have a guard around the blade. Look for models which have a useful clamping mechanism to the left of the blade to hold the paper in place while it is cut. Rotary (rolling) trimmers have a circular blade, held in an enclosed housing, which runs horizontally along a metal support bar. As the blade is never exposed, rotary (rolling) trimmers are extremely safe and are widely used in schools, and photographic darkrooms where lighting may be dim.

BABS
Not available in the USA

WEB PLUS ROTARY TRIMMER
Cutting lengths: 360mm (14 in.), 460mm (18 in.), 670mm (26 in.), 1000mm (39 in.), 1300mm (51 in.)
A range of trimmers with self-sharpening high carbon steel blades which can cope with any thickness up to a maximum of 1.7mm ($1/16$ in.). These models incorporate a unique front gauge and a magnetic back gauge for convenient repeat trimming of measured sizes without alteration of the settings. The beds of the trimmers are printed with paper size and registration guides.

WEB PREFECT PLUS+ GUILLOTINE
Cutting lengths: 360mm (14 in.), 460mm (18 in.), 610mm (24 in.)
Prefect Plus+ guillotines incorporate the same front gauge for the repeat trimming of off-cuts as the Plus+ range. The Sheffield steel blade is suitable for a wide range of surfaces including board, cloth, leather and other light craft materials. The guards on these models are completely transparent to give full visibility of the work in progress.

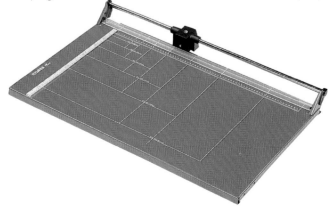

The mid-range Dahle rolling trimmer, 720mm (28in.).

SIMPLEX GUILLOTINE

Cutting lengths: 350mm (13¾ in.), 360mm (14 in.)

Faster cutting is achieved by using an automatic clamping guillotine to hold the paper firmly in place. These two models are the first small cutters on the market to incorporate a simultaneous clamping and cutting action controlled by the blade handle.

SOLID GUILLOTINE

Cutting lengths: 360mm (14 in.), 550mm (21 in.), 700mm (27½ in.), 800mm (31½ in.), 1100mm (43½ in.)

A top-quality range of precision guillotines. They are gauged on both sides of the blade, the front one being dial-set to within 2mm (3⁄32 in.) for repeat trimming of measured sizes. All sizes cope easily with papers, boards, plastics, lino, felt, rubber, foil and similar industrial and craft materials. The largest two stand models have foot-operated clamps to assist when handling hardboard, plywood and light metals.

BEROL

PAPER TRIMMER

A good quality, economically priced, sturdy rotary trimmer for paper and card. The paper guide is marked in inches, centimetres and international paper sizes. Continuous roll feed and backstop attachments are available.

BLUNDELL HARLING

Not available in the USA

ROLOCUT SAFETY TRIMMER

Cutting lengths: A4, A3, A2, A1, A0, 1500mm (60 in.)

A high-quality trimmer for the drawing office or photography studio. The A4, A3 and A2 sizes have a 3mm (⅛ in.) thickness capacity and are suitable for cutting paper, film, mounting board, photographic paper, card and tissue paper. The A1, A0 and 1500mm (60 in.) versions have a 1mm (1⁄24 in.) thickness capacity so cannot cope with mounting board or thick card. The cutting wheel is made from hardened steel and runs on a single guide rail; its housing is moulded in two halves which can be split apart to facilitate easy replacement of the blade. The bed of the trimmer is calibrated in millimetres and international paper sizes and is fitted with an adjustable backstop and a plastic clamp strip.

DAHLE

DAHLE CUT-CAT HOBBY TRIMMER

Cutting lengths: 320mm (12½ in.), 460mm (18 in.)

Described as 'hobby trimmers' by the manufacturer, these make a good choice as a personal tool for home use. They are compact and light to handle with table areas marked in centimetres and standard photographic sizes, good for use in the darkroom. Both models can cut materials up to 0.5mm (1⁄48 in.) in thickness and are ideal for small quantities of paper and single sheets of light card.

DAHLE ROLLING TRIMMER

Cutting lengths: 360mm (14 in.), 460mm (18 in.), 720mm (28 in.), 960mm (38 in.), 1260mm (49½ in.)

These are ideal for clean accurate cutting of all papers (including photographic), card, film and plastic sheets up to a thickness of 1.5mm (1⁄16 in.) for the first three sizes and 1mm (1⁄24 in.) for the last two. The trimmers are supplied with a raised stop edge calibrated in centimetres and DIN (inches are marked on the table area), and an automatic clamping device of transparent plastic. An adjustable backstop can be fitted (as can a paper roll dispenser) but is not supplied as standard.

DAHLE LIGHT BOX TRIMMER

Cutting length: One only 460mm (18 in.)

This type of trimmer is particularly useful for working with transparencies and films, or any work where back lighting is essential. It consists of a small mains-powered lightbox specially adapted with a steel support bar to carry a rotary cutting head along one long edge. The trimmer has a thickness capacity of 1.5mm (1⁄16 in.) and is provided with an automatic clamping device, helpful when dealing with slippery plastic-based materials, and a calibrated stop edge at right angles to the blade. A good tool for photography or reprographic studios.

Dahle lightbox trimmer for use with transparencies and film.

DAHLE GUILLOTINE – HOBBY CUTTER

Cutting lengths: 250mm (9¾ in.), 320mm (12½ in.)

Similar in application and economic price to the Hobby Trimmer, these small size guillotines are ideal for home use. They are supplied with a hand pressure clamp for stabilizing the sheet as it is cut, a safety guard, two scale bars marked in millimetres and a table area marked with standard photograph sizes. They have a maximum thickness capacity of 0.5mm (¹⁄₄₈ in.) and will deal well with small quantities of paper or light card.

DAHLE GUILLOTINE

Cutting lengths: 360mm (14 in.), 550mm (21 in.), 700mm (27½ in.), 815mm (32 in.), 1060mm (42 in.)

For larger studio use Dahle manufacture the most comprehensive range of hand-operated guillotines on the market. All except the smallest model have a thickness capacity of 3.5 mm (³⁄₃₂ in.) which allows, for instance, 35 sheets of 70 gsm paper to be trimmed at once. They are supplied with safety guards, adjustable backstops, calibrated stop edges marked in centimetres, DIN and inches and either an automatic or hand-operated clamp. The larger models, capable of dealing with heavy boards, have helpful foot clamping devices to free both hands for the exact adjustment of the material to be cut. These robust machines can accurately trim all conventional studio materials and also tackle foils, felt, foam rubber, acrylic sheets, balsa-wood, plastics, leather and so on.

INGENTO

Not available in the UK

INGENTO PAPER CUTTER

Cutting lengths: 12 in., 15 in., 18 in., 24 in., 30 in.

A robust cutter with a self-sharpening steel blade capable of dealing with paper, heavy cardboard, cloth, leather, plastics and even light sheet metal. The hardwood bed of the cutter is scored with ½ in. squares and is fitted with an adjustable paper guide.

INGENTO GT PAPER CUTTER

Cutting lengths: 12 in., 15 in., 18 in.

The wood composition bed of this cutter is finished with a durable grey lacquer coating and scored with a ½ in. grid. A recessed rule is also supplied, calibrated in both inches and millimetres. The cutter has non-slip rubber feet, an adjustable paper guide and a self-sharpening steel blade. As an additional safety feature the blade can be locked when not in use. It will cope with most materials in studio use.

INGENTO TABLE-MOUNTED CUTTER

Cutting lengths: 30 in., 36 in.

A heavy-duty cutter for trimming wide papers and boards. The cutting assembly is mounted on a sturdy wooden table with a drop shelf to catch offcuts. Only the 36 in. model has a foot-operated hold-down bar, helpful when manoeuvring large sheets, but the 30 in. model has detachable legs and will pack flat.

Note that all three Ingento cutters do not have blade guards.

ROTATRIM

Not available in the USA

ROTATRIM M SERIES

Cutting lengths: Seven from 305mm (12 in.) to 1374mm (54 in.)

RotaTrim offer reliable, general-purpose trimmers, capable of cutting virtually every flexible sheet material in general use up to a maximum thickness of 3mm/⅛ in. (1.5mm/¹⁄₁₆ in. for 1067mm/42 in. and 1374mm/54 in. models.) The self-sharpening tungsten steel blade glides smoothly on twin support bars for extra rigidity and the melamine baseboard has a raised rule for easy measuring. A continuous roll feed and a bench stop for repetitive cutting to pre-set lengths can be fitted and all models are available in foot- or hand-operated electrically powered versions.

ROTATRIM TECHNICAL SERIES

Cutting lengths: Six from 650mm (26 in.) to 2150mm (85 in.)

Heavy-duty rotary trimmers built to withstand the particular stresses of cutting extremely thick (up to 4mm/³⁄₁₆ in.) or tough materials. They feature a single 38mm (1½ in.) square steel support bar and a cutting head which automatically adjusts to varying material thicknesses. The sheet cannot slip due to the clamping action of the twin spring-loaded pressure rollers on either side of the blade. A manual clamping strip is also provided.

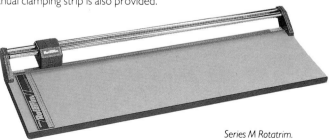

Series M Rotatrim.

ERASERS

Many erasers are not made of rubber any more, but of varying grades of vinyl, plastic and even glass fibre. Several are designed to perform an optimum service for one particular situation, say, removing drawing ink from drafting film or pencil lead from tracing paper. Others work in conjunction with liquid additives or solvents. The shape varies from the traditional rectangular block to pencil-thin erasers enclosed in wood, wrapped in paper or held in plastic. Others come in chuck form for insertion into electrically driven units which set up the necessary reciprocal motion to achieve the desired result.

CARAN D'ACHE

Caran d'Ache manufacture various rubber and vinyl erasers for pencil and ink removal.

EDDING

R10 (LARGE), R20 (STANDARD)
Plastic erasers with no abrasives for removing pencil marks, each contained in a plastic sleeve.

DR15 (LARGE), DR20 (STANDARD)
Combination erasers for removing pencil and ink, colourpen and copying pencil marks.

BR20 – A pencil eraser with a brush at the other end for removing dust.

ER20 – A pencil eraser supplied in a closeable plastic case.

FR10 – Erases pencil and film leads as well as foil and OHP inks.

FABER-CASTELL

7030, 7030-20 – Standard white and extra soft pencil erasers.

7061 – A dual eraser for ink and pencil.

7530 – A kneadable, soft compound eraser.

211 – An artists' eraser made from artgum, a compound of crepe rubber and oil which erases and dry cleans the surface.

1101 ERASING SHIELD
An erasing shield assisting in the cleaning of small areas within detailed work.

1954 MAGIC RUB
A vinyl eraser which absorbs the pencil marks into the particles which come away from the eraser as it is used. It can also be used with moisture to remove waterproof ink from film.

18 92 20 – TG-K combination eraser. The solvent impregnated in the green end assists in the removal of waterproof inks from acetate and drafting film. The white end erases pencil lines and also removes any residual solvent left by using the green portion.

18 81 20 – A white vinyl pencil eraser with a plastic sleeve drawn on for protection.

1965 – A sack filled with granules of 'Magic Rub' used for cleaning larger areas of film and cloth.

1960 – A 'Magic Rub' eraser with a peelable paper wrapping for removing ink from drafting film or pencil lines from drawing paper.

30103 – A glass-fibre eraser which is particularly useful for removing ink and hard pencil marks. Refills are also available.

JAKAR

5334 – A set of three erasers for removing pencil, ink, and ball-pen ink.

5321(9) – A glass-fibre eraser in a strong plastic barrel with a tapering metal tip. Refill elements are available.

ROTRING

LARGE AND SMALL PENCIL ERASERS: B20 551 120, B30 551 130
A soft white eraser with no added abrasives. The

pencil marks are rolled up into the rubbings which are easily removed from the drawing.

LARGE AND SMALL INK ERASERS: T20 551 220, T30 551 230

Removes ink from tracing paper, drafting film or master copies in a non-abrasive way that does not damage the surface which can immediately be redrawn on without any further preparation.

COMBINED INK AND PENCIL ERASER: TB20 551 320

A combination of the two above: two-thirds for non-etching inks and one-third for pencil erasing.

'BI-RASOR' HOLDER

A double-ended holder for two replaceable erasers for the precision erasure of both pencil and ink lines. Refills are available.

ERASING MACHINES

ECOBRA

A mains-driven eraser which will handle small, detailed alterations or large area removal. The air-cooled motor will work continuously for hours if required. The rapid-clamping chuck takes a very wide range of erasers each of which is

available in five degrees of hardness. Each of the erasers is 180mm (7⅛ in.) long and available in boxes of 12.

EDEC

A mains-driven eraser which comes supplied with five eraser points. It switches on automatically when held in the erasing position and switches off when returned to the rest position.

MOTORASER

A lightweight electric erasing machine which can hold a variety of different eraser plugs, ranging from red (medium) and pink (soft) for pencil to dark grey for ink. For heavy-duty erasing the switch can be set so that the machine runs continuously.

UNO

MODEL A

An economy mains-driven eraser whose shaded pole motor operates quietly so as not to distract other occupants in the studio. The motor will stop if too much pressure is applied and will immediately restart when the pressure has been released. The case is sturdy and impact resistant. The chuck will give way if the eraser is dropped so that the motor spindle will escape damage.

SHARPENERS

Two methods of sharpening drawing tools are used to suit different needs. For fine, detailed artwork a hard pencil with a long sharp point is needed to give absolute accuracy and visual control over the work. To obtain this, it is best to use a knife and sandpaper block rather than a pencil sharpener (see p.52).

For softer graphite pencils or coloured pencils this technique may be difficult as the leads are too brittle to retain a long, sharp point for long. For this type, then, use a traditional pencil sharpener which gives a shorter conical point. Although

metal alloy models are often more expensive than plastic ones they are generally more useful and long-lasting as the blades can be replaced when they become too blunt to be effective. Those which have an attached container to collect the shavings are handy to have by your desk so that a trip to the waste bin is not called for every time your pencil is blunt. Lead pointers differ from sharpeners in that they do not shave off any of the wood casing, just sharpen the lead itself to a fine point. These are particularly useful for mechanical pencils.

DRAWING A BOX WITH ROUNDED CORNERS

1 Either (a) Construct an exact square within the corner using a T-square and set square (triangle). Bisect the angle by drawing a straight line between the diagonally opposite corners of the square.

Or (b) Position the pencil point of a compass on to the corner and the needle point on to one of the straight lines. Draw a wide arc through the corner. Repeat the procedure on the other side of the corner so that the arcs intersect. Using a straight-edge, draw a connecting line between the corner and the point where the arcs intersect.

2 Draw an ordinary box accurately with a T-square and set square (triangle). If using method (a), make sure the square is exactly the same size at each corner of the box. Method (b) is unsuitable if you are going to ink in the box as the compass needle will leave holes in the paper which could interrupt the flow of the pen nib. Place the compass point on the diagonal which now bisects each corner. Draw in a curve which meets the sides of the box. The size of the curve is dependent upon the position of the compass needle on the diagonal.

3 When inking in the box always draw the curved corner first, then the straight lines; you can then alter the position of the straight lines slightly if necessary to achieve a smooth join.

DIVIDING A LINE INTO EQUAL PARTS

1 Using a parallel motion (parallel straight-edge) or T-square and a sharp pencil, draw a horizontal line. Measure and mark off the length of the line to be divided.

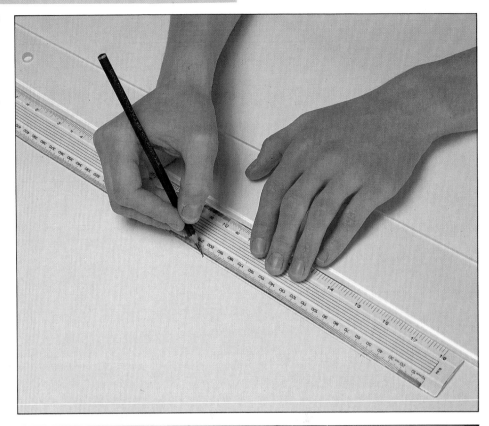

2 Now draw a straight line at an acute angle to the first, passing through the left-hand point. On this line mark the number of divisions required in units that are easy to measure. If for example you wish to divide your line into five portions, mark off 5cm (2 in.) from the point of intersection.

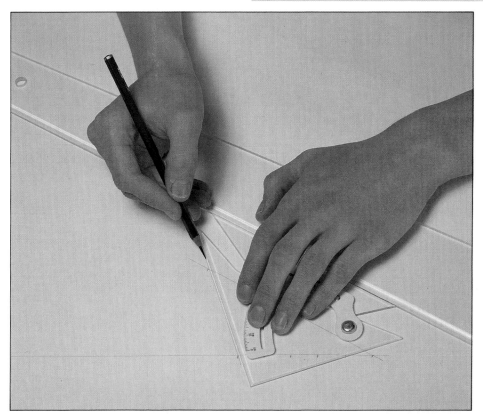

3 Now rest an adjustable set square (triangle) against the T-square. Adjust the sloping edge so that it connects the last mark on the angled line to the right-hand point on the horizontal line. Draw this line in.

4 Slide the set square (triangle) along to the left until it touches the next mark on the angled line. Draw another line parallel to the first. Do this for each of the marks. Where these lines cross the horizontal gives the equal parts needed.

DRAWING A SET OF PARALLEL LINES WITH A COMPASS

To draw a set of accurate, evenly spaced parallel lines use a compass as a convenient measuring instrument. This is less time consuming than using a ruler to measure the distance each time and reduces the risk of error.

1 Set the compass to the required measure against a ruler.

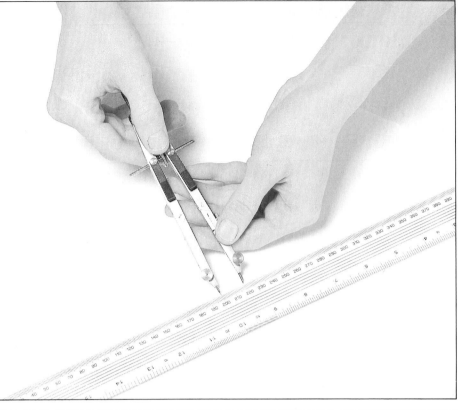

2 Using a set square (triangle) and T-square draw a vertical line at the left-hand side of the page and a horizontal one across the top. Place the compass needle on the point of intersection and make a mark with the pencil against the vertical.

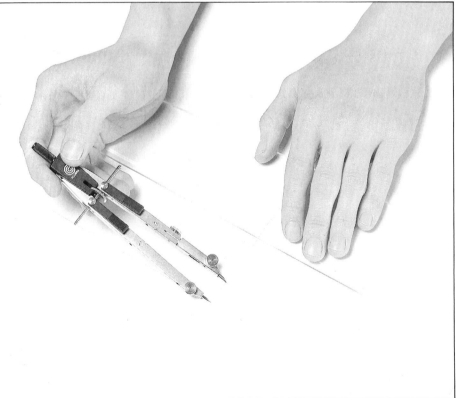

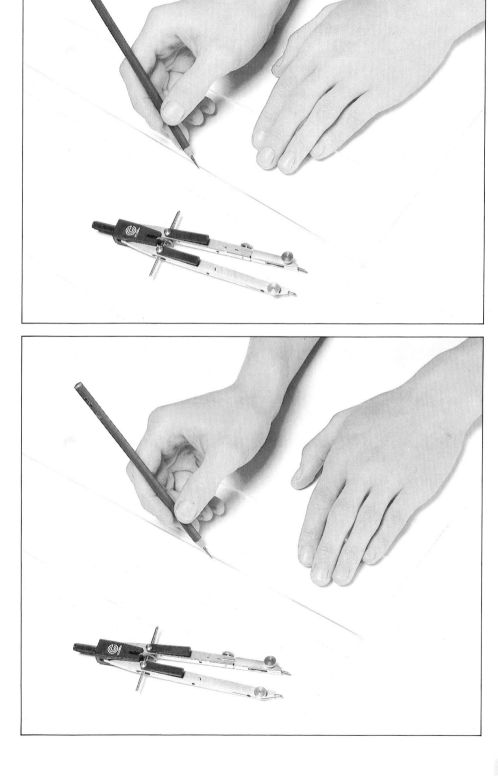

3 Draw in the second horizontal line at this mark using the T-square.

4 Continue this procedure down the page until the desired number of lines has been ruled.

USING STENCILS

1 When using lettering stencils, rule in the baseline and x height lightly with a sharp non-repro blue pencil before you begin. Place the stencil in position and mark off another line where the bottom of the stencil touches the paper. Use these three guides to align your letters.

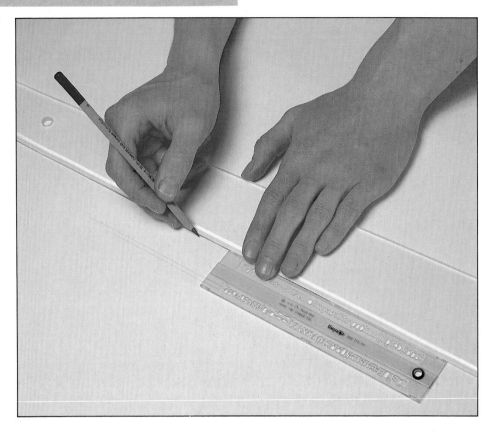

2 Space letters evenly by trial and error using a pencil first and only go over them in ink when you are satisfied. Generally, the tendency is to leave too much space between the letters; close spacing always look better than wide.

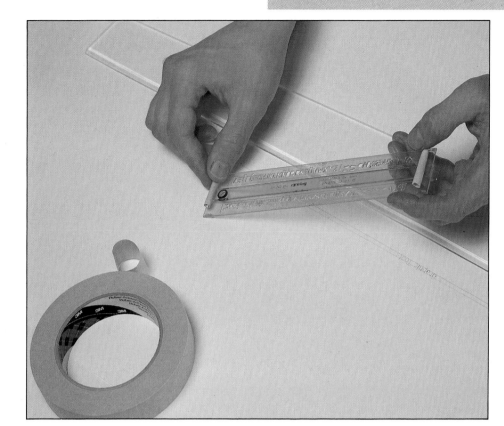

3 If you are using ink with a stencil which does not have bevelled edges or ink bosses, attach small lumps of rolled-up sticky masking tape under each end to raise the stencil from the drawing surface and prevent smudging.

4 Keep the pen at a constant 90° angle to the paper to ensure accuracy. This is easier using a lettering joint.

DRAWING CURVES

Flexible curves and french curves are useful for drawing a variety of shapes. Like templates, they should have bevelled edges for ink work without smudging.

I Do not try to draw more than one part of a complicated curve at any one time. Always draw the line smoothly without changing the speed of the pen. This applies to drawing a line along a straight-edge too.

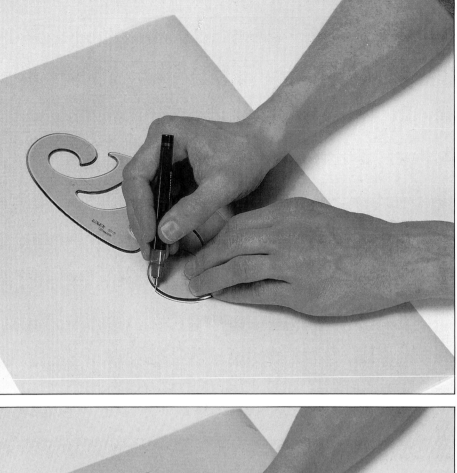

2 Position the next part of the curve carefully and find out if they join exactly by testing with a pencil line. Then ink in, overlapping the ends by a few millimetres to create a smooth join.

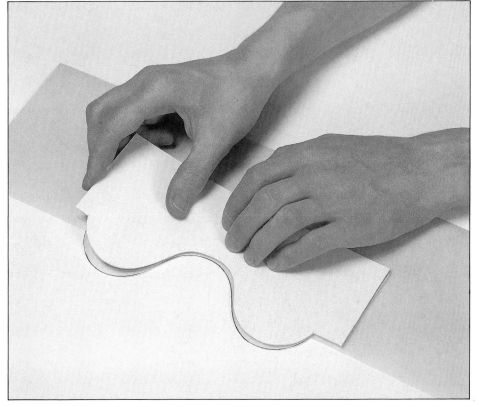

CUTTING YOUR OWN CURVED TEMPLATE

If you need to create the image of a composite curve more than once, a french curve is not really suitable. It is easier, in the long run, to create your own template.

1 Draw the shape required on to heavy drafting film, and on two pieces of fairly thick card. Cut out all three shapes carefully with a sharp knife. Glue one side of one of the card shapes and stick it to the drafting film. The edge of the film should overlap the card by about 10mm (³⁄₈ in.). Stick the second card shape to the other side of the film in a similar fashion so that you have created a sandwich with the film protruding slightly.

2 Finally, rub down the edge of the drafting film with fine sandpaper (glasspaper) to even out any roughness in the curve. You now have a bevelled edge which can be used with drafting pens.

PENCILS, CHARCOALS AND PASTELS

Pencils are produced in a range of grades and forms for both quick sketching and precise drafting needs. This section presents the major types, and attempts to clarify the difference between products which, at first glance, resemble each other closely, including chalks, pastels, charcoal and crayons.

PENCILS

Coloured pencils and (right) a Conté watercolour pencil.

The term 'lead pencil' is essentially misleading. These drawing tools are not actually constructed from lead metal but from a mixture of carbon and graphite, bound together with water and clay, then shaped into sticks and baked in a kiln at very high temperature. These 'leads' are then bonded to pre-cut wood slats, usually of cedar, which provide strength while remaining soft and supple enough for easy, smooth sharpening. This manufacturing process allows the addition to the mixture of various other substances, such as waxes, resins and shellacs, which add particular strength or smoothness to the finished pencil. The finest leads, used in mechanical and clutch pencils (lead holders), are made from a special blend of high-quality graphite and polymer resins.

Coloured leads are an amalgam of a water-soluble or insoluble pigment, a filler (usually clay or talc), a wax-like lubricant and a gum binder. Three main types are available. Those with thick, relatively soft, leads are waterproof, lightproof and do not erase or smudge easily. Manufacturers often produce these in a wide range of shades. A similar pencil, in smaller colour ranges, is produced with a finer, non-crumbling lead for detailed work. Lastly come pencils with water-soluble leads, which can be used in conjunction with water to give washes of colour.

The quality and quantity of the materials used in the manufacture of pencils affects their grading for tone and strength and the quality of the mark produced. As the proportion of clay in the mixture increases, the pencil becomes harder. A graphite 'lead' pencil gives grey shiny marks, a carbon/charcoal pencil matt black marks and a Conté pencil slightly greasy matt black marks. Two systems are used to grade hardness: the Conté system employs numbers and the Brookman system letters (BB, F, HB etc). In artists' or draftsmen's pencils, B describes softness (9B being the softest), and H hardness (10H being the hardest). This grading system provides a guide to choosing the most suitable tool for any particular job. A soft pencil will not remain sharp for long and is therefore not practical

for technical drawing, while a very hard pencil, which retains a needle point for a greater length of time, is useless for shading large areas of a tonal drawing. For laying out guidelines on artwork or technical drawings, where a feint but very accurate line is required, a reasonably hard pencil (4H or harder) should be used. Care should be taken to maintain a sharp needle point at all times but the pencil should not be pressed hard into the paper or board as this is likely to create an indentation which is difficult to remove.

As a general rule, the softer types of pencil should be used on paper which has a degree of grain or 'tooth' to pick up and retain the looser graphite particles, while the smoother surfaces such as line board (illustration board) or art board (bristol board) are only suitable for harder pencils. If the surface is excessively shiny a special pencil with a waxy quality – such as a chinagraph (china marker) – is needed in order to make any impression at all. Another valuable tool for anyone using pencils is an extending holder which, as its name implies, serves to lengthen partly used pencils, prolonging their life considerably.

Of particular interest to designers and draftsmen has been the development in recent years of mechanical and clutch pencils (lead holders) with retractable leads. These eliminate much time-consuming sharpening and provide precisely accurate line widths for technical drawing needs. They consist of a metal and/or plastic barrel containing a sleeve which holds the lead in place. This is released and propelled forward by pressing a button at the end of the barrel or, sometimes, by simply shaking the pencil. In a clutch pencil (lead holder), the lead is usually rather thicker than in a mechanical pencil and its tip is held by a clutch lock. The exposed tip of a mechanical pencil is encased in a shoulderless metal sheath, similar to a drafting pen, which allows use of the tool with stencils, drafting guides and straight-edges. Many of the newest types of lead for these products now give a line which is dense enough for direct reproduction without having to be overdrawn in ink.

BLACKLEAD PENCILS

Note: This list includes charcoal pencils and chinagraphs (china markers).

BEROL

VENUS DRAWING

Grades: 14 grades 6B to 6H
A top-quality pencil for professional use, easily recognized by its distinctive green 'crackle' finish. An excellent subtle and responsive tool for tonal drawings, this is also available with an eraser tip.

TURQUOISE DRAWING

Grades: 17 grades 6B to 9H
Especially designed for use by draftsmen, this top-quality graphite pencil reproduces well, is smudge resistant and easy to erase.

TURQUOISE FILMOGRAPH

Grades: Five grades E1 (soft) to E5 (hard)
Designed for drafting on all types of film, this range has a special plastic-based 'lead' which reproduces well but can be removed cleanly with a Filmograph eraser (see p. 26).

BLAISDELL CHARCOAL PENCIL

Grades: Three grades, extra soft, soft, medium
Another alternative to traditional charcoal sticks, these are clean and convenient to handle due to their paper wrapping which unwinds progressively to reveal the point.

BLAISDELL MARKER

Colour range: black, red, blue, green, brown, crimson, yellow, white
Similar to the Blaisdell Charcoal Pencil in its paper wrapping, this has a wax core for use on smooth glossy surfaces. It is also useful for detailed areas of wax-resist work.

CARAN D'ACHE

TECHNOGRAPH

Grades: 17 grades 6B to 9H
High-quality pencils for general and technical drawing.

BLACK BEAUTY

Grade: One grade only
A pure graphite crayon which gives a smooth matt black line.

FABER-CASTELL

CASTELL 9000

Grades: 17 grades 8B to 7H
The famous and very popular range of top-quality drawing pencils giving good opacity and clean erasability. The leads are very smooth and sharpen easily but are resistant to point breakage. Grades 8B to 5H are suitable for blueprints, 8B to 3H for photocopying and HB to 6H for use on matt drafting film.

GOLDFABER

Grades: 12 grades 5B to 5H
An economically priced good-quality drawing pencil suitable for most general drawing and sketching.

GRAPHITE PURE

Grades: Three grades HB, 3B, 6B
As their name implies, these are thick, solid leads of pure graphite, without a wood casing, although they sharpen as easily as a pencil. Unlike similar charcoal sticks they have a smooth un-gritty feel and are particularly recommended for free expressive drawing and sketching out ideas.

PITT CHARCOAL

Grades: Five grades extra soft, soft, medium, hard, extra hard
Charcoal is a popular and traditional drawing medium (see pp. 48-9), ideal for studies, sketches and finished drawings where a soft, hazy effect is desired. Smudging is almost bound to occur, so a fixative is essential (see pp. 112-19).

GLASS WRITER

Colour range: black, red, blue, green, yellow, white
A round, soft pencil, soluble in spirit (alcohol), for marking on all smooth surfaces such as plastic, glass and metal.

KOH-I-NOOR

Not available in the UK

KOH-I-NOOR SKETCHING PENCIL

Grades: Three grades 2B, 4B, 6B
A soft-leaded pencil with a flat, oval shape. An ideal tool for wide line drawing, broad coverage or free calligraphic work.

KOH-I-NOOR 'NEGRO' PENCIL

Grades: Four grades No. 1 (softest) to No. 4 (hardest)
A particularly smooth lead giving a dense black line suitable for reproduction. It can be erased easily without smudging.

Blacklead pencils, one (left) with eraser tip, and a chinagraph (china marker).

A selection of blacklead pencils.

REXEL

DERWENT GRAPHIC
Grades: 20 grades 9B to 9H
An extremely high-quality pencil for professional use, produced in the widest range of grades. Its distinctive matt black finish is a further reason for its popularity in design studios.

FIVE STAR PENCIL
Grades: 17 grades 6B to 9H
These high-grade pencils are slightly more economically priced than the Derwent Graphic, and are also available with an eraser tip.

DERWENT SKETCHING PENCIL
Grades: Three grades soft, medium, hard
A chisel-tip drawing and sketching pencil, which will provide a wide variation of tones, lines and shades.

ROYAL SOVEREIGN GRAPHICS
Not available in the USA

RS800
Grades: 14 grades 6B to 6H
A popular and distinctive range of precision drawing pencils offering consistency and smoothness.

CARBON PENCILS
Grades: Six grades 3B to 2H
Especially suitable for use on cartridge or 'not' surfaced papers (cold-pressed papers) with a definite 'tooth', these pure carbon pencils produce an intense matt black line. Good for both quick roughs and finished drawings.

CHARCOAL PENCILS
Grades: Three grades soft, medium, hard
Unlike traditional charcoal sticks, these have an outer wood casing – good for keeping your hands clean – and reproduce charcoal effects without the powdering and dusting normally encountered with this medium. Charcoal pencils are ideal for roughing in the outlines of gouache, oil or acrylic paintings as they produce a darker line than graphite, and for finished drawings.

CHINAGRAPH/CHINA MARKER
Colour range: black, red, blue, green, brown, yellow, white
A wax-based pencil useful for many marking jobs around the studio on any surface with a high gloss, such as glass, acetate overlays, transparencies or prints. The line is water-repellent but can be removed with a dry cloth.

STAEDTLER

MARS LUMOGRAPH 100
Grades: 19 grades EE, EB, 6B to 9H
Similar to other top-quality ranges for the professional, these pencils offer slow wear and high opacity with good resistance to point breakage, making them popular with designers.

MARS DYNAGRAPH 100 50
Grades: Six grades N0=HB, N1=F, N2=H, N3=3H, N4=5H, N5=7H
A range with a plastic-based lead specially formulated for use on drafting films.

COLOURED PENCILS

BEROL

VERITHIN
Colour range: 38 colours, plus gold and silver
As their name implies, these professional-quality pencils have extra thin leads which can be sharpened to a needle point for fine detailed work. The pigments are very sensitive to the drawing surface, giving draftsmen a degree of control over the mark similar to that produced by a blacklead pencil. This makes them useful for bringing colour into black and white drawings or adding points of detail to illustrations executed in a broader, more expressive style. Available singly or in wallets of six, 12 and 24 colours.

PRISMACOLOUR
Colour range: 60 colours
These pencils have large diameter leads giving soft, smooth marks which are waterproof and light-resistant. There is a particularly useful selection of eight different warm and cold greys.

CARAN D'ACHE

PRISMALO I AND PRISMALO II
Colour range: 40 colours
Two co-ordinating ranges of high-quality coloured pencils with water-soluble yet strong leads which can be diluted with water to give unlimited blending opportunities. Prismalo I have thin leads for detailed work while Prismalo II have extra soft thick leads for larger coverage.

FABER-CASTELL

LOTUS-COLOUR PENCILS

Colour range: 36 colours
Medium-soft pencils giving dense, highly pigmented marks. Faber-Castell pencils are particularly noted for their improved lead strength and resistance to point breakage. Available in sets of 12, 24 and 36 pencils.

POLYCHROMOS ARTISTS' COLOURED PENCILS

Colour range: 72 colours
High-quality oil crayon leaded pencils which give a smudge-, water- and fade-resistant line on cardboard, wood and textiles as well as on normal drawing surfaces. They are soft and supple enough for intense covering but will sharpen easily to a point. The pigments can be dissolved or removed with turpentine and are non-toxic. Available singly or in sets of 12, 24, 36, 60 and 70 colours.

ALBRECHT DÜRER ARTISTS' COLOURED PENCILS

Colour range: 36 colours
Fine-leaded, non-fading, fully water-soluble pencils, these can be sharpened to a point for detailed work or used in combination with water and a brush to create washes of colour. A useful feature enabling a crayon drawing to be converted, either in part or in its entirety, into a watercolour. Available in sets of 12, 24 and 36 pencils.

COL-ERASE PENCILS

Colour range: 24 colours
These are coloured pencils with the unusual feature of being completely erasable using the special eraser tip provided on the end of each pencil. They have fine, non-crumbling leads which sharpen to a needle point, making them ideal for engineering drawings, blueprints, typographic renderings and all situations where accuracy of detail is required. Available singly or in sets of 12 and 24 pencils.

REXEL

DERWENT ARTISTS' PENCILS

Colour range: 72 colours
A superfine quality artist's drawing pencil with a thick, soft lead, ideal for subtle combinations of tones and tints. The pigments are extremely lightfast which makes these pencils an excellent dry colouring medium for finished artwork. Available singly or in tins of 12, 24, 36 and 72 colours.

DERWENT STUDIO PENCILS

Colour range: 72 colours
These are designer-quality coloured pencils with fine leads capable of retaining a point for more detailed work. Very popular among designers for their versatility and subtle colour selection, their matt black finish co-ordinates with the Derwent Graphic blacklead pencil range. The tips are colour-coded for easy identification. Available singly or in tins of 12, 24, 36 and 72 colours.

DERWENT STUDIO BLOCKS

Colour range: 72 colours
These 8mm (⅜ in.) square solid sticks of colour, matched exactly in both colour and material to the Studio Pencil range (see above), are designed for colouring larger areas. They are clean to handle and not wax-based.

DERWENT WATERCOLOUR PENCILS

Colour range: 36 colours
A fine-leaded pencil similar to the Studio range but containing a water-soluble pigment which can be diluted with a wet brush to form a wash. Combines the precision of a pencil with the versatility of watercolours. Available singly or in tins of 12, 24 and 36 colours.

SCHWAN-STABILO

STABILOTONE

Colour range: 51 colours, plus gold, silver and copper
A versatile new drawing tool, this combines the qualities of a coloured pencil, a crayon and a watercolour. Although smaller and chunkier than the average pencil, it sits comfortably in the hand and sharpens easily with the special Stabilo sharpener, and has a thick (10mm/⁷⁄₁₆ in.) lead giving highly concentrated, rich colour delivery over large areas. As such, it can be used for quick sketches and layouts in much the same lively way as a marker but in many ways is even more versatile and obviously there are no problems of drying out. It will create the subtle tonal effects of a pencil, will lay colours over one another – enabling the use of sgraffito techniques – or produce blended washes when used with water and a brush. A similar pure graphite pencil is marketed as part of the Stabilotone range. Available singly or in sets of 10, 30, and 54 pencils.

STABILO THIN LEAD COLOURED PENCILS

Colour range: 36 colours, plus gold and silver
An easy to sharpen thin-leaded pencil giving an accurate, controlled line on silk, linen, leather and wood as well as paper. The points are resistant to

Coloured pencils, one (centre) a watercolour pencil.

wear and breakage and the pencils can be used on either dry or wet surfaces, giving excellent lightfast results on both. Available singly or in sets of six, 12, 18, 24, 30 and 36 colours.

STABILO 'ALL' PENCILS
Colour range: Seven colours, plus graphite
A soft-leaded pencil with a special dense pigment which will write on all surfaces, including those with a high gloss such as plastics, metal and glass. Although waterproof, it is easily erased.

STAEDTLER

MARS LUMOCHROM 104 COLOURED DRAWING PENCILS
Colour range: black, red, blue, green, brown, violet, orange, light yellow, carmine
Though only available in a small range of colours, the plastic formulation of the leads of these pencils gives water-, smear- and fade-proof lines which are easy to erase.

MECHANICAL AND CLUTCH PENCILS/LEAD HOLDERS

There is now such an enormous range of mechanical and clutch pencils (lead holders) on the market that a purchase for the first-time buyer, or even the professional with some experience, can be fraught with difficult choices. Here we define a few of the characteristics of each category as a guide to making a more informed choice.

In simple terms, the main difference between a mechanical and a clutch pencil (lead holder) is that the clutch or collar mechanism which grips the lead is contained within the barrel in the mechanical pencil while it remains outside the barrel at its neck in the clutch pencil (lead holder). The latter usually carries much thicker leads of about 2mm and is good for sketching and drawing. It also makes a good coloured lead holder, as these can be easily changed, and is particularly useful when carrying a blue lead as a non-repro pencil for artwork.

The mechanical pencil takes much finer leads, down to 0.2mm, and has an extended metal sleeve which holds and protects the lead as it protrudes from the barrel. This lead guard can be either fixed or retracting (one which retreats into the barrel as the lead is used up). The retracting type is good for protecting softer leads, particularly highly flexible film leads. Whatever kind is chosen, the lead guard must be at least 3.5mm long at its shortest point (the standard thickness of a ruler) if it is to be used with stencils and drafting guides where some clearance is required. As a general rule, a fixed guard type of pencil provides greater stability and accuracy for this work.

There is also an extensive and confusing array of leads from which to choose these days. These can be classified into three basic ranges. Graphite leads are suitable for general drawing, sketching, layout and and design work on all papers (including tracing) and boards. Leads for use on drafting film are usually polymer based and give a harder, more resistant structure and a more consistent dense matt black line for reproduction. Special plastic-based polymer leads for use on plastic drafting film are also available from many manufacturers. These are graded differently from ordinary pencils using an alternative system of numbers (1 to 5) and letters (prefix letters vary from manufacturer to manufacturer) – 1 denotes the softest and 5 the hardest lead. These give a good reproducible line which is virtually impossible to smudge but can be removed easily using special erasers.

There are two important points to remember when purchasing and using one of these pencils. Firstly, you should never attempt to use anything but the diameter of lead for which the pencil was designed. Secondly, the most expensive is not necessarily the best: an economically priced product may well fulfil your needs.

Most manufacturers of mechanical pencils also produce a range of suitable leads, in various grades and diameters, for use on both paper and film. These are normally quite interchangeable so that it is not essential to buy the leads which correspond exactly to each make of pencil so long as they are of appropriate size. As with ordinary pencils, it is perhaps best to experiment with one or two types in order to discover which accords best with personal preference and drawing style.

BEROL

TURQUOISE TECH

Line widths: Four widths 0.3mm, 0.5mm, 0.7mm, 0.9mm

A professional-quality mechanical pencil with a fixed sleeve. The lead is automatically advanced as it is used up, a useful quality when doing precision work where stopping to replenish the lead by hand would prove to be an irritating interruption.

This range also has a useful eraser supplied under the end button and a cleaning wire for clearing any possible blockages which may occur in the mechanism.

TURQUOISE HALF-SLIDING SLEEVE

Line widths: Three widths 0.3mm, 0.5mm, 0.7mm

This pencil is similar in many respects to the Turquoise Tech, but has an automatically retracting half-sliding sleeve which protects the lead as it is used up.

TURQUOISE 10

Line width: One width only 2.0mm

This is a clutch pencil (lead holder) with a sturdy push-button mechanism which advances the lead when necessary. This model also features a lead sharpener for easy repointing.

PCL 2000

Line widths: Four widths 0.3mm, 0.5mm, 0.7mm, 0.9mm

A recent innovation, the PCL 2000 incorporates a special spring-loaded mechanism which helps to protect the lead from breakage when exposed to excessive downward pressure on the drawing surface. When this occurs the lead is automatically retracted, only returning to its normal position if the pressure is released.

Berol also market a range of Polymer, Graphite and Filmograph (plastic-based) leads in various widths for use with these and other manufacturers' products.

CARAN D'ACHE

FIXPENCIL

Line widths: Three widths 0.5mm, 2.0mm, 3.0mm

These are sturdy mechanical pencils, particularly in the larger widths, very suitable for heavy-duty use or any situation where rough treatment is likely to occur.

EDDING

EDDING P7/S

Line width: One width only 0.5mm

Edding market these mechanical pencils in sets of seven, containing leads of seven different grades. They all have 4mm fixed lead guards and are supplied with cleaning wires. For anyone thinking of equipping themselves with such a range, this would make an ideal economical and robust choice.

EDDING P8

Line widths: Two widths 0.5mm, 0.7mm

Another good-quality, low-cost basic pencil supplied with cleaning wire and eraser and a fixed lead guard. Its all-metal internal mechanism helps to ensure trouble-free use.

FABER-CASTELL

TK-MATIC

Line width: One width only 0.5mm

A completely automatic mechanical pencil with a unique continuous pumping mechanism which eliminates any need to advance the lead by hand except when a new one is required from the reservoir.

This model is supplied with an eraser and cleaning wire under the endcap.

APOLLO

Line width: One width only 0.5mm

A fine-lead mechanical pencil with completely retractable sliding sleeve to protect against point breakage. This means, however, that it cannot be used with rulers or other drafting guides but is very suitable for general sketching, drawing and writing.

CONTURA XL

Line widths: Two widths 0.5mm, 0.7mm

An economically priced, good general-purpose pencil with a fixed sleeve and push-button mechanism. This model can also be used with drafting guides.

Both Apollo and Contura XL are supplied with extra large erasers under the endcap.

CASTELL TK FINE

Line widths: Four widths 0.3mm, 0.5mm, 0.7mm, 0.9mm

This is a high-quality but still economically priced fixed-sleeve drafting pencil. Each width is colour coded, according to ISO standards, around the push button and is supplied with an extra large eraser.

CASTELL TK FINE L

Line widths: Four widths 0.3mm, 0.5mm, 0.7mm, 0.9mm

A high-quality drafting pencil for professional use. It has a fixed sleeve, ISO colour-coded push button and a variable indicator which identifies the grade of lead being used.

ECONOMY CLUTCH PENCIL

Line width: One width only 2.0mm

As its name implies, this is a low-priced but reliable clutch pencil (lead holder). The push button has an inbuilt sharpener for easy repointing.

UNIVERSAL CLUTCH PENCIL

Widths: for use with 2.0mm to 3.15mm leads

A holder which will accept a variety of lead widths, particularly useful for grades 4B to 8B which tend to be thicker than average.

Faber-Castell also produce a range of Super Polymer leads, TK-Colour leads (red and blue) and TK Filmar leads for use on drafting film.

PENTEL

P200 SERIES AND PS SERIES

Line widths: P200 Series available in four widths 0.3mm, 0.5mm, 0.7mm, 0.9mm; PS Series available in two widths 0.3mm, 0.5mm

The basic mechanical pencils in the Pentel range have an all-brass construction and a special internal mechanism which advances each size of lead by an amount appropriate to its diameter. The P200 Series has a fixed 4mm long sleeve for technical drawing while the PS Series, identical in every other way, features a sliding sleeve (from 5mm to 3mm). Both are equipped with erasers.

PG500 SERIES

Line widths: Four widths 0.3mm, 0.5mm. 0.7mm, 0.9mm

This range has an unusual shape for a mechanical pencil and very much resembles a technical pen in both appearance and good, well-balanced feel. None of the working parts are exposed during cleaning, which is accomplished by unscrewing the front cone section, making accidental damage unlikely. The drafting point is shoulderless and conforms to the required clearances for standard drafting guides. The design also has an eraser under the endcap and a lead hardness indicator.

Pentel also market a similar pencil in a Student range. Although identical in mechanical characteristics, this is economically priced due to the different materials used in the design of the barrel housing, and would make a good-quality cost-conscious first buy.

PF SERIES

Line widths: Three widths 0.5mm, 0.7mm, 0.9mm

The cream-coloured barrel of this range denotes its special recommendation for use on coated polyester and polypropylene films. For this purpose, the 0.5mm and 0.7mm sizes are both fitted with sliding sleeves to protect the flexible film leads. Once retracted to 3mm, a click on the end button will restore the sleeve to its full working length of 5mm.

Pentel also produce a full range of leads for both paper and film use in various diameters and hardnesses.

PILOT

H22 PROFESSIONAL SERIES, H58 SUPER PROFESSIONAL SERIES AND H60 SUPER PROFESSIONAL SERIES

Line widths: Four widths 0.3mm, 0.5mm, 0.7mm, 0.9mm

The H22 Series is a basic, good-quality range available at an economical price. It has a sturdy 4mm fixed lead guard and a push-button mechanism and makes a good choice for general drawing or use with drafting guides. The H58 and H60 Series are similar but incorporate a few extra features – a lead hardness indicator and a better balanced barrel design which gives more comfortable use over a longer period for the professional. The H60 has a white barrel denoting its special use with film leads but in all other respects has an identical mechanism.

H55 HALF SLIDING SLEEVE SERIES

Line widths: Three widths 0.3mm, 0.5mm, 0.7mm.

This pencil has a sleeve which retracts from a maximum of 5mm to a minimum of 3mm, giving the lead a longer life when in use. This pencil can be employed with thinner drafting guides but those with bevelled edges could prove difficult to use.

H100/H200 SERIES

Line widths: Two widths 0.3mm, 0.5mm

This range has fixed 4mm sleeves but these can be retracted completely using the Pilot double knock mechanism to protect the drawing point and your pocket when the pencil is not in use.

H1585 SHAKE OR PRESS AND H1010 THE SHAKER

Line width: One width only 0.5mm

Both these pencils feature Pilot's dual lead-feed mechanism. The lead can be extended in measured increments using the conventional push-button system or by simply shaking the pencil with a flick of the wrist. This is certainly convenient in situations where any change in the grip on the pencil would be an irritating interruption. The Shake or Press version has a 4mm fixed lead guard and so is probably more generally useful than the Shaker which has a retracting sleeve whose maximum length is only 2mm. This model does, however, have a see-through window in the barrel which keeps a check on the remaining lead.

ROTRING

ROTRING TIKKY F AND TIKKY S
Line widths: Tikky F available in three widths 0.3mm, 0.5mm, 0.7mm; Tikky S available in one width only 0.5mm
An economical choice for a good, unfussy, general-purpose fine-lead pencil. The range offers an option between a 4mm fixed sleeve (Tikky F), for use with drafting guides, and a fully retracting sleeve (Tikky S) for clean, neat sketching and drawing.

ROTRING T
Line widths: Three widths 0.3mm, 0.5mm, 0.7mm
The Rotring T has a semi-retracting sleeve which

retreats from 5mm in length to a minimum of 3.5mm, making it suitable for use with stencils while retaining the protective qualities of the sliding lead guard.

STAEDTLER

MARS MICROGRAPH 770 FINELINE HOLDERS AND MICRO F 775 FINELINE HOLDERS
Line widths: Four widths 0.3mm, 0.5mm, 0.7mm, 0.9mm
Both these ranges of professional pencils have reliable precision mechanisms and fixed lead guards for use with stencils. The major difference between them is that the Micrograph has a metal finger grip, a lead hardness indicator and a metal internal mechanism for longer, more durable wear.

MARS TECHNICO 780C and 785C LEADHOLDER
Line width: One width only 2.0mm
Popular and widely used clutch pencils (lead holders) with either a metal (780C) or plastic (785C) finger grip and an inbuilt sharpener in the endcap. These are ideal for sketching with softer graphite leads or for handling the wide range of Mars Lumochrom coloured leads and are often used in the studio as a non-repro blue lead holder.

1 Koh-i-Noor clutch pencil (lead holder) Technicolor leads; 2 Staedtler Mars 780 clutch pencil (lead holder); 3 Tombow AX, 4 Pentel P200 series, and 5 Rotring Tikky Springer mechanical pencils; 6 leads for Pentel mechanical pencil; and for Koh-i-Noor (7) and Mars 780 (8) clutch pencils (lead holders).

CHARCOAL, CHALKS, PASTELS AND CRAYONS

Willow charcoal sticks.

Charcoal has a long and distinguished pedigree as a drawing medium, having been employed extensively by artists over many centuries, and will be familiar to most people as a basic and indispensable tool in the armoury of professional and student alike. It has versatility, variety and availability in its favour, and puts a diverse range of techniques at the fingertips of any artist.

Willow wood has, over the years, been used most extensively for natural charcoal but, during the last two centuries, many experiments took place using other types of wood: vine was found to be particularly successful and has acquired a high reputation for producing exceptional quality, fine charcoal. This gives not only a responsive line but one which is also easy to correct as marks can be quickly dusted, or even blown, from the drawing surface.

Compressed charcoal is made by combining powder-ground charcoal and a binding agent into short lengths, giving tougher, less breakable sticks. This makes them more convenient to handle in many ways but less easy to erase. Charcoal pencils (see Pencils, pp. 40-47) are also made from compressed charcoal but have an outer wrapping of wood or rolled paper for cleaner handling. The points can be easily sharpened – making them ideal for detailed work – but, obviously, a variety of line widths cannot be produced.

It is this variety that makes traditional charcoal such a versatile medium for both line and tone drawings, particularly for work done on a large scale where a broader treatment is required. Preliminary outlines can be laid down freely and then either removed easily or painted over at a later date. Charcoal can give both a precise mark using the tip of a stick or larger areas of graduated tone using a broad side stroke. Further tonal effects can be achieved by cross-hatching or smudging with a stump, a putty rubber

(kneaded eraser) or a brush dipped in clean water. A putty rubber (kneaded eraser) is also invaluable for picking out highlights. Like pencils, charcoal is produced in a range of grades; with practice the different hardnesses can be utilized in creating a variety of tones. Willow charcoal (the most popular kind) can usually be obtained in three or four grades (extra soft, soft, medium and hard), in two lengths of 75mm (3 in.) and 150mm (6 in.) and in a variety of diameters, the thickest being about 12mm (½ in.). Vine charcoal is most commonly sold in 150mm (6 in.) lengths only.

Charcoal will make a mark on most drawing surfaces but it is best to use a paper with a heavy tooth where its crumbling consistency can be exploited to the best advantage in picking up the grain of that surface, giving a characteristic textured quality to a drawing. The fragility of the medium does have its disadvantages, however. Mistakes can be removed easily – but so can marks which were deliberate; therefore it is essential to fix a drawing immediately upon completion using a thin coat of a suitable spray varnish (see Adhesives, Tapes and Sprays, pp.112-119).

Natural chalks, as their name suggests, are naturally occurring soft mineral deposits of varying colour which have been used for centuries as a convenient drawing tool. A deposit of carboniferous shale gives black, while red is formed by iron oxide and white by chalk or gypsum. Red and black can be used in combination to form rich shades of brown, and white is invaluable for highlighting. Chalks can be used in a similar way to charcoal for both line and tone drawing: a precise mark may be made with the tip, especially when dipped in water to produce a solid dark line, but it is also possible to soften their effect and create tones by rubbing and blending, or to lay down solid areas of colour using bold side strokes. By the eighteenth century, the supply of high-quality natural chalk was dwindling to such an extent that manufacturing expertise was devoted to producing a fabricated version of similar quality which could take its place. During the nineteenth century, the man-made product almost completely replaced the natural product and is what we most commonly refer to today as 'chalk'.

Fabricated chalks and pastels, like compressed charcoal, are made by combining dry powdered pigments and a binding agent into a paste which is then formed into a stick. By controlling the proportion of pigments to binder, a large range of both colours and hardnesses can be produced. The larger the proportion of binder used, the harder the stick will be and the duller the colour will become. The softest and most friable sticks therefore produce the most brilliant colours and are ideal for a broad, bold style of working. The word 'pastel' is most commonly ascribed to this type while the harder varieties, used for smaller scale detailed work, should be termed 'chalks'.

It is not easy to mix colours using pastels (and this obviously cannot be done away from the drawing surface as with paints) so it is advisable to develop a technique of building up tone and tint variations by laying down areas of colour alongside or over one another. This technique obviously requires a larger range of available colours than would be necessary with paints, and the development of a more systematic working method. As mentioned above, the colour strength of the pastel can be varied according to its composition. Most manufacturers now produce a range of strengths from 0 to 8, the palest tint being 0. A beginner in the use of pastels would do best to select one light, one medium and one dark tone of each colour only and lay these out in a methodical way before starting. Useful beginners' combination sets are now available.

Pastels should be used with a degree of delicacy and care at first, especially if you are unused to the medium. Too heavy-handed a technique will only clog the grain of paper and make further applications of colour over the top almost impossible. Interesting tonal and textural effects can be achieved by varying the width, length and direction of the stroke made (using cross-hatching for instance)

rather than by too much vigorous rubbing and blending with the finger. Corrections are best made by dusting gently with a good-quality brush or lifting particles with a kneadable putty eraser. Pastel drawings should always be fixed immediately upon completion (see pp.112-119 for suitable products).

Oil pastels have a larger proportion of a greasy binding agent in their composition. This makes them more lightfast and resistant to rubbing and, unlike ordinary pastels, they often require no fixing. They are easier to blend on the drawing surface without producing a muddy, overworked effect – a common fault when using this medium – by using a turpentine wash. Dip a brush, cloth or rag, or even your fingertip, into the turpentine and paint it on the surface – this dissolves the binding agent and spreads the pigment across the surface.

The quality of the drawing surface is extremely important when using any sort of pastel. Because of their powdery nature a ground with a defined grain is needed to retain the loose particles of pigment. Many Ingres type papers are produced specifically for use with pastels (see Paper, pp.104-5), and have a variety of depth and pattern of texture. Paper which has a mid-tone, rather than white, is particularly interesting to use as the tint of the ground can be incorporated to effect into the general colour scheme of the drawing. Other suitable surfaces to use with this medium are stretched canvas, vellum or glasspaper (sandpaper).

Crayon is a word often applied, inaccurately, to what we call a coloured pencil. The term should properly be used to describe a short length of solid viscous pigment which has been made using a fatty binding medium. Crayons are available in two basic ranges – water-soluble and water-resistant, which have a particularly oily or waxy base. Both can be used on practically any surface and should be non-toxic. Oil crayons are similar to oil pastels but are generally even less friable, more easily blended and do not smudge. A lithographic crayon is a well-known example of an oil crayon. A rub with a soft cloth will fix them quite simply. Wax crayons are useful for any sort of wax-resist work. Water-soluble products can be blended with water and a brush so in many ways act as a convenient solid block of watercolour.

Caran d'Ache Neocolor I wax crayons (top), and Conté à Paris oil crayons.

BEROL

CASCADE
Colour range: black, red, blue, light blue, green, light green, brown, crimson, orange, purple, yellow, white
Large diameter soft wax crayons giving a dense and richly pigmented line. There is little problem from either grittiness or fragmentation with these particular wax crayons which are available singly or in sets of 12.

VERITHIK
Colour range: Ten colours
Standard pencil diameter sticks of colour with a thin plastic coating to give clean handling. The pigments are brilliant and intense but very smudge resistant, making them ideal for use in any situation where immaculate presentation or easy storage are required. Available in wallets of ten colours.

ARTWORKER
Colour range: black, red, dark blue, light blue, dark green, light green, brown, magenta, orange, red 8, ultramarine, burnt umber, deep yellow, lemon, white
A professional-quality square-shaped crayon produced in an unusual range of brilliant colours. They have a smooth, non-flaking consistency and would make a suitable, easy-to-handle choice for any beginner in this medium. Available in sets of 16 crayons.

AQUASTICK
Colour range: 12 colours
These are round-section, medium diameter water-soluble crayons offering the choice between standard drawing techniques and watercolour wash techniques when used with clean water and a brush. Available in sets of 12 sticks.

CARAN D'ACHE

NEOPASTEL
Colour range: 24 colours
This is a popular range of round-section artists' crayons favoured for their responsiveness and easy blending. Although soft in consistency, they produce little messy dust, and cover the surface evenly and cleanly. Available singly or in sets of 12 and 24 crayons.

NEOCOLOR I AND NEOCOLOR II AQUARELLE
Colour range: 30 colours

Both these ranges have acquired a high reputation among professionals for their good covering and blending characteristics. They are both light-resistant and can be used on practically any surface. Neocolor I has a waxy, oily base, is water-resistant and has a hard to medium consistency. Neocolor II is softer and more malleable, is water-soluble and offers the unlimited possibilities of watercolour style blending. Available singly or in sets of ten, 15 and 30 colours.

CONTÉ À PARIS

CONTÉ COMPRESSED CHARCOAL
Grades: 4B (extra soft), 3B (very soft), 2B (soft), B (medium soft), HB (medium)
This range of five grades of charcoal is suitable for all kinds of drawing and sketching.

CONTÉ CRAYONS
Colour range: black, white, sanguine natural, sanguine 18th century, sanguine Watteau, sanguine Medici, bistre
The traditional and popular range of square-section artists' crayons from France – so well known in fact that the name has become synonymous with this type of crayon. Easy to use and giving a smooth, relatively dust-free responsive feel, they are well established as a favourite among artists, illustrators and designers alike. White and black are produced in three grades of HB, B and 2B.
Conté also produce wood-cased pencils in similar shades as a complement to the crayons. These tend to have a slightly more chalky consistency.

FABER-CASTELL

PITT CHARCOAL
Grades: extra soft, soft, medium, hard, extra hard
Round-ended sticks of good-quality compressed charcoal produced mainly, although not entirely, from carbon black. They are available in cushioned boxes of 12 sticks.

NATURAL CHARCOAL
Line width: Varies from approximately 4mm to 12mm
A useful range of entirely natural charcoal, although obviously the degree of hardness for such a natural product cannot be defined as precisely as is possible for compressed charcoal. These charcoals are available packed in folding boxes of six sticks.

POLYCHROMOS PASTELS

Colour range: 72 colours

These are high-quality, soft, easy blending pastels with a high proportion of pigment to binder, producing brilliant and luminous colours. Nonetheless, they offer good adhesion to the drawing surface, fade resistance and stability when used with fixatives (see pp. 112-19). They have a square shape – convenient to prevent rolling – which gives both fine and broad strokes when necessary. Available in air-cushioned sets of 12, 24, 36 and 72 pastels.

Useful to note are the three specialist ranges of brown and grey shades. The brown set contains ten shades from light to dark plus black and white. Each grey set (cold and warm) contains two each of six shades at intervals of 20 per cent between black and white.

PITT ARTISTS' CRAYONS

Colour range: sepia, roman, van-Dyck, raw umber burnt, bister, sanguine unburnt light, sanguine unburnt dark, white, black unburnt, black burnt

Anti-rolling square-shaped pastels produced in the traditional brown colour spectrum. They are fade resistant and adhere well to the drawing surface but are recommended particularly for use on softer, textured papers. Similar pigments are produced in a pencil form with an outer coating of wood and these can be used for detailed work while the crayons are reserved for shading larger areas. The white and black crayons are available in both soft and medium grades.

GRUMBACHER

GRUMBACHER SOFT PASTELS

Colour range: 144 colours

Perhaps the largest available range of high-quality soft pastels. They are popular both for this immense selection of tints and for their consistency which gives good uniform coverage and subtle blending. Each stick comes with a paper sleeve, helping to keep hands and work surfaces clean, and combination sets are packaged in either cardboard or plastic interlocking trays. Available in sets of 12, 24, 30, 48, 90 and 144 pastels.

NUPASTEL

Colour range: 96 colours

Square-section pastels having a less friable consistency than most others of this type, thus allowing for the easy creation and blending of subtle and delicate shades. The large range of rich pigments gives good coverage on most textured papers. Available in sets of 12, 24, 36, 48, 60, 72 and 96 colours.

PRANG

PRANG CRAYONEX CRAYONS

Colour range: 48 colours

A usefully large range of solid wax crayons which will draw on any surface and can be repointed using a standard pencil sharpener. The colours are brilliant and non-toxic, and available in sets of 16, 24 and 48 colours.

REMBRANDT

SOFT PASTELS

Colour range: 180 colours

These pastels are pleasant to use, with strength of colour, optical brilliance and permanence.

Available in worksets of 15, 30, 45 (landscape and portrait), 60, 90 (both portrait) and 180 (landscape and portrait) colours.

SAKURA

CRAYPAS

Colour range: 25 colours

Round sticks of colour which are something of an intermediary between pastels and crayons. The pigments are vivid and brilliant but have the slightly more oily consistency of a crayon. Using a stump or fingertip they can be blended on the drawing surface. Their clean handling qualities and economical price make them popular with beginners in this medium. Available in sets of 12, 16 and 25 colours.

SCHWAN-STABILO

CARB-OTHELLO

Colour range: 60 colours

This range is called 'coloured charcoal' by its manufacturer, a term which quite adequately describes its chalky nature. It is an extremely popular, versatile and recommended product, since it is available as both a wood-cased pencil for fine line work and, in a more limited range of 36 colours, in the form of a solid square chalk for larger or bolder areas. The colours are rich and lightfast and lend themselves easily to blending, shading and intermixing. Both are available singly or in sets of 12, 24, 36, 48 and 60 colours.

SHARPENING PENCILS

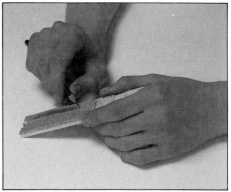

1 Hold the pencil firmly with your hand about halfway down the stem. Place the scalpel (X-Acto) blade about 15mm (⅝ in.) from the pencil tip and cut on a slight slope towards the lead. Always cut away from your body, rotating the stem after each stroke and shaving off only a small quantity of wood and graphite at a time.

2 When about 8 to 10mm (¼-⅜ in.) of lead has been exposed, rotate it slowly against a fine sandpaper (glasspaper) block to achieve a point. Repeat this motion against a piece of cartridge (drawing) paper or smooth dust from the point with a soft tissue.

USING GRAPHITE PENCILS

1 When accuracy and detail are required, use a pencil with a hard lead (2H to 5H) and hold it upright. Soft leads smudge easily and create a darker but less crisp line.

2 Flat shading with graphite pencils is most easily achieved by using medium to soft leads (2B to 6B). Hold the pencil far down the stem and almost horizontal to the paper. Move over the surface with very light, even strokes.

3 Hard edges and highlights can be produced by rubbing out with a soft eraser.

4 Masking off areas with masking tape or masking film can protect areas yet to be worked on, as well as creating a hard edge to a graphite drawing.

I Lay down an area of pencil, and work it with a torchon. The absorbent nature of the torchon will pick up the graphite particles and spread them into the artwork.

2 Alternatively, shave graphite dust from the pencil, and pick up the particles on the torchon. Use this as a means of creating a broad pencil.

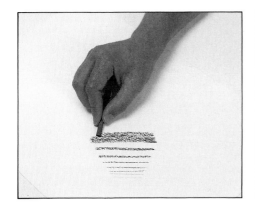

I Charcoal gives black, very soft lines. Used lightly it picks up the surface texture of almost any paper.

2 Large areas are covered by gentle shading, then blending using a cottonwool (absorbent cotton) pad or your finger.

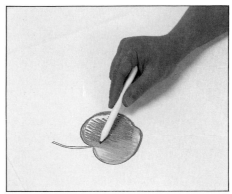

3 Shaded areas can be highlighted by using a kneadable eraser or white chalk. The eraser is also useful for lightening and blending.

4 Alternatively, use a torchon to blend the charcoal particles, in the same way as described for graphite pencils above.

**USING COLOURED
PENCILS**

1 Shaded areas and texture can be produced by cross-hatching techniques. Use drawn multidirectional lines and do not attempt to blend the different colours.

2 Restricting hatching to a single direction creates a sketchy appearance. Use different coloured pencils to create subtle changes in tone.

3 Using water-soluble coloured pencils enables you to achieve what is, in effect, a combination of watercolour and pencil. Lay down an area of coloured pencil.

4 Work the pencilled area with a fine brush and water. Apply colour to small areas at a time, then work them, then lay on more colour to build up a drawing.

I Lay down the outline of the image in oil pastel.

2 This line image can then be worked as described for water-soluble pencils on p.54. Blend and then work the areas of colour using a paintbrush, cottonwool bud (Q-tip swab) or tissue moistened with solvent.

3 Areas of oil pastel can be laid down on a sheet of paper, to create a 'paint palette'.

4 Colours can also be mixed away from the drawing surface and applied using a cottonwool bud (Q-tip swab), dipped in solvent.

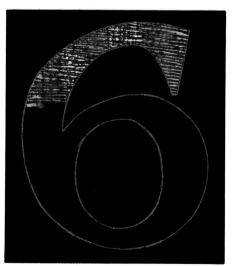

5 Cover the surface of a sheet paper in wax crayon. A number of different colours can be used. Over this put down a layer of black acrylic paint. When the paint is dry, scratch it away in a design to reveal the coloured crayon underneath.

**USING COLOURED
PASTELS**

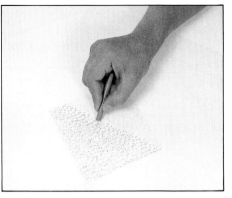

1 Lines drawn with coloured pastel are soft-edged. Short, unblended strokes and/or dots create a pointilist effect.

2 For larger areas of flat colour, scrape pastel dust from a stick with a scalpel (X-Acto knife).

3 Moisten a paintbrush or cottonwool bud (Q-tip swab) with white spirit (paint thinner), and use this to spread the colour.

4 When the solvent evaporates, the area can be worked on further.

5 Colours can be blended together during drawing by smudging with your fingertip or a tissue. Continue to work on the area until the desired effect is achieved.

1 To produce an area of flat colour, scrape some dust from a pastel stick, mixing colours if required. Prepare the drawing surface by dusting with talcum powder.

2 Pick up the pastel dust using a cottonwool (absorbent cotton) pad and dab on to the paper. Keep the colour density even, and smooth off excess with a tissue.

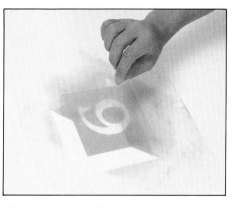

3 Hard edges and highlights can be created by removing areas of pastel with a kneadable eraser.

4 Alternatively, mask off larger areas before you lay down the initial colour.

5 Lines drawn with conté sticks are soft-edged and smooth.

6 For a broad line, or large areas of even colour, lay the stick on its side, and draw it across the paper.

MARKERS

The advent of markers and their increasing popularity among designers have made quite a change in studio techniques and practices over recent years. Convenient to use, markers are responsive to all kinds of drawing styles, offering endless applications and, as manufacturers provide an even wider choice of nib sizes and compatible colour ranges, they are now employed extensively at all stages of the design process, from layout to finished artwork.

STUDIO MARKERS

Markers can be divided into two distinct groups – water-based and spirit (alcohol)-based – the latter giving good intermixing qualities but being insoluble in water and having a relatively short life due to the fast evaporation of solvents. Water-based markers can be rendered over one another to create a layered effect rather than blending together in one wash. Both kinds of marker dry up quickly if the caps are left off so care must be taken to replace these after use. However, a new development is the valve action felt tip in which ink from the reservoir is only released by a valve when the tip is pressed on to the drawing surface. Ink supply stops when this pressure stops, so preventing drying out when the cap is removed.

Two different processes are now employed in the construction of the drawing nibs for markers. The nib of a felt tip is made from either wool, a synthetic material or a combination of the two and is often chamfered so that it can produce fine, medium and broad lines. These are usually used for layout work. Fibre tips, varying from supple to firm, can give either medium or fine lines but have extended lives as they are made from more hard-wearing resin-bonded synthetic fibres. This type is more often used for detailed, precise work.

With a little practice, it is possible to produce very high-quality visuals using markers, approximating very closely to photographs or illustrations in other media. The characteristic 'bleed' of spirit (alcohol)- based markers can be used to advantage when mixing washes of colour freely on the page while more detailed line work can be achieved by combining spirit (alcohol)- and water-based products.

BEROL

WATERCOLOUR
Line width: Varies from approximately 1.0mm to 5.0mm
Colour range: black, red, blue, green, light blue, light green, grey, orange, yellow, pink, purple
A chisel-tipped marker for papers. The colours are water-based, so will not bleed and can be overlaid to create different shades and tones.

PERMANENT MARKER
Line width: Varies from approximately 1.0mm to 5.0mm
Colour range: black, red, blue, green
Similar in character to the Watercolour marker but can permanently mark almost any surface, this is available with either a chisel or bullet tip.

BOARDWRITER
Line width: Varies from approximately 1.0mm to 6.0mm
Colour range: black, red, blue, green, brown
A water-based marker with a chisel tip specially developed for use on white laminate display boards. The ink will wipe off with a damp cloth.

TOUGHPOINT
Line width: Varies from approximately 1.0mm to 4.0mm
Colour range: black, red, blue, green, brown, yellow
The bullet-shaped acrylic nib of this marker was designed for particularly heavy-duty use on both abrasive and smooth surfaces.

VALVEMARKER
Line width: Varies from approximately 1.0mm to 6.0mm
Colour range: black, red, blue, green, brown, orange, yellow, purple
Berol's unique valve action shuts off the ink supply when the marker is not in use, even with the cap off. Although originally intended for industry, this feature makes the Valvemarker ideal for use around the designer's studio. The ink is permanent and will function on most surfaces.

MAGNUM
Line width: One width only 13mm
Colour range: black, red, blue, green
An extra-broad permanent felt tip ideal for poster work and large coverage.

FLO-MASTER STANDARD AND FLO-MASTER KING SIZE
Colour range: transparent black, transparent red, transparent blue, semi-opaque silver
A new development, this extremely versatile refillable valve action marker with a selection of interchangeable nibs (bullet, chisel and wedge

shapes are available for both sizes) allows one tool and one type of ink to complete all aspects of a single job. The Standard version has an ink capacity of 8ml which is increased to 18ml for the King Size. Refill inks and cleanser are supplied.

COLOURPEN, COLOURSTICK AND COLOURBRUSH

Line width: Varies from approximately 0.5mm to 4.0mm

Colour range: black, red, blue, green, light blue, light green, brown, orange, yellow, pink, purple, grey

An economical, usefully co-ordinating range of water-based fibre tips with different nib characteristics for various applications. The Colourpen has a tapered tough nylon fibre tip for detailed work on small areas while the Colourstick and Colourbrush are designed with broader tips for larger coverage. The Colourbrush, which has an extended supple polyester fibre nib is particularly versatile and can generate both fine and broad lines in much the same way as an artist's brush. All three types are available singly or in wallets of six and 12 pens.

PRISMACOLOR ART MARKERS

Line width: Approximately 1.0mm for Fine nib; varies from approximately 1.0mm to 5.0mm for Broad nib

Colour range: 118 colours, metallic gold and silver

An ingenious double-ended spirit (alcohol)-based marker with a fine nib at one end and a broad, wedge-shaped nib at the other – perfect for ensuring exact colour match between the detailed and broad areas of a drawing. The colours will not bleed and are available in both bright, vivid tints and subtle shades for realistic rendering of tones.

Useful sets of 12 co-ordinating colours are packaged for particular needs, for example, Architects' Colours, Wood Colours, Warm Greys, Cold Greys and Portrait Colours. All markers are available singly or in sets of 12, 24, 48, 72 and 120 colours.

CARAN D'ACHE

FIBRALO MARKERS FINE, MEDIUM AND LARGE

Line width: Varies from 0.5mm to 1.0mm for Fine; approximately 1.0mm for Medium; approximately 2.0mm for Large

Colour range: 40 colours in Medium width; ten colours in Fine and Large

The Medium width is the most familiar and well used of these art markers and, like the Fine pen, gives smooth-flowing water-resistant ink. The

Fine and Large pens can be bought in wallets of ten, the Medium is available in sets of six, ten, 15, 24, 30 and 40 colours.

CHARTPAK

AD MARKER

Line width: Varies according to tip used, from approximately 0.9mm to 6.0mm

Colour range: 200 colours

An adaptable long-lasting design marker supplied in a prolific range of intense colours. The basic barrel and ink reservoir can be used with any one of four interchangeable points – fine line, bullet, wedge and brush – making it a very versatile tool, suitable for the detailed and broad aspects of any job. Available singly or in sets of 30 colours.

EBERHARD-FABER

DESIGN ART MARKER

Line width: Varies according to tip used, from approximately 0.4mm to 6.0mm

Colour range: 96 colours with oblique chisel (regular) tip; 48 colours with bullet tip; 48 colours with fine tip

This is a slim metal-bodied co-ordinating range of spirit (alcohol)-based markers in three different nib styles – a useful feature for quick changes between outline and in-filling work. Each colour in the range is supplied with a highlight, middle tone and shadow value for easy rendering of tonal drawings. Complementary to these markers is the Eberhard-Faber Colorless Blender, containing a solvent which aids precise shading and tonal graduations in work done with spirit (alcohol)-based markers. It can be used to mix and blend colours on the page or to reduce the intensity of any individual colour.

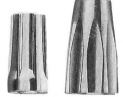

EDDING

EDDING 600 GRAFIK ART MARKER

Line width: Varies from approximately 1.0mm to 7.0mm

Colour range: 80 colours

A spirit (alcohol)-based design marker which has proved a firm favourite with those professionals who have discovered the range. It is comfortable to use and has a firm, precise, chisel tip. The lifespan of these markers can be extended considerably by replacing this tip. Also available is the Edding 600 Blender, a colourless solvent marker used to shade, intermix or brighten all colours.

EDDING 650 GRAFIK PAINTER

Line width: Varies from approximately 3.0mm to 7.0mm

Colour range: 20 colours, including white
Unlike a more traditional marker, the Grafik Painter's very rounded, thick bullet tip produces viscous, opaque colours of a pasty consistency which can be used on nearly all materials including rough or uneven surfaces. The paint dries quickly and is rubproof and waterproof. It is a versatile drawing tool, closer in feel to a crayon or pastel than a marker, and is well suited to freely executed drawing and sketching.

The Edding 950 model is similar but has a 10mm tip and is available in black, red, blue, yellow, white.

EDDING 3000 and 3300/2000 and 2200

Line width: Varies from 1.5mm to 3.0mm (bullet tip) for the 3000; from 2.0mm to 6.0mm (oblique chisel tip) for the 3300

Colour range: 20 colours
These are similar to the Grafik Art Markers but are completely refillable with Edding T25 and T100 bottled inks, and have replaceable tips. The colour range of permanent inks is smaller, but they will write on practically any surface.

EDDING 500, 800 AND 850

Line width: Varies from 2.0mm to 7.0mm for the 500; from 4.0mm to 12.0mm for the 800; from 5.0mm to 20.0mm for the 850

Colour range: black, red, blue, green, yellow, orange, brown, violet, pink, light blue
Identical to the 3000 and 3300 in almost every respect, these markers have chunkier aluminium barrels and very robust broad wedge tips for large lettering and poster work and industrial use. Except for the 850, which is only produced in the first four colours, the range in such broad markers is usefully comprehensive.

EDDING NO. 1 AND NO. 2

Line width: Varies from 2.0mm to 5.0mm (oblique chisel tip) for the No. 1; from 1.5mm to 3.0mm (bullet tip) for the No. 2

Colour range: black, red, blue, green, yellow, orange, brown, violet, pink, light blue
Again utilizing Edding's replaceable tip construction and refillable reservoir, these are handy pocket models with shorter tapered barrels and highly permanent inks.

EDDING 1300 AND 1200

Line width: Approximately 3.0mm for the 1300; varies from 0.5mm to 1.0mm for the 1200

Colour range: 48 for the 1300; 24 for the 1200
These are useful companion fibre-tip pens, in the medium and fine widths, to the Grafik Art Marker. Due to their water base they will not bleed into areas laid down by the broader pen, and will produce strong, intense colours.

EDDING 1250

Line width: Varies from approximately 0.75mm to 3.0mm

Colour range: black, red, blue, green, yellow, orange, brown, violet, pink, light blue, light green, grey
This pen could also be used in conjunction with the Grafik Art Marker as it, too, is water-based. It has an oblique chisel tip, unusual in a fine grade marker, which makes it ideal for lettering, ruler work and in-filling solid areas of intense colour.

EDDING 1380

Line width: Entirely variable

Colour range: black, red, blue, green, yellow, orange, brown, violet, pink, light blue, light green, grey
The supple nylon brush tip of this pen makes it a very flexible instrument for rendering brush drawings, rough sketches and layouts. The water-soluble ink can be diluted into washes across the page using the pen or another brush.

EDDING 750 AND 751

Line width: Varies from 2.0mm to 4.0mm for the 750; from 1.0mm to 2.0mm for the 751

Colour range: 15 colours, including white; five metallic colours, five metallic silver with coloured outlines; five fluorescent colours
A large capacity valve-action marker with replaceable tip, and an excellent 'cap off' life. The ink is highly permanent, rubproof and waterproof, giving an opaque lacquer type finish, but the pens must be shaken well before use to ensure thorough mixing of the solvents and pigments.

EDDING 250

Line width: Varies from approximately 1.5mm to 3.0mm

Colour range: black, red, blue, green, yellow, orange, brown, violet, pink, light blue
Designed for laminate display boards, this model contains special ink that can be removed from non-porous surfaces with a dry cloth but will act like a normal permanent marker on all porous surfaces. It is usefully fine for such a boardmarker.

EDDING 200 AND 215

Line width: Varies from 1.0mm to 5.0mm for the 200; from 1.0mm to 3.0mm for the 215

Colour range: yellow, orange, pink, light blue, light green
Long-life fluorescent markers designed for highlighting important copy. The 200 is a chunky pocket model with an oblique chisel tip; the 215 is finer for use on small closely printed text.

FABER-CASTELL

TEXTLINER AND TEXTLINER 2000

Line width: Varies from 1.0mm to 5.0mm
Colour range: yellow, orange, red, pink, blue, green

A versatile range of fluorescent highlighting markers designed with a convenient non-roll flat barrel and a large ink capacity. The blue marker will not reproduce on most photocopies while orange can be used over ink-written text without smudging. Red and blue can also be used on NCR-type papers. A companion fine-tipped version, the Textliner 2000 (2.0mm tip), is also available, in yellow, orange and green. .

PENOL 100

Line width: Varies from 1.0mm to 10.0mm
Colour range: black, red, blue, green

A permanent extra-broad marker equipped with a 10 × 10mm square-section felt tip. It will write on both porous and non-porous surfaces.

The Penol 1000 is identical but has a 11 × 18mm felt tip.

PENOL 700 and 750

Line width: Varies from 0.5mm to 3.0mm (bullet tip) for the 700; from 1.0mm to 4.0mm (chisel tip) for the 750
Colour range: black, red, blue, green

A range of permanent markers for use on card, metal, plastic, foil, films and most other surfaces.

PENOL PAINT MARKERS 50, 51, 52

Line width: Approximately 2.0mm for medium 50; approximately 1.2mm for fine 51; approximately 0.8mm for superfine 52
Colour range: Nine colours, including white; six metallic colours; eight silver and gold metallic with coloured outlines

This range of markers features an acrylic-based paint-like medium which is totally permanent and opaque so that one colour can be laid down over another. They are water resistant and will paint on almost any surface. The outline marker, packaged under the title of 'Paint Festival', produces an opaque stroke with coloured outlines only if used on paper. When used on a smooth surface it produces a metallic finish with a shimmering tint of colour.

LETRASET

PANTONE COLOUR MARKERS

Line width: Varies according to tip used, from approximately 0.4mm to 6.0mm
Colour range: 203 colours with broad tip; 104 colours with fine tip

The Pantone range offers the widest choice of colour marker in the world. The range covers both broad and fine tip pens and ties in with other products in the Pantone Matching System (see The Pantone System, pp.123-5). The marker has a slim, comfortable squared-off barrel which helps to stop the pen rolling from the work surface, and a double seal twist-off cap to prevent drying out. (White caps for broad tips, black caps for fine tips.) The broad-tipped version is spirit (alcohol)-based and the fine tip water-based, enabling detailed work to be carried out over broad backgrounds without intermixing or bleeding. Both bright and pastel shades are provided along with 34 different greys for monotonal work.

MARVY

Not available in the UK

MARVY ART AND DESIGN WATERCOLOR MARKERS

Line width: Varies from approximately 0.5mm to 1.0mm for Fine; approximately 1.0mm for Medium
Colour range: 60 colours

Non-toxic, water-based markers giving good pigment intensity. They are smooth to use and provide a usefully comprehensive selection of both bright and subtle colours, including a set of eight different greys for tonal shading. Available in sets of 8, 12, 18, 24, 36, 48 and 60 colours. (Fine available in sets of 24, 36, 48 and 60 colours.)

MARVY BRUSH MARKER

Line width: Entirely variable
Colour range: 60 colours

A brush-type marker in a pleasingly wide selection of water-based colours. The tip gives a soft, manoeuvrable feel but is durable enough for sustained use without feathering.

MECANORMA

MECANORMA ART MARKERS

Line width: Varies from 1.0mm to 6.0mm
Colour range: 92 colours, including 11 warm greys, 11 cold greys, 8 'wood tones', 24 pastel shades

Wedge-tipped, spirit (alcohol)-based, permanent markers giving transparent, uniformly flat tints which can be superimposed and mixed. A tight-fitting cap gives good protection against premature drying out. The 'wood tone' set is particularly useful for visualizing architectural drawings.

Available singly or in sets of 24.

EXTRA-FINE TIP ART MARKER

Line width: Approximately 1.0mm
Colour range: 24 colours
Containing exactly the same permanent, superimposable inks as the ordinary Art Marker range, these have unusually fine, precise tips for detailed work and outlining. Can be used separately or in conjunction with the 92 wedge-tipped Art Markers. The extra fine-tipped versions have white caps to distinguish them easily in use from the black caps of the wedge-tips.

NIJI (YASUTOMO & CO LTD)

INSTA-BRUSH

Line width: Entirely variable
Colour range: black, red, blue, green, brown, orange, yellow, lime, grey, pink, sky blue, purple
Another pen which combines the advantages of a marker with the feel and versatility of a brush, this type is particularly responsive to different drawing techniques. It has a resilient nylon tip giving water-based quick-drying ink. Available singly or in a set of eight colours.

METALLIC MARKERS EXTRA FINE AND SMALL NIB

Line width: Approximately 0.6mm for Extra Fine; approximately 1.0mm for Small Nib
Colour range: gold, silver, blue, green, pink, lavender, non-metallic white
Metallic waterproof ink which dries instantly on virtually any surface. Extra Fine is available in gold and silver only.

HI-BALL

Line width: Varies from 0.8mm to 3.0mm for chisel tip
Colour range: blue, pink, yellow
A convenient double-ended pen combining a highlighter with a ballpoint, particularly useful when checking copy or printed matter. The ballpoint writes with black ink and the chisel-tipped highlighter uses one of three fluorescent colours.

PENTEL

PENTEL PEN N50

Line width: Varies from 1.0mm to 2.0mm
Colour range: 12 colours
A tough, durable and waterproof bullet-point marker suitable for both rough and smooth surfaces. The cap clicks conveniently on to the end of the barrel while the pen is in use. The Pentel N60 has a chisel point and is only available in black, red, blue and green.

PENTEL FELT PEN F50

Line width: Varies from 1.0mm to 5.0mm
Colour range: black, red, blue, green, brown, orange, yellow, violet
A chunky wedge-shaped felt tip ideal for all general-purpose marking. The ink is permanent and waterproof. An extra broad version, with a line width of 3.0mm to 9.0mm, is available in black, red, blue and green.

PENTEL PAINT MARKERS MEDIUM AND FINE POINT

Line width: Approximately 2.0mm for Medium point; approximately 1.0mm for Fine point
Colour range: 15 colours, including gold, silver and copper
Valve-controlled markers containing a quick-drying opaque medium for use on plastic, glass, rubber or metal.

PENTEL WHITE MARKER

Line width: Approximately 2.0mm
Another valve-action felt tip, this time offering very opaque quick-drying white ink on rubber, metal, glass or plastic.

PENTEL COLOUR PEN

Line width: Approximately 0.7mm
Colour range: 36 colours
A useful range of water-soluble fine fibre-tipped pens, producing bright intense colours for use on their own or in conjunction with spirit (alcohol)-based markers. They can be obtained singly or in sets of six, 12, 18, 24 and 36 colours.

PENTEL SIGN PEN

Line width: Approximately 1.0mm
Colour range: 12 colours
Pentel's original fibre pen, of a similar nature to the Colour Pen but with a slightly broader tip.

PENTEL SEE-THRU MARKER

Line width: Varies from 1.0mm to 3.0mm
Colour range: orange, yellow, light green, pink
A wedge-shaped transparent ink highlighter which is fine enough for either underlining or over-marking on small print.

PILOT

SUPER COLOUR MARKERS

Line width: Approximately 1.0mm for Fine (SC-F bullet tip); approximately 0.9mm for Fine (SC-FII bullet tip); varies from 2.0mm to 4.5mm for Broad (SC-B chisel tip)

Colour range: black, red, blue, green, purple, brown, orange, yellow

Universal, general-purpose permanent markers with a large ink capacity which will write on almost any surface. The broad version is also available with a short chunky barrel for carrying in a pocket.

SUPER COLOUR MARKER SC-6600

Line width: Varies from 3.0mm to 10.0mm
Colour range: black, red, blue, green

A refillable and long-lasting industrial marker with a jumbo chisel tip. The quick-drying, permanent, oil-based ink will write on practically any surface.

SUPER COLOUR PAINT MARKERS

Line width: Approximately 0.8mm (plastic tipped – see Ballpoints and Rolling Writers, pp. 77-9) for Extra Fine; approximately 1.2mm for Fine; approximately 2.0mm for Medium; varies from 1.0mm to 4.0mm for Broad (chisel tip)
Colour range: Ten colours, including white; eight metallic colours, including silver and gold

A very similar range to the Faber-Castell Penol Paint Markers (see p. 63), containing permanent opaque type ink which will write on practically any surface. Also available are unusually broad (10.3 × 17.0mm felt tip) super jumbo gold and silver markers, using the same ink.

COLOUR PENS AND COLOUR BRUSH

Line width: Varies from 0.5mm to 4.0mm, according to tip used
Colour range: 24 colours

Two versions of the Colour Pen are available, one with a fine bullet tip varying from 0.5mm to 1.0mm, and one with a chisel-shaped tip giving a stroke varying from 0.5mm to 4.0mm. Entirely compatible with these is the Brush Pen which has a flexible polyester tip. These three products combine to provide a comprehensive co-ordinating range of water-based pens for detailed work and medium coverage. They can be obtained singly or in vinyl pouches of three, four, six, eight, ten, 12 and 24 colours.

ROYAL SOVEREIGN

Not available in the USA

MAGIC MARKER STUDIO COLOURS

Line width: Varies from 1.0mm to 7.0mm
Colour range: 123 colours

The leading and most popular marker among professional graphic designers today. Its chisel-shaped oblique felt tip and spirit (alcohol)-based ink are good for both subtle colour combination in flat washes and a variety of line effects. The colour range makes it the ideal marker for presentation visuals and layouts. Can be bought separately or in sets of 12 colours.

SLIMGRIP

Line width: Varies from 1.0mm to 7.0mm
Colour range: 48 colours

This marker is a slimmed-down version of the Studio Colour range, retaining the four-way chisel point but incorporating a larger ink capacity in its extended barrel. For those who do not like the 'chunky' feel in the hand of the Studio Colours, this could be a good alternative.

MMIO

Line width: Approximately 0.4mm
Colour range: black, red, blue, green, orange, yellow, purple, pink

The water base of this fine line marker is incompatible with the spirit (alcohol) base of the Studio Colours and Slimgrip ranges so preventing intermixing or 'bleed'. This makes it ideal for rendering outlines or detailed work before filling in with a broader nib.

SCHWAN-STABILO

STABILAYOUT

Line width: Varies from approximately 1.0mm to 5.0mm
Colour range: 70 colours

Although having a smaller colour range than Magic Markers, these high-quality wedge-shaped markers are often adopted for use by professionals. As their name suggests, they are particularly useful for layouts and visuals. They have a large ink capacity and, being water-based, a good 'cap off' life and intense ink which will not penetrate most papers. Due to its flat shape, the marker will not roll away and the colour coded barrels make identification easy. Can be bought singly, in wallets of 25, or worksets of 20 colours.

STABILO PEN 68

Line width: Varies from approximately 0.4mm to 4.0mm
Colour range: 50 colours

A fibre-tip pen which is complementary to the Stabilayout range for more detailed work. The large selection of colours in this fine to medium width is not common, making it a popular range with designers, and its slim barrel makes it usable with compasses. Like Stabilayout it has a good 'cap off' life and, although it dries immediately on paper, the ink can be loosened with water. Available singly or in metal tins of ten, 15, 20, 30, 40 and 50 colours.

STABILO BOSS

Line width: Varies from 1.0mm to 5.0mm
Colour range: red, blue, green, yellow, orange, pink, turquoise, lilac
Styled to the same specifications as the Stabilayout range, this is a fluorescent highlighting marker, useful for emphasizing words and phrases in copy. The inks are transparent and will not damage text material.

STABILOPLAN BOARD MARKER

Line width: Varies from approximately 1.0mm to 5.0mm
Colour range: black, red, blue, green, brown, violet
Although retaining the familiar Stabilo external shape, this marker has a bullet tip and is especially designed for use on write-on wipe-off boards. The special inks dry quickly but are easy to remove using a rag or cloth.

STAEDTLER

MARSGRAPHIC 3000 LAYOUT MARKER

Line width: Entirely variable
Colour range: 60 colours
A versatile brush-type layout marker with a soft foam tip, this contains fast-drying, water-based ink which will not smudge or bleed. The large range includes basic colours plus toning pastel shades, skin tones and a selection of greys. Available singly or in sets of 10, 30 and 60 colours.

MICROLINE S 331

Line width: Approximately 0.40mm
Colour range: black, red, dark blue, light blue, dark green, light green, orange, yellow, violet, brown
Corresponding to the same basic colour range, these fine markers provide useful tools for detailed line work on layouts and sketches produced with the Marsgraphic 3000.

TOMBOW

DUAL BRUSH PEN

Line width: Varies from 0.5mm to 1.4mm for fibre tip; entirely variable for brush tip
Colour range: 72 colours
A double-ended pen with both a fibre tip and a flexible brush tip, generating a wide range of line widths in identical colour shades. The water-based ink will not smear and is supplied in a particularly large reservoir to give extended life to both tips. The colour selection, including 16 shades of grey, is very comprehensive for a pen of this kind, making it a particularly useful tool for layout work and presentation visuals.

FINE LINE MARKERS

Fine fibre-tipped pens have advanced technologically to such a degree of precision and accuracy that they are now produced to the high standards required of drafting pens and are being marketed as their competitors. Some of these products now combine the advantages of a marker (non-clogging instant ink flow, no maintenance, convenience) with the precision required for technical drawing. However, it is necessary to be vigilant when choosing to use these pens for finished artwork. The ink must be dense enough to reproduce well and the tip must not spread, otherwise accurate and consistent line width cannot be guaranteed. Apart from these reservations, this type of pen is ideal for rendering small type and accomplishing precise roughs and layouts, as well as for writing and sketching.

EDDING

EDDING 1800/1880 PROFIPEN

Line widths: Three widths 0.10mm, 0.30mm, 0.50mm
Colour range: black, red, blue, green
Designed with stencils and straight-edges in mind, this disposable pen is popular with designers for both accurate drawing and writing. The pigmented ink is waterproof and lightfast.

FABER-CASTELL

TECPEN

Line widths: Three widths 0.20mm, 0.50mm, 0.70mm
Colour range: black, red, blue, green
An inexpensive disposable drawing pen which

produces precise lines which do not bleed. This pen is particularly useful for accurate layout work as, in conjunction with a special adaptor, it can be attached to a compass.

NIKKO

FINEPOINT SYSTEM AND NEW FINEPOINT SYSTEM

Line widths: Six widths from 0.10mm to 0.80mm

Colour range: black, red, blue, green
Manufactured particularly for designers and draftsmen, and available in a comprehensive choice of line widths, this range is ideal for use with variously sized lettering guides and templates. The special formula ink does not dry up in the pen. The New Finepoint System pens are identical but have permanent ink (black only) for use on film, and are ideal for dyeline work.

FINEPOINT 99-L

Line width: Approximately 0.30mm
Colour range: black, red, blue, green
Although exact line width is not guaranteed, the ink in these pens is reproduceable and will not dry up, even when the pen is left uncapped.

PENFORAL PEN

Line widths: Three widths 0.20mm, 0.30mm, 0.50mm
Colour range: black, red, blue, green
A slimline pen with a high line consistency which will not dry up even if left uncapped.

ROTRING

VARIOGRAPH

Line widths: Four widths 0.2mm, 0.3mm, 0.5mm, 0.7mm
Colour range: black, red, blue, green
Although available in fewer line widths, these pens are comparable to the Tombow range with many of the same characteristics and give a long service life. The replaceable fibre tip is adjustable for both writing and drawing by twisting the nib section and a spare tip is carried in the colour-coded end stopper. The pen is suitable for use with stencils and drafting guides and is refillable in a few seconds by standing the reservoir upright in the special Rotring ink bottles.

FINOGRAPH

Line widths: Three widths 0.20mm, 0.30mm, 0.50mm
Colour range: black, red, blue, green
This fine line fibre tip uses pigmented lightfast,

waterproof ink which produces excellent line quality, is erasable on tracing paper and drafting film and reproduces well. It is not refillable and the tip cannot be adjusted but the pen is suitable for use with drafting guides.

TOMBOW

TOMBOW LINE SYSTEM PG

Line widths: Seven widths from 0.18mm to 0.70mm

Colour range: 16 colours
A system of refillable fine line markers, very similar in appearance to a traditional drafting pen. The special fibre tip is held in a stainless steel tube, allowing use of the pen with stencils and drafting guides, and its length can be adjusted to compensate for wear or personal drawing style using the cone key in the end of the cap. A spare tip is supplied in the barrel end of each pen. Refilling is easily accomplished by standing the reservoir end of the pen upright in the special Tombow ink bottles. The 16 water-based ink colours now available for these pens makes them suitable for a diverse range of applications.

Tombow inks should only be used with Tombow markers.

TOMBOW PG-SX

Line widths: Seven widths from 0.18mm to 0.70mm

Colour range: black only
The grey barrel of this Tombow Liner denotes its compatibility with the special Tombow Pigment Ink PG-IP which is quick-drying, dense, waterproof and erasable on tracing paper, making it suitable for reproduction purposes. It is similar in all other respects to the basic PG range.

FILLING AN AREA USING MARKERS

To fill an area evenly with flat colour you must work fast, constantly moving backwards and forwards over previously laid down colour in order to keep it wet. Practise on scrap paper, using a simple square shape.

1 With a broad, wedge-shaped marker, lay a strip of colour down first the left-hand margin, then along the top edge. Work downwards and outwards from these points in diagonal overlapping strips to keep them wet.

2 When you get about halfway across the square put in another strip along the bottom edge. Continue working upwards from the bottom left-hand corner in diagonal strokes until you reach the right-hand edge.

MARKER TECHNIQUES

1 Use masking tape to create edges to an area to be filled with marker. Work boldly across the masked area.

2 Carefully peel away the tape. The edge will not be absolutely crisp as the marker will bleed slightly under the tape.

3 Work in this way if you want a solid patch of colour, or two areas of colour next to each other.

4 Create a tonal effect or blend the colours using a cottonwool (absorbent cotton) pad soaked in solvent. This technique will work for spirit (alcohol)-based markers.

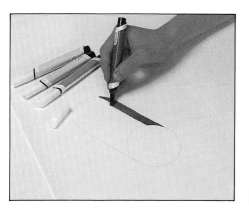

I Use streaks of warm or cool greys to build up a feeling of solidity on three-dimensional objects. Have at least four or five different tones laid out ready in sequence from light to dark.

2 Work quickly so that areas of different tones blend into each other while they are still wet, avoiding harsh lines where the different colours meet.

3 Use a fine fibre-tipped pen to delineate outlines or detailed parts of a drawing. If you are using spirit(alcohol)-based markers, the fibre-tipped pen should be water-based (and vice versa) to prevent bleeding and intermixing.

4 To give added realism, highlights can be added at the final stage using a white pencil or white gouache. The pencil would give a softer effect while gouache produces a sharp, bright highlight for shiny or metallic surfaces.

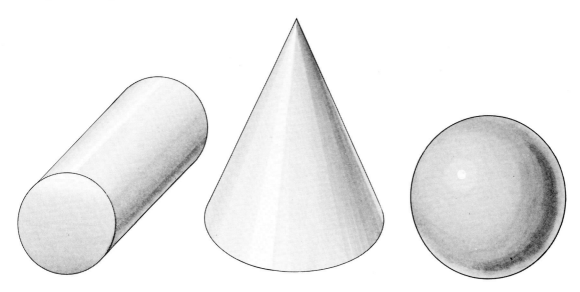

PENS AND INKS

The graphic designer today can select from a wide choice of pens and nibs (and there is a correspondingly broad range of suitable inks), choosing the ideal tool to achieve any desired effect. This section looks at these products, and advises on their suitability for different design needs.

PENS AND NIBS

Calligraphy pen and a selection of nibs.

Quills and reed pens (now largely replaced by steel-nibbed dip/technical pens) are not widely available but can still be obtained in specialist art shops. Although not durable (due to the softness of the tip), quills are particularly adaptable as they can be cut at the right angle to suit individual requirements and produce a pleasing variety of line qualities. Cutting and trimming a quill requires a degree of skill but with a little practice, and a sharp craft knife, a useful drawing tool can be made quite simply. Reed pens have limited uses as, unlike quills, they are somewhat insensitive to the drawing surface, but the oblique line characteristic of this type of pen can be very effective when used in conjunction with a more delicate or subtle pen-and-ink technique.

Dip (technical) pens and mapping pens are cheap and easy to obtain, sensitive and versatile drawing instruments consisting of a simple plastic or wood holder with any one of a number of interchangeable steel nibs. The available range includes many specialist nibs – copperplate, script and lithographic – all of which can be used with a variety of different inks. In these pens, the ink must never be allowed to dry on the nib, which should be cleaned after each use, and the finer nibs should be replaced as soon as they show signs of splitting or losing sensitivity.

Fountain pens (those in which the ink is sucked up through the nib into a reservoir) are ideal as a self-contained, sturdy and portable drawing tool, especially when sketching out of doors. Again, these pens have the advantage of interchangeable nib widths, the most common choice being between broad, medium and fine. As well as the large range produced by stationers for handwriting, several manufacturers are now adapting their products for use by the artist and designer. Particularly handy are those which can use waterproof ink, such as the Osmiroid range. The Parker and Pelikan ranges do not as yet include this feature but are, nevertheless, good-quality, reliable drawing pens. Rotring are also now marketing a series of 'ArtPen' sets, a cartridge-containing holder with one of three styles of nib: for sketching, lettering or calligraphy. Similar ranges are produced by Berol, Edding, and other manufacturers.

Calligraphy pens are similar in character to ordinary dip (technical) pens but have carefully shaped squared-off nibs in a selection of line widths, enabling the calligrapher to produce different lettering styles such as round hand or italic. Specialist free-flowing calligraphy inks are available for use with these pens. Rotring produce a calligraphy pen in their 'ArtPen' series, and Rexel's William Mitchell range is a large assortment of high-quality pens for all styles of writing. Each set comes with a holder and a selection of nibs in varying widths. Types available include Italic (left and right hand), Round Hand (square cut and left oblique), Script, Scroll, Decro, Poster and Five line nibs.

DRAFTING PENS

The drafting or technical pen has now become an indispensable part of any designer's toolkit. It is fundamentally a precision instrument used in any situation where a consistent line quality and thickness is required. The fine metal filament, encased in an outer sheath and tipped with a hard-wearing point (a variety of materials are used for this) allows a uniform supply of ink to reach the drawing surface and standard line width to be achieved. They are ideal for use with stencils.

Although now such an everyday object in a designer's studio, a drafting pen is a delicate and complicated mechanism and care and attention are necessary to maintain trouble-free operation. They are prone to drying up and ink encrustation (so regular cleaning is a must) and can be easily damaged if dropped or mistreated. Some designers add sketching and writing to their list of uses but a specific pen should be kept for these purposes as the sensitive points could be damaged by the heavier or more uneven pressure used.

The range of pens offered by manufacturers is now very wide, with a variety of line widths, points and inks available for different drawing surfaces: all major manufacturers now conform to the international (ISO and DIN) line width specifications and use the same colour codes for these. The two internationally recognized width standards available are defined as 'Series 1' and 'Series 2'. The increment factor of Series 1 corresponds to that for 'A' paper sizes (making this the most popular choice in Europe), this relationship ensuring that the line width remain standard when drawings are reduced or enlarged to any DIN size. This is one of the reasons for their increasing use by and popularity with professionals. The line widths in Series 2 (more popular in the United States) increase in tenths of millimetres from 0.10mm to 0.60mm and in fifths of millimetres between 0.60mm and 2.00mm.

Within such a wide range, two broad categories can be defined: those that use disposable ink cartridges, eliminating much of the messy and time-consuming cleaning procedure, and those that use refillable ink reservoirs, offering more convenience and cost-effectiveness when working with a number of different inks. The ideal drafting pen allows the designer to concentrate on his work rather than on pen maintenance, and gives a smooth, even glide over the drawing surface. Individual replacement components for pens can usually be bought separately, while the larger manufacturers' ranges also offer combination work sets containing various nib sizes and compatible attachments – good value if you are about to equip yourself with these pens for the first time.

Two particularly useful attachments for drafting pens are a universal compass adaptor with a standard screw thread, allowing the use of compatible drafting pens with many precision drafting instruments, and a lettering joint. This is a jointed holder, again with a standard thread, which maintains the nib of the pen at a 90° angle to the drawing surface when using stencils, templates or lettering guides. All of the larger manufacturers, such as Faber-Castell, Rotring, Staedtler and Letraset, provide these products, and also produce work

stands, compact units which hold pens upright, ready for instant use. These are particularly useful in a cramped studio where space is at a premium. Higher priced stands often incorporate a humidifier which prevents the ink drying out when the pen is on the stand.

DR MARTIN

DR MARTIN'S DESIGNER TECHNICAL PEN

An unusual technical pen with a one-size flexible plastic point which can generate both a fine and a broad line or can be used to fill in larger areas. Developed specially for use with both types of Dr Martin's watercolours (see Paints, pp. 88-9), it is non-clogging, has a refillable cartridge and a see-through nib to check colour and ink flow. Excellent for use on slides, transparencies, gelatin-coated surfaces and films.

ECOBRA

Not available in the USA

ECOBRA TS

Line widths: Three widths 0.35mm, 0.50mm, 0.70mm

The first completely disposable drafting pen, this uses pigmented, waterproof and lightfast ink, which is sufficiently black and dense for photocopying, microfilming and dyeline printing. This model does not have a thread for use with compass attachments.

FABER-CASTELL

TG1-S

Line widths: 16 widths from 0.10mm to 2.00mm, Series 1 and 2

The basis of the Faber-Castell range with the distinctive green barrels, these are very easy to dismantle and clean and have a good cap seal incorporating elastic silicone balls to prevent drying out. A precise, reliable, general-purpose technical pen with a refillable reservoir and stainless steel alloy point for use on paper, board, vellum and tracing paper.

TG1-H

Line widths: 16 widths from 0.10mm to 2.00mm, Series 1 and 2

This range has tougher tungsten carbide points for heavy-duty use on drafting film where a high degree of resistance to wear is required.

TG1-J

Line widths: 10 widths from 0.13mm to 2.00mm
The white barrels and caps of these pens denote the special jewel points designed, again, for use on drafting film but giving particular smoothness with virtually no wear. They are also well suited to use on vellum and tracing paper.

KOH-I-NOOR

RAPIDOGRAPH 3165 TECHNICAL PEN

Line widths: 13 widths from 0.13mm to 2.00mm, Series I
A standard drafting pen with a hard chrome stainless steel point for use on all papers and cloth. It features a longer, more streamlined barrel for comfort and balance, and a quick-release double seal cap.

RAPIDOGRAPH 3165 JEWEL PEN

Line widths: 13 widths from 0.13mm to 2.00mm, Series I
Extending the capabilities of the standard Rapidograph 3165, this pen has a self-polishing abrasive resistant jewel point for use on coated (glossy) drafting film. The drawing nib section is also made of extremely hard acid-resistant material.

LEROY (KEUFFEL & ESSER CO)

Leroy lettering equipment offers a high-quality co-ordinating system for easy lettering and symbol drawing. The system consists of a drawing nib section used either with a standard holder or, in conjunction with specialist adaptors, with Leroy lettering templates. The adaptors eliminate the usual smudging problems found when using pens with templates or straight-edges since they keep the pen point well away from the template itself. The letters are described using a tracer pin which then transmits the shape through a tracer arm to the pen point. This is a particularly useful piece of equipment when a large amount of hand-rendered but neat lettering material is required on drawings and plans.

LEROY 61 0070 STANDARD PEN AND 61 3075 STANDARD PEN HOLDER

Pen available: In 12 sizes (not metric)
A corrosion-resistant durable nib section which fits both the Pen Holder and Scribers and is especially suited to small lettering jobs and freehand work. The Holder has a simple clamp mechanism to facilitate quick insertion and removal of the nib.

LEROY 61 0051 RESERVOIR PEN SECTIONS

Available: In 10 sizes (not metric)
A drawing point section similar to a standard drafting pen, threaded for use with any Scriber or in its own barrel. It has a refillable cartridge and a stainless steel tip. These pens are also available with extra durable jewel tips.

61 0003 ADJUSTABLE SCRIBER

Produces vertical and slanted lettering by using an adjustable tracer arm. Leroy's own pen sections or standard metric sizes are easily inserted and can be quickly changed during use.

61 0015 ADJUSTABLE SCRIBER

Similar to the 61 0003 model, this is specially designed for large templates.

61 0020 HEIGHT AND SLANT CONTROL SCRIBER

Adjustable to form characters either vertical or slanting at any angle up to 45° forward and any height from 60 to 150 per cent of the template character while the width remains unchanged.

LETRASET

KERN PRONTOGRAPH $\overline{m}$, $\overline{m}$ Hm

Line widths: Nine widths from 0.13mm to 2.00mm, Series I
A reservoir-type pen available with either a hard chrome-plated point or gold-plated tungsten carbide point for extra wear (Hm range). Both the nib and the filament inside it have smooth, rounded ends, helping to give this pen an even glide across the drawing surface and a constant ink flow. Design features include a square barrel to prevent the pen rolling off the desk, a spanner (wrench) in the barrel end for unscrewing the nib, and a soft plastic seal in the cap to prevent drying.

KERN PRONTOGRAPH Va, Va Hm

Line widths: Nine widths from 0.10mm to 1.20mm, Series 2
Similar in construction and characteristics to the $\overline{m}$ range, these conform to Series 2 standards.

PELIKAN

GRAPHOS

Like the Rotring Graphos system, this is a highly versatile drawing ink fountain pen with special, easily interchangeable steel nibs for every kind of high definition drawing. The ink always flows uniformly from the nib and the rate of flow can be varied by changing the feed. The holder and an assortment of nibs are available singly or in various different work sets.

A Series – fine ruling nibs, 0.1mm to 0.7mm
T Series – broad ruling nibs, 0.8mm to 6.4mm
N Series – right-hand slant nibs for square end lines, 0.8mm to 4.0mm
Z Series – left-hand slant nibs for square end lines, 0.8mm to 3.2mm
R Series – tubular nibs for lettering with stencils, 0.3 to 3.0mm
S Series – fine freehand drawing nibs, soft, medium soft, hard, extra hard
O Series – round nibs for round end lines, 0.2mm to 3.2mm

PENTEL

CERANOMATIC

Line widths: Six widths from 0.13mm to 0.70mm
This pen takes its name from the extremely hard, durable ceramic material which forms the tip of each nib, giving long-lasting performance on most drafting surfaces. Dye-based ink replaces pigment-based ink in its disposable cartridges and it is suitable for use with standard drafting guides and compass attachments.

PILOT

CERAMIC PEN

Line widths: Four widths 0.25mm, 0.35mm, 0.50mm, 0.70mm
A technical pen with a ceramic drawing point which takes the concept of the disposable cartridge even further. The entire drawing point section and ink reservoir are discarded each time the ink is exhausted, rendering washing out unnecessary and any degree of wear on each tip minimal. Although it can be used on drafting film, the manufacturer recommends care when handling and processing drawings on this surface. Although it fits standard lettering templates and stencils it cannot be used with compass attachments as it does not possess a standard thread on the drawing point section.

ROTRING

The Rotring company were the inventors of the drafting pen and theirs are the most well-used of any make around the world. Although available in fewer line widths than Faber-Castell, their large range covers both the main categories of refillable reservoir and capillary cartridge pens and includes specialist items and accessories for particular technical drawing needs.

ISOGRAPH

Line widths: Nine widths from 0.13mm to 2.00mm, Series 1
The basis of the Rotring range, a refillable reservoir pen with a push-on twist-off sleeve around the ink helix which allows easy cleaning without having to empty the reservoir or dismantle the drawing point section. The point is hard chrome-plated steel with a shoulder which prevents ink from running underneath flat rulers or stencils.

ISOGRAPH F

Line widths: Nine widths from 0.13mm to 2.00mm, Series 1
The gold lettering and fitments of this pen indicate its suitability for drafting on film with non-etching inks. On no account should etching inks be used in the Isograph F as these will damage the pen. The drawing point is fitted with a tungsten carbide tip which is resistant even to extremely abrasive surfaces, such as heavy-duty drafting film.

RAPIDOGRAPH F ISO

Line widths: Nine widths from 0.13mm to 2.00mm, Series 1
The capillary cartridge version of the Isograph F, incorporating the same features.

ISOGRAPH P

Line widths: Nine widths from 0.13mm to 2.00mm, Series 1
Again equipped with a wear-resistant tungsten carbide tip, but specially adapted for use with etching ink on plastic uncoated drafting film. Etching inks are for use in solvent-proof drafting pens only (the grey holder of this pen is also particularly resistant to solvent) and should only be removed with a special cleaner supplied by the manufacturer, not with water.

RAPIDOGRAPH ISO

Line widths: Nine widths from 0.13mm to 2.00mm, Series 1
The newest part of the Rotring range, this uses a capillary cartridge, incorporating both the ink helix and reservoir in one unit. Each time a cartridge is changed any ink deposits in the capillary system are disposed of, eliminating much of the maintenance procedure necessary with other pens. The Rapidograph ink contains a special additive which delays the drying process in the drawing point while not affecting the short drying time on any normal drawing surface.

The nib of the Pentel Ceranomatic.

OTHER ROTRING MODELS

The Variant (Series 2 only) is the original Rotring drafting pen with a hard chrome-finished tubular tip. The comparable etching ink pen is the Foliograph. They are still in production but now largely replaced in the studio by the Isograph and Isograph P.

The Varioscript is especially designed with a shoulderless tubular tip for use with lettering stencils.

GRAPHOS

A very versatile drawing pen suitable for technical and freehand drawing, stencil lettering and illustration work. It consists of a universal holder with ink feed plus any one of three styles of interchangeable nib for different drawing needs: ruling nibs (A) for fine lines, ruling nibs (T) for broad lines or poster work, and tubular nibs (R) for lettering and stencilling.

Available in a wide range of line widths and character heights, and combining the best features of a technical pen with an old-fashioned dip (technical) pen, the system has proved very popular in drawing offices.

STAEDTLER

MARSMATIC 700

Line widths: Nine widths from 0.13 to 2.00mm, Series 1

Marsmatic 700 is a fully integrated drafting system similar in character to those produced by Faber-Castell or Rotring. The basic Staedtler drafting pen offers steady, non-clogging, regular ink flow. The unique Marsmatic spring-seal eliminates the need to shake the pen which starts instantly even after several months out of use. Ideal for all general-purpose drafting requirements on papers and boards.

MARSMATIC 707 DURANITE

Line widths: Nine widths from 0.13mm to 2.00mm, Series 1

The tungsten carbide points of these pens, which show practically no wear on abrasive surfaces, are specially designed for use on drafting film.

MARSMATIC 709 DURAGLIDE

Line widths: Seven widths from 0.13mm to 1.00mm, Series 1

For use on drafting film with a matt surface and on tracing paper. These jewel-tipped points glide smoothly without scratching, even in the finer line widths, and offer extra durability and hardness on heavy-duty drafting film, and during constant heavy use.

CALLIGRAPHY PENS

Italic calligraphy pens, similar in construction to a marker and with none of the problems associated with steel-nibbed dip (technical) pens – flooding of the nib, or ink flicking on to the paper – are now being produced. This makes them a particularly useful tool for preparatory exercises and roughs.

BEROL

ITALIC PEN

Line width: Approximately 0.5mm
Colour range: black, red, blue, dark blue, green, brown
An oblique chisel nib fibre pen producing smooth thicks and thins.

BRAUSE

BRAUSE LETTERING NIBS

Line widths: Nine widths from 0.5mm to 5.0mm
These exceptional quality flat chisel edge lettering points are especially recommended for italic and broad edge pen letterforms.

EDDING

1255 CALLIGRAPHY PEN

Line widths: Three widths 2mm, 3.5mm, 5mm
Colour range: black, red, brown
A squared-off fibre nib using waterproof ink.

PLATIGNUM

SILVERLINE PEN

A standard size fountain-type pen which accepts a variety of lettering, italic, left-hand and oblique nibs. Although economically priced, they are of high quality and are not prone to clogging.

PETITE PEN

Although only 112mm (4½ in.) long when capped, this pen has a surprisingly large ink capacity and is compatible with the full range of nibs produced for the Silverline Pen.

ROTRING

ARTPEN SKETCHING

Line widths: Two widths fine, extra fine
A reliable pen for illustrators and artists, this can be used for fine linework or broader sketching.

ARTPEN LETTERING

Line widths: Three widths medium, broad, extra broad
Superior ink flow facilitates shading, outlining and cross-hatching, making this ideal for headlining.

ARTPEN CALLIGRAPHY

Classic calligraphy pens, available in three line widths, these all have the smooth writing action of a traditional fountain pen.

SPEEDBALL

SPEEDBALL PENS

Pens equipped with nibs in four different shapes (square, round, flat, oval) for various lettering and drawing techniques. They have a larger ink capacity and better ink flow due to the built-in nib reservoirs.

SPEEDBALL FLICKER LETTERING PENS

Lettering pens with gold-plated reservoirs that are hinged to open easily for care and cleaning. Available with round nibs only.

SPEEDBALL STEEL BRUSH

A fountain lettering pen closer in feel to using a brush than a pen. It will give a free-flowing line without dripping ink.

PLOTTER PENS/ POINTS

All numerically controlled drafting machines and plotters require a precision nib similar to a manual drafting pen but, if possible, even more reliable as they have to be trusted to run without constant supervision and at considerable speed. Like drafting pens, they must be properly maintained and regularly cleaned to prevent clogging.

These are available from several manufacturers; differences between makes are often slight.

BALLPOINTS AND ROLLING WRITERS

Many designers have now taken to sketching and writing with a ballpoint or rolling writer where formerly they would have used a dip (technical) or mapping pen. These offer a more convenient ink delivery via the metal ball in the point or, in the case of rolling writers, the cushioned plastic ball tip. Rolling writers are generally more popular as metal ballpoints tend to be insensitive to both the drawing surface and the hand of the user, and consistent ink flow is not necessarily guaranteed. The ink in ballpoints is also prone to blotting and smudging, although it has a very good, almost unlimited, 'cap off' life.

Also useful in this field are plastic-pointed writers, similar to fibre pens but with a hard plastic tip fed by water-based ink. Both these and rolling writers will work at any angle where a ballpoint will only function when gravity, and the action of the rotating ball, are pulling the ink downwards towards the tip. They are much more hard-wearing than fibre tips, especially in the finer widths, as the points will not spread or kink with heavy use. All three types of pen are particularly suitable for making carbon and photocopies and have the advantage of being widely available in stationers, office suppliers and art shops.

BEROL

Berol produce an exhaustive range of economically priced pens for both writing and drawing, covering practically every eventuality. The distinctive Berol family 'look' features a textured finger grip on the barrel and a snap-on cap with an airtight seal to prevent drying out.

BALL PEN

Line widths: Fine approximately 0.5mm; Extra Fine approximately 0.3mm
Colour range: black, red, blue
A ballpoint pen which features a tungsten carbide ball in a brass housing, giving prolonged, reliable use and a high-quality lightfast line, particularly with black ink.

ROLLERPEN
Line width: Approximately 0.8mm
Colour range: black, red, blue, green
A durable rolling writer which makes excellent carbon copies and is smooth to use.

SMOOTHWRITER
Line widths: Fine approximately 0.5mm; Medium approximately 0.8mm
A ball pen which can be used with drafting guides and straight-edges due its elongated nib section.

STRONGPOINT
Line width: Approximately 0.8mm
Colour range: black, red, blue, green
A very durable and long-lasting plastic-nibbed pen popular with graphic designers for type mark-up and general writing purposes.

NOTEWRITER
Line width: Approximately 0.8mm
Colour range: black, red, blue, green, orange, purple
A good value plastic-tipped product intended for all casual writing.

LABELLING PEN
Line width: Approximately 0.8mm
Colour range: black, red, blue, green
Intended as a labelling pen, this item has advantages for use around the studio as it will give a reasonably fine line on a variety of surfaces such as glass, cloth, plastic and wood. Its plastic tip has good resistance to drying out if left uncapped for a short period.

The Berol Notewriter (left) and Edding 1600 plastic-tipped writers.

EDDING

Like Berol, Pilot and Pentel, Edding offer an enormous choice in these kinds of pens. The difference between models, for all manufacturers, is sometimes very slight and the ultimate decision, after a little trial and error, is mainly personal preference.

EDDING K9
Line width: Approximately 0.7mm
Colour range: blue only
A refillable basic ballpoint pen, supplied in various coloured barrels, for general office use.

EDDING 55 SIGNPEN
Line width: One width only 0.3mm
Colour range: black, red, blue, green
This popular and economical pen with the familiar striped barrel has a metal-framed plastic tip, making it suitable for use with straight-edges and templates (from 1.6mm/^{1}/16 in.), as well as for general sketching and writing.

EDDING 88 AND 89 OFFICE LINERS
Line widths: Two widths 0.75mm, 0.3mm
Colour range: black, red, blue, green
A useful and adaptable plastic-tipped writing pen. The 89 has a particularly fine nib for delineating small letters and figures.

EDDING 780 MARKER
Line width: One width only 0.8mm
Colour range: five metallic colours; five metallic gold with coloured outlines; five metallic silver with coloured outlines
This has a metal sheath to the plastic tip to protect and maintain the fineness of the line, making it one of the few metallic pens which can be used with a template. Like the 752, it contains opaque waterproof ink.

EDDING 2100 SIGNPEN, 2100 PERMANENT
Line width: One width only 0.3mm
Colour range: black, red, blue, green
For general writing and sketching, this plastic-tipped pen is a comfortable and economical choice. The permanent version is unusually fine for such a product and contains rubproof and waterproof ink, particularly useful for work on plastics, glass and foils.

EDDING 1600 SERIES
The Edding 1600 Series by itself provides a large range of plastic-tipped writers. These are particularly economical, after the initial outlay, as they are refillable with a variety of cartridges.

FABER-CASTELL

ROLLER PEN 2000
Line width: One width only 0.8mm
Colour range: black, red, blue, green
A pen which incorporates the best features of both the ballpoint and the rolling writer. It uses the liquid ink of the latter but is designed with a super-smooth metal ball tip for harder wear.

PENTEL

BALL PENTEL
Line widths: Fine 0.8mm; Extra Fine 0.6mm; Super Fine 0.4mm
Colour range: Fine available in black, red, blue, green, brown, orange, light green, pink, violet; Extra and Super Fine available in black, red, blue, green
A popular and widely available rolling writer with the familiar green barrel, this is a good all-round economical pen for sketching and writing.

PENTEL ROLLER MARKER

Line width: One width only 0.8mm
Colour range: black, red, blue, green
An up-market version of the Ball Pentel with a satin finish, brushed-chrome body. These are refillable with disposable ink cartridges.

SUPER BALL

Line width: One width only 0.6mm
Colour range: black, red, blue, green
A metal-tipped rolling writer distinguished by its blue barrel. The Super Ball's performance is long-lasting in general use and, like the Ball Pentel, it contains water-soluble non-toxic ink.

ULTRA FINE

Line width: One width only 0.4mm
Colour range: black, red, blue, green
A particularly fine pen with a durable plastic point, this also uses water-soluble ink.

FOUNTAIN PENTEL

Colour range: black, red, blue, green
Although this pen has a flexible plastic nib, shaped like a traditional fountain pen, this model works on the same principle as a rolling or plastic-tipped writer, combining the advantages of both.

PILOT

Pilot produce a large number of rolling writers and ballpoints for all sections of the market. Their BL, BLL, and BLT ranges offer a choice of more expensively styled pens for personal use but many of their products are ideally suited for use by the graphic designer.

BALL LINER

Line widths: Two widths 0.3mm, 0.4mm
Colour range: black, red, blue, green, purple, brown
Equivalent to the Pentel range (see pp. 78), this is a useful general-purpose rolling writer tipped with a cemented carbide alloy ball for smooth, flexible writing and sketching. It uses water-soluble ink.

HI-TECPOINT 05

Line width: One width only 0.3mm
Colour range: black, red, blue, green, violet, brown, pink, light blue
A smooth-flowing, lightweight rolling writer with an ultra-fine microball tip enclosed in a stainless steel tube (similar to a drafting pen) which allows use of the pen with a 5mm (3/16 in.) template. Unlike a fibre tip, the point will not wear or spread, staying fine until the ink is exhausted. Excellent for all detailed work, including multiple carbon copies.

HI-TECPOINT 07

Line width: One width only 0.5mm
Colour range: black, red, blue, green
Identical to the Hi-Tecpoint 05 but the slightly wider tip can be used with a 7mm (1/4 in.) template.

HI-TECPOINT V5

Line width: One width only 0.3mm
Colour range: black, red, blue
A new liquid ink type extra-fine rolling writer. It is longer lasting due to the enlarged ink reservoir which has a see-through window to check the ink supply, and has a higher resistance to drying out (45 days or more) if the cap is left off.

FINELINER SW-PP

Line width: One width only 0.3mm
Colour range: black, red, blue, green, violet, brown, orange, yellow
An economical and hard-wearing fine pen which utilizes Pilot's multi-channel plastic tip and water-soluble ink. The pen produces a smooth line, and the tip does not spread, even with continued use.

ULTRA FINE PERMANENT SC-UF

Line width: One width only 0.3mm
Colour range: black, red, blue, green, violet, brown, orange
An unusual and conveniently large range of colours in an ultra-fine pen which uses permanent ink. It has a similar tip to the Fineliner but can write on any clean surface.

EXTRA FINE SC-G-EF

Line width: One width only 0.5mm
Colour range: gold, silver
Pilot were the originators of gold and silver paint markers and these are the extra-fine plastic-tipped versions in their comprehensive range. The permanent paint is waterproof and can be used on any clean surface.

CONTRAST MCE/300

Colour range: black, red, blue, green, violet
Another plastic-tipped pen which writes a brilliant silver, this produces a coloured outline to the stroke. This can only be used on porous surfaces, such as paper, material or wood, but is useful for decorative writing, illustration work, greetings cards and imaginative visuals.

INKS AND DYES

DRAFTING PEN INKS

Capillary cartridge drafting pens use their own compatible ink cartridges, which should never be refilled from a bottle but discarded as soon as they are empty. Inks for reservoir-type pens are available in filler bottles from most manufacturers and come in a selection of colours as well as black. The pen should always be washed out thoroughly before changing either the make or colour of the ink. Cold water is usually sufficient for this but specialist pen cleaners can be used to remove both etching and non-etching inks if the pen has become totally encrusted. Some drawing inks contain a high proportion of shellac which can dry out quickly and clog the fine filament inside the stylo of a drafting pen; this makes them inappropriate for these pens. The most suitable ink is one that is easy-flowing but quick-drying, with good adhesion to the drawing surface, and non-erasable with pencil erasers so that guidelines can be removed from finished work. Some inks can be erased from tracing paper and film using special chemical-impregnated erasers supplied by the manufacturer. Some water-based dyes, rather than true ink, do not have sufficient viscosity for technical pens, causing the dye to flow too freely from the stylo and flood the drawing. These should be avoided if possible.

DRAWING INKS

Ink is an extremely versatile medium which can be applied using many different tools and is suitable for most drawing surfaces. Inks termed 'artists' drawing inks' are waterproof, smudge-proof and have good adhesion properties. They can be used successfully on paper, board,

vellum and synthetic surfaces, and even for staining untreated wood. They make an excellent medium for line drawing, wash illustration and lettering work. Waterproof inks are transparent, can be mixed with each other and overlaid to create an infinite variety of shades and tones. Because they contain shellac (a kind of resinous substance used in varnishes), waterproof inks dry quickly to a glossy film which can sometimes crack or flake. They tend to evaporate if left uncapped, especially in hot weather, but can be thinned again using a very small quantity of distilled water. All brushes and pens which have come into contact with them should be washed immediately work finishes because, once dry, the ink is very difficult to remove. In case of accidents, dried ink can be dissolved in washing soda or methylated spirits (denatured alcohol): this method should not be used repeatedly however, as equipment, especially brushes, can be damaged by these solutions.

Pigmented inks and dyes consist of suspensions of finely ground, water-insoluble coloured materials. They can also be waterproof but dry to an opaque matt finish and have better lightfast properties. As they often contain no shellac, and therefore do not clog so easily, they are particularly recommended for use in airbrushes.

Black drawing inks, sometimes called Indian inks, are produced in a wide variety of different forms to suit different graphic techniques. There is often very little to choose between them except for their degree of opacity and covering power. Specialist calligraphy ink, for example, needs to be exceptionally free-flowing so should not be used where dense coverage over large areas is required as it will produce a grey, semi-transparent effect. Writing inks for dip (technical) and fountain pens are often water-soluble and can be used in wash illustration to create interesting tonal effects – a black ink, when splashed with water, can give a variety of blue and indigo hues.

All inks should be shaken or stirred well before use as the pigments tend to sink to the bottom of the bottle.

ARTONE
Not available in the UK

ARTONE 723 FOUNTAIN PEN INK
Size: 56 ml (2 oz.) bottle
Colour range: black only
This is a free-flowing, non-waterproof ink, particularly recommended for sketching and calligraphy, but it can also be used in any fountain pen. It gives a deep black and is non-clogging.

ARTONE SEPIA FOUNT INK
Size: 56ml (2 oz.) bottle
Colour range: sepia only
A non-waterproof fountain pen ink giving a rich brown colour. Good for any lettering and calligraphic work and for sepia drawings.

DR MARTIN'S

DR MARTIN'S PEN WHITE
Size: 28ml (1 oz.) bottle
An opaque white ink for drafting pens which will remain dense even if used over other inks, dyes or marker colours. It will adhere well to untreated acetate. It should not be used in pens of less than 0.25mm nib width. Good for very accurate corrections on artwork.

DR MARTIN'S TECH WATERPROOF INKS
Size: 28ml (1 oz.) bottle
Colour range: 14 colours
A free-flowing ink for line work, lettering and calligraphy but should not be used in fountain pens. Available in sets of seven or 14 colours.

FABER-CASTELL

HIGGINS PIGMENTED INKS
Size: 29ml (1 oz.) plastic bottle with dropper
Colour range: lemon, red, carmine, magenta, yellow, blue, green, violet, brown
Waterproof, opaque inks which dry to give a flat matt appearance. The vibrant colours will not fade under light and can be mixed with each other to create a variety of shades. They can be diluted for use in an airbrush or drafting pen and are suitable for calligraphic work and illustration.

HIGGINS COLOURED DRAWING INKS
Size: 29ml (1 oz.) plastic bottle with dropper
Colour range: 17 colours, including white
A good range of bright, transparent, waterproof drawing inks. They can be blended with each other to produce new shades, dry rapidly and are ideal for use with brush, dip pen or airbrush on any sized paper or board.

HIGGINS SUPER WHITE
Size: 29ml (1 oz.) bottle
A non-transparent, water-soluble medium designed for highlighting and opaquing with airbrushes and brushes.

HIGGINS COLOURED DRAWING INKS
Size: 23ml (¾ oz.) plastic bottles
Colour range: yellow, red, violet, blue, green, brown
A range of waterproof inks intended for use on drafting film, tracing paper and drawing papers. They are opaque and less fluid than other waterproof inks and so are not suitable for use in drafting, fountain or dip (technical) pens.

HIGGINS CALLIGRAPHY INK
Size: 74ml (2½ oz.) bottle
Colour range: black, sepia
A free-flowing ink developed for lettering work with calligraphy pens, quills, fountain pens and so on. Black is waterproof but sepia is water soluble.

HIGGINS BLACK MAGIC DRAWING INK
Sizes: 23ml (¾ oz.), 38ml (1½ oz.) 250ml (9 oz.) bottles
Colour range: black only
A lightproof ink that dries quickly to give an intense black semi-matt finish. Ideal for drafting pens and airbrushes for use on most surfaces, including tracing paper and drafting film.

HIGGINS T-INK
Size: 23ml (¾ oz.) plastic bottle
Colour range: black only
T-Ink is an excellent medium for any work requiring high-quality photographic reproduction as it has a matt, non-reflective finish. It resists cracking, flaking or peeling on the drawing surface and will not clog in drafting pens or airbrushes.

FW

FW WATERPROOF DRAWING INKS
Size: 28ml (1 oz.) glass bottle with pipette
Colour range: 13 colours, including black
A range of non-clogging inks that can be used on most surfaces with brushes, dip (technical) pens, drafting pens or airbrushes. The colours are rich and vivid, extremely lightfast and smooth to handle. Popular with designers and illustrators for high-quality work. Available singly and in sets of 12 colours (excluding black).

KOH-I-NOOR

KOH-I-NOOR RAPIDOGRAPH DRAWING INK

Sizes: 21ml (¾ oz.) plastic bottle with pouring spout; 28ml (1 oz.) plastic bottle with pipette; 225ml (8 oz.), 450ml (1 pt) plastic bottles
Colour range: black only
An intense black ink for use in drafting pens on paper, film and tracing cloth. Although free-flowing, it dries quickly and adheres well to the drawing surface.

KOH-I-NOOR RAPIDRAW INK

Sizes: 21ml (¾ oz.), 450ml (1 pt) plastic bottles with pouring spout
Colour range: black only
An exceptionally black ink giving a uniformly dense, opaque image with excellent adhesion properties. It is particularly recommended for use on drafting film, for work subjected to heavy handling, or for work requiring high-quality photographic reproduction.

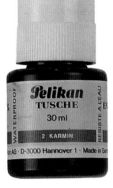

PEBEO

COLOREX TECHNIC INKS

Size: 45ml (1½ oz.) bottle with dropper
Colour range: black, white, sepia, process blue, ultramarine blue, magenta, yellow, orange, emerald green, violet
These inks contain pigments and have an acrylic resin base. They dry very quickly (a few seconds) leaving a supple, opaque and totally waterproof surface. They are also lightfast and indelible, and with good adhesion properties can be used on a wide variety of surfaces, including plastics. The inks can be mixed with each other and with water to extend the colour range, and as they do not clog can be used in airbrushes, drafting pens, and with traditional drawing and painting tools.
    A cleaning fluid (Technic Cleaner) is available.

PELIKAN

PELIKAN WATERPROOF DRAWING INKS

Sizes: 28ml (1 oz.) glass bottle with pipette (all colours); 225ml (8 oz.), 850ml (32 oz.) glass bottles (black only)
Colour range: 17 colours, including black
A popular and versatile range of transparent, vivid colours. They are waterproof, flow freely and do not clog in drafting or ruling pens. They can be mixed with each other and with watercolours to achieve intermediate shades, and

diluted with distilled or boiled water for washes. Recommended for work which will be reproduced.

PELIKAN DRAWING INK Z

Size: 28ml (1 oz.) bottles with pipette
Colour range: black, red, blue, green, yellow, violet, brown
Developed for use in drafting pens with a special formulation which prevents drying in the pen without delaying drying time on the drawing surface. They give a waterproof, opaque finish which is good for reproduction and can be used successfully on drafting film, line board (illustration board) and hard surfaced papers.

PELIKAN FT, FL DRAWING INK

Sizes: 23ml (1¾ oz.) filler bottle; 28ml (1 oz.) glass bottle with pipette; 225ml (8 oz.) glass bottle with pouring spout
Colour range: black only
Formulated to give extra adhesion on matt drafting film, tracing cloth and hard surfaced papers, this ink has a high degree of opacity, dries quickly and is waterproof. It can be used in all technical pens. FL ink gives a super black line of even greater opacity and is recommended for use in technical pens of 0.25mm or above.

PELIKAN FOUNT INDIA

Size: 35ml (1¼ oz.) plastic bottle
Colour range: black only
A dense black drawing ink for fountain pens which flows freely and will not leave sediment in the pen. It is water-based, making it an ideal, easy-to-handle wash medium for producing a wide range of grey tones.

PELIKAN 4001 FOUNTAIN PEN INK

Size: 65ml (2⅓ oz.) bottle
Colour range: black, blue-black, royal blue, red, green, sepia
A good ink for all lettering and fountain pens. It is non-clogging and flows freely but gives an intense, reproducible line. The blue-black ink gives interesting wash effects. They are also ideal for sketching and fine line work.

ROTRING

ROTRING DRAWING INK

Sizes: 23ml (¾ oz.) plastic bottles with dropper spout; 30ml (1 oz.), 250ml (9 oz.) bottles (black only)
Colour range: black, blue, red, green, yellow, brown, white
Special inks for use in drafting pens, funnel pens and ruling pens, these are free-flowing and produce high-quality dense lines which give

excellent results in reproduction. They can be mixed with each other, are waterproof, smudge-proof when dry, non-erasable and adhere well to tracing paper, drawing paper and line board. White ink can also be used on photographic negatives and slides. All except white are available in the form of capillary cartridges for the Rotring Rapidograph pens.

ROTRING F, FL DRAWING INKS

Sizes: 23ml (¾ oz.) plastic bottles with dropper spout; 250ml (9 oz.) bottles
Colour range: black only
Intense, very opaque non-etching inks for drawing on matt drafting film. They dry fast, will not smudge, run or flake and are resistant to fingermarks. They also give good lightproof coverage suitable for reproduction. FL ink has a latex base for even better adhesion to the film surface but has a slightly longer drying time. Use this type for any drawing which is likely to be subjected to constant handling.

Both types are designed for use in drafting pens, graphos and ruling pens but FL ink should not be used in a pen with a nib width of less than 0.25mm.

ROTRING DRAWING INK P

Size: 30 ml (1 oz.) glass bottle with pipette
Colour range: black, blue, red, yellow, green, violet
For a permanent image on uncoated drafting film use this non-erasable etching ink. It is waterproof, smudge-proof and lightfast for clean, accurate results in reproduction. It should only be used in solvent-proof drafting pens, or in ruling or graphos pens.

ROTRING DRAWING INK K

Size: 30ml (1 oz.) glass bottle with pipette
An etching ink particularly suitable for use on both clear and matt drafting films giving a dense, opaque image for reproduction. Very useful for preparing overhead transparencies on acetate. Use only with graphos-type drawing pens.

ROTRING CLEANING FLUID AND CLEANING FLUID P

Efficient solvents for cleaning drafting pens, especially when encrusted with dried ink. Soaking components overnight should clear most blockages. Cleaning Fluid P should never be used for anything but etching ink drafting pens.

ROYAL SOVEREIGN

MAGIC COLOR

Sizes: 28ml (1 oz.) glass bottle with pipette; 220ml (7 oz.) plastic bottle with dropper spout

Colour range: 24 colours
A non-shellac-based, non-clogging, opaque ink designed especially with airbrushes in mind. It is waterproof when dry, is lightfast to a degree, and dries to a smooth even finish. Colours can be mixed readily and are also suitable for use with drafting pens and brushes, and are popular with airbrush artists. The pipette in the cap of the smaller bottles is useful for noting exact proportions when mixing colours.

Dilutant lacquer and cleaning fluid are available for use with Magic Color.

MARABU BUNTLACK AEROSOL SPRAY COLOURS

Size: 300ml (10 oz.) can
Colour range: 28 colours; four fluorescent colours (lemon, red, blue, green); five metallic colours (silver, rich gold, pale gold, Ducat gold, copper)
These aerosol spray colours can be used on almost any surface to give a totally weatherproof, matt silk finish. They are ideal for exhibition and display work and the colours can be used successfully on plastics, glass, metal, cement, stone and many natural materials. All except Ducat and pale gold can be used on expanded polystyrene.

WINSOR & NEWTON

WATERPROOF DRAWING INK

Size: 14ml (½ oz.) glass bottles
Colour range: 22 colours
A very popular range of waterproof drawing inks (not least for their attractive packaging), available in a pleasingly wide selection of colours, which can be mixed with each other and diluted with water. They dry quickly and flow freely so are most suitable for use with brushes and dip pens on a wide variety of surfaces: sized paper, board, vellum and acetate. Colour intensity can be built up in layers but the inks are not completely lightfast and will fade significantly if exposed to natural or artificial light.

GOLD AND SILVER DRAWING INK

Size: 14ml (½ oz.) glass bottles
These inks are non-waterproof and opaque. They must be shaken or stirred thoroughly before use as the metal content (bronze and aluminium) tends to settle to the bottom of the bottle. They can be applied to a range of surfaces using a brush or dip (technical) pen only.

LIQUID INDIAN INK

Size: 300ml (10 oz.), 14cc (½ oz.) glass bottles
An excellent medium for all lettering work, this consists of the calligrapher's traditional black Chinese Stick Ink in a water solution.

USING A RULING PEN

1 With the blades close together fill the pen using a dropper or brush so that the ink comes about 13mm (½ in.) up from the point. Adjust the width of the point by turning the screw. Test the pen on a piece of scrap paper, adjusting the screw each time until you achieve the line thickness you require.

2 To draw a rule, place the straight-edge slightly below the required position for the line. With the adjusting screw facing away from you, put the point in position on the line and tilt the pen backwards slightly so that the flat blade rests against the straight-edge. There should be a small gap between the pen and the straight-edge to prevent flooding. Your fingers should rest lightly on the straight-edge.

CALLIGRAPHY PEN TECHNIQUES

Well-executed hand lettering can be used instead of dry transfer for a neat appearance on finished artwork. To write with an italic hand, first draw lines representing the baseline, x height and cap height of the letters. Hold the pen at the same angle throughout, and make the strokes in the order indicated. Try to establish a rhythm as you work.

Foundational hand

Italic hand

1 Trying to butt two lines together neatly is almost impossible and will result in a blob or lines of uneven thickness. To draw clean, square corners for boxes and borders always rule beyond the corner by 2 or 3mm (⅛ in.) and paint out the excess lines with opaque white.

2 Ink lines can be scratched off artboard or line board (bristol board or illustration board) using the tip of a sharp blade. Work slowly and methodically, with light, short strokes.

3 To correct larger areas, it is better to redraw the item on a separate sheet of high-quality smooth art paper, trim neatly and paste this down over the original mistake.

4 Stubborn stains on artwork can be removed using liquid bleach and a cottonbud (Q-tip swab). Do not flood the area but dab lightly with small strokes. Finally, go over the area with clean water. This technique can obviously only be used on white surfaces.

5 Ink mistakes or unwanted lines can be removed from tracing paper or drafting film using special chemically impregnated erasers.

6 Wet ink blots on artwork can be removed using blotting paper. Moistening the paper between your lips will help to ensure that the blot does not spread. You will be left with a small grey stain, which can be removed using another method.

PAINTS AND BRUSHES

Although pencils are invaluable for the quick sketching out of ideas, and markers can be used for both initial roughs and finished presentations, paints can be very useful for producing accurate representations of how a finished piece of design will appear. This section looks at the different types of paints and brushes (including airbrushes) on the market.

PAINTS

Graphic design is an activity in which the finished result is usually attained by a photomechanical printing process. Paints and similar media are used purely for the preparation of visuals and camera-ready artwork. In other words, using paint media is not an end in itself but simply one step on the way to the finished, printed result.

The main studio stages in the preparation of a design idea prior to its being printed are:

1 initial 'roughs', 'scamps' or 'thumbnails'
2 'finished' or 'client presentation' visuals
3 'camera-ready' artwork

The first step is, as it suggests, the jotting down of first ideas. This is probably done with pencil, crayon or felt-tip pen. Depending on the kind of work being done, and also the particular preference and style of the designer involved, paint may be used. Paint, though, really comes into its own with the second stage. This involves producing an accurate facsimile of how it is intended that the finished, printed job is to look. Many other media are also used but paint products are certainly widely useful.

Much the same thing can be said about the preparation of camera-ready artwork. Any part of a piece of design which is not strictly typographic or photographic is going to rely heavily on paint of one kind or another. Although some illustrative work is done using pencil and/or ink, most work of this kind depends on paint.

WATERCOLOUR

Watercolour paints impose upon the user the most 'honest' approach. The pigment washes on the paper are transparent and translucent. In other words, they are not opaque: what goes down on the paper can always be seen, even when covered over with other washes of colour.

These paints are manufactured with very finely powdered pigment, bound with gum arabic into an emulsified state, and are available in several forms. The purest kind is the dry cake which contains the highest proportion of pure pigment but needs a lot of brushing with water to release the colour.

Pans and half-pans contain lozenges of pigment mixed with glycerine or honey to keep the paint moist. Because of the keeping qualities and the sensibly portable and useful boxes they come in, pans offer the most convenient and accessible form of watercolour. Boxes of colour of this type are especially useful for outdoor work or in other locations away from the studio.

Tubes are particularly convenient for mixing large amounts of paint for denser washes on greater areas. They do not, however, have the glycerine additives of the pans and will dry out quickly if the cap is left off. Some dry out completely, even with the cap on, over a period of time.

Watercolours are also available in concentrated liquid form in bottles complete with an eyedropper. These are useful for larger areas of wash but they do lack the simplicity and the almost infinite subtlety available with pans or tubes. They also tend to be more fugitive.

Watercolours often come in two standards: 'artists'' quality and 'students'' quality. The students' range is generally smaller, the more expensive pigments are excluded from the selection available and the colours tend not to be so strong or durable as the artists' colours. But they are cheaper and represent a most viable introduction to a satisfying but rather difficult technique.

Some manufacturers – Winsor & Newton, Rowney and Grumbacher, for example – also grade their paints according to their degree of permanence: class AA = extremely permanent; class A = durable; class B = moderately durable; class C = fugitive.

DR MARTIN'S

SYNCHROMATIC TRANSPARENT WATERCOLOURS
Colour range: 39 colours
These are watercolours already in liquid form

which makes them easy to use. This particular range is notable for the transparency of the colours and is particularly useful on photographic papers and for flat washes on illustration board. They are suitable for use straight from the bottle and, of course, mixed with the colours from other bottles, but they can be diluted with water to give subtler tones.

RADIANT CONCENTRATED WATERCOLOURS

Colour range: 42 colours

Although somewhat less transparent than the Synchromatic range, these bottled colours are much more concentrated, enabling a higher degree of lustre and brilliance to be attained. All the colours may be diluted with water and freely mixed with one another.

LUMA WATERCOLOURS

Colour range: 80 colours

Another concentrated, bottled pigment. They are of exceptional strength, giving an intensity more often associated with opaque media. The range of 80 colours is very comprehensive. Like all liquid watercolours, they are as easy to apply by pen or airbrush as they are by paintbrush.

WINSOR & NEWTON

ARTISTS' WATERCOLOURS

Colour range: 87 colours

A range of colours with a large pigment content. These are available in pan, half-pan and tube form.

COTMAN/LONDON WATERCOLOURS

Colour range: 39 colours

This is a 'students'' quality range. All 39 colours are available in tube, and 24 of the colours are also available in pan, form.

ACCESSORIES

Boxes are available which hold either pans or tubes. Each box has two mixing surfaces and a thumb ring underneath.

Various mediums and varnishes are also available for increasing the flow, transparency and gloss of the colours. Masking fluids enable parts of the painting surface to be rendered impervious to pigment; the masking fluid can be rubbed off after the work is completed.

Similar ranges of products are available from Rowney, Reeves, Grumbacher, Pelikan and other manufacturers but Winsor & Newton offer the most comprehensive range of paints and accessories.

GOUACHE

The only essential difference between watercolour and gouache is that the latter is opaque or semi-opaque. The pigments used in the manufacture of these paints are much the same as those used for watercolours but they are mixed with Chinese white to give added brilliance, smoother flow and greater covering power. This allows large areas of consistent, flat colour to be laid, enabling work to be photographed and reproduced with ease. Because of the added white, the colour looks lighter dry than wet, achieving a chalky appearance as light is reflected from the fine particles of white.

In high-quality ranges of gouache colour, the pigments are very finely ground, allowing them to be used, with care, in a pen or an airbrush.

WINSOR & NEWTON

DESIGNERS' GOUACHE COLOURS

Colour range: 80 colours

A very brilliant and full range. They are graded, in terms of permanence, on the same AA, A, B and C scale as watercolours. In addition, they have an opacity rating: O = completely opaque; R = reasonably opaque; P = partly transparent; T = transparent (applying only to some of the yellows).

Two whites are offered. Zinc white gives the cleanest and most lightfast tints and, therefore, is recommended for mixing with other colours to produce lighter tints of them. Permanent white gives greater opacity but is not recommended for mixing with other colours as it reduces the colour fastness of many of them.

POSTER GOUACHE COLOURS

Colour range: 53 colours

This range was originally produced for outdoor use on account of the boldness of the colours. But because they are cheaper to produce than the Designers' range, they are more popular and practical for students or for teachers to use in the classroom.

PROCESS BLACK AND PROCESS WHITE

These two opaque colours are particularly useful for camera-ready artwork as the white gives a true white and the black is truly black in that, unlike most black paints, it contains no blue.

These two colours can be used freely in an airbrush when diluted and will mix to produce a wide range of greys.

ACCESSORIES

Winsor & Newton produce a useful range of additives for extending the performance of gouache paints.

To prevent subsequent smudging, add Acrylic Gloss or Acrylic Gel. These render the paints virtually waterproof, add a slight gloss to the finish and allow impasto effects to be built up. Aquapasto, as the name suggests, allows thick layers of paint to be built up without cracking but it does decrease the opacity of the colours.

Adding Nacryl Acrylic Medium increases the adhesive powers on acetate or other shiny surfaces.

Art Masking Fluid protects any part of the work which is to remain uncovered after painting. It can be removed by peeling or rubbing when the surrounding paint is dry.

Several other manufacturers, including Pelikan and Reeves, produce gouache paints; Winsor & Newton's products, however, are the most widely available in several countries.

ACRYLIC PAINTS

Acrylic paints have become enormously popular over the last 20 years. This is probably explained by the fact that they are extraordinarily versatile. They can be used on almost any surface: virtually the only unsuitable surface is an oil-primed one. The paint, once applied, dries quickly and is waterproof. While the paint is still wet, however, it remains water soluble and can continue to be worked on, like any other paint. Remember that paintbrushes should be washed before the paint dries. Impasto effects are possible as acrylic paints do not crack easily. They can be used very much like watercolours in that washes can be laid over each other, allowing all the brilliance of the other transparent medium (the only drawback here is that the edges of such washes cannot be subsequently softened with water as the wash is waterproof once dry).

The only obvious disadvantage is their covering power. Even used straight from the tube or pot more than one application is likely to be required if true opacity is to be achieved.

GRUMBACHER

GRUMBACHER HYPLAR ACRYLICS
Colour range: 38 colours
A range available in 60ml (2 oz.) tubes, with Mars Black and Titan White also available in 150ml (5 oz.) tubes. A good range of Mediums, Varnishes and Gels are available to make the most of this flexible medium.

LIQUITEX

A very full range of colours offering brilliance, luminosity and durability, and available in various sizes of tube and jar. The colours from tubes dry with a slight gloss and those from jars dry with a matt finish.

Various additives and mediums are available. Gloss Medium and Varnish gives a highly reflective surface and increased transparency to the colours. On its own, it can be used as a final gloss varnish.

Matte Medium gives increased transparency but with a matt finish. Matte Varnish is what its name implies, and mixed with Gloss Varnish the precise degree of sheen desired can be controlled.

Retarding Medium slows down the drying time of acrylic paint, and Gel Medium, in addition to slowing drying time, also enables heavy impasto effects to be built up.

WINSOR & NEWTON

ACRYLIC COLOUR
Colour range: 34 colours
The manufacturers claim that this range has been improved recently by increasing pigment strength, stabilizing the consistency and increasing the adhesive and durability properties. All colours are available in either 60ml (2 oz.) tubes or 250ml (8 oz.) pots. Titanium White and Ivory Black are also available in 120ml (4 oz.) tubes.

A range of additives and accessories similar to the Liquitex products described above is also available.

OIL

Oil painting is not normally associated with graphic design but some illustrators certainly use this medium. As the photomechanical techniques of printed reproduction will work from virtually any source material there is no reason why this particular technique should not be used more frequently.

A restriction is that oil paints are slow drying and this is not compatible with the kinds of deadlines facing most designers! All the other paint types discussed in this chapter allow a comprehensive piece of illustrative work to be done almost as fast as the artist can put it down. Obviously some drying time is required but probably no more than 30 minutes at most in normal circumstances; with oils the drying time can be several days. But this disadvantage is offset by realizing that the paint is workable for a considerable period of time. Whereas watercolour dries almost immediately (unless in large wet washes) and gouache or acrylic take little longer, you can leave an area of oil paint for hours, then return to modify it.

As a technique, it probably has a wider range of colours, primers, mediums, drying oils, solvents and varnishes than any other. Winsor & Newton's Artists' Oil Colours probably offer the most comprehensive range of high-quality goods. This is complemented by their cheaper 'Winton' range. Liquitex and Grumbacher also offer good ranges of colours and accessories.

Nonetheless oil painting is a minority concern to the graphic designer. An immense library of books has been written on this medium and the interested reader is referred to them.

BRUSHES

Truly it can be said of brushes: you get what you pay for. A large, high-quality, sable brush can cost over $200. The same size brush in synthetic hair can be bought for less than $10.

Basically, there are two types of brushes: hard/stiff and soft/springy. Hard brushes are usually made of hog hair bristle, although synthetics are available. These brushes are generally used in oil painting but can be used for acrylics, particularly, and gouache.

The soft brushes are made of various kinds of hair and also synthetics. The best hair is sable: the best sable is 'Kolinsky' and these are the ones that cost a great deal of money. Kolinsky sable is the very tip-most hairs at the end of the tail of a species of Asiatic mink found only in remote parts of Siberian Russia and Northern China. Other, less exotic, kinds of sable are available and are not so expensive, although still not cheap, and for most purposes these are perfectly adequate.

Sable hair is notable for being both very soft and also springy. Rather more springy, but not so soft, are ox-hair brushes. Some designers prefer the greater springiness even though these brushes do not achieve such a fine point as sable. As a general rule, though, a good brush for most design work, retouching, and so on, should have a long slim shape and taper to a fine point to give greatest control over and ease of flow with, opaque colours and drawing inks.

A good blending brush, looking rather like a shaving brush, can be made of badger hair and is very good for handling large flat washes.

Of the natural hair brushes, the cheapest generally available is camel, although this is frequently squirrel! These brushes are soft and hold the pigment well, but they have little or no spring.

Other natural hair brushes are the increasingly familiar Chinese or Japanese bamboo brushes. These achieve a very fine point, hold a great amount of liquid but have little or no spring at all.

Brushes are also available in several different shapes:

Brights – short, curved-in, flat brushes
Flats – straight and longer than brights, these hold more pigment
Rounds – the 'traditional' watercolour brush shape
Fans – a widely spreading, thin, flat brush
Sky – oval-shaped, full brushes good for laying broad washes
Lettering – long, straight brushes holding a lot of pigment, useful for one long uninterrupted stroke

All brushes should be looked after carefully. Oil brushes should be cleaned initially in white spirit (paint thinner),

then in cold water and soap. Watercolour and gouache brushes should be rinsed in cold water then washed in soap in the palm of the hand until all trace of pigment has gone.

Acrylic brushes must be washed in cold water immediately after use and then given the soap and water treatment. Short of this rather lengthy procedure, rinsing the brush in cold water, filling it once more with cold water and hanging upside down will allow any residue pigment to leach down to the tip of the brush and simple rinsing in cold water then completes the job.

All brushes should be stored dry, either standing upwards or lying flat. They should never be enclosed when wet as mildew can set in. There are some risks from moths so a mothball in the container used for storing the brushes is advisable.

Most brushes are available in a range of sizes starting at 00, very small and fine, 0, 1, 2, 3 and through to 12 or 14 which is quite large. Some flat brushes are sized in millimetres or inches.

ARTEC

Series 360 – camel hair watercolour brushes
Series 610 – synthetic, round watercolour brushes
Series 640 and **Series 650** – synthetic hair, flat, one-stroke brushes
Series 500B, **500F**, **500R 515** – natural bristle brushes for oil and acrylic work
Series 520 – a natural bristle fan blender

GRUMBACHER

Series 178 – fine, round, sable brushes for watercolour; especially useful for retouching

Series 6142 – flat, sable line brushes for watercolour
Series 579 and **582** – pure white bristle oil and acrylic brushes
Series 1131 – a round-section, flat-ended stencil or stippling brush made from quality bristle
Series 197 – watercolour brushes, made from the finest sable, with a full-bodied shape for both wash and detailed work
Series 55 – 'sky' brushes made from sable for laying broad washes
Series 9455 – medium-length sable lettering brushes with a clean, square end. **Series 9355** are similar but have longer handles
Series 289 – bamboo watercolour brushes with long tapered points made from textured hair

SIMMONS
Not available in the UK

Series 760-3 – long-handled 'brights' for oil and acrylic work, made from Simmons White Sable, a synthetic fibre that performs like traditional natural sable but is considerably lower in price. It is easy to clean and holds pigment well
Series 761-R – long-handled 'rounds' for oil and acrylic work, also made from White Sable
Series 748L – White Sable fan brushes for blending and textured effects
Series 785 – White Sable watercolour brushes
Series 40 – Natural bristle brushes for oil and acrylic work, in flat (F), bright (B) or round (R) shapes

WINSOR & NEWTON

Winsor & Newton offer a very wide and large selection of all types of brushes from the most expensive sable (Series 7) through less expensive sables (eg Series 3A, 12, 14 and 33) to inexpensive synthetic brushes, and various bristle brushes for oil and acrylic work.

AIRBRUSHES

Airbrushes have always been an essential tool for photographic retouchers and technical illustrators but in recent years they have also achieved an astonishing popularity in other fields of commercial graphics. A good airbrush artist can reproduce precisely an array of photographic effects and create many more which photography can never hope to match. Airbrushing gives a brilliance and clarity of colour, combined with subtle use of light and shade, which even the best photography cannot achieve, and can show realistically what, in reality, it would be impossible to construct for the camera, such as 'cut away' illustrations and exploded views. The airbrush has also acquired a reputation for the imaginative execution of illustrations in the fields of science fiction and advertising, as well as being employed extensively in ceramics and stained glass, and in the automotive industry. Some airbrushes can even carry abrasives instead of pigments and are used to erase paints and inks without smudging.

Although there are several different types of airbrush on the market, the basic principle of operation remains the same in all cases. Compressed air is fed through a narrow channel into a nozzle chamber containing a long needle where it meets liquid pigment from a reservoir under normal atmospheric pressure. This mixture is then expelled through the nozzle as an atomized spray. This is termed an 'internal mix' airbrush. In an 'external-mix' airbrush the air and pigment come together outside the nozzle or fluid assembly; this makes the spray inherently more coarse and gives a stippled dot pattern. This method is not nearly so common and is only used for particularly viscous, heavy-duty media such as enamel-based paints or ceramic glazes. Different types of pigment require different air pressures to atomize them effectively. The heavier and more viscous the medium, the higher the pressure required. Between 25 and 30 pounds per square inch (p.s.i.) is sufficient for inks, dyes, watercolours and thinly reduced gouache but 40-50 p.s.i. is necessary for acrylics, enamels and lacquers.

Two basic types of airbrush are available: those with a single action, and those with a double action lever control mechanism. The double action lever meters exactly the proportions of air and pigment delivered to the spray nozzle, allowing you to change line value and density without stopping the spraying process. Downward pressure on the lever regulates the amount of air passing into the chamber while backward movement increases the flow of pigment by withdrawing the needle from the nozzle. With a single action lever airbrush (the simplest and cheapest type), only the flow of air can be controlled and the mix cannot be adjusted during use. The spray pattern can only be altered by changing the distance between the airbrush and the work being sprayed. This type obviously does not provide the degree of control necessary for detailed work but makes a good tool for a novice user or for airbrushing large areas and backgrounds.

Before purchasing an airbrush, think carefully about the applications for which it is needed. The size, type and fineness of the line desired and the materials to be sprayed are important in determining your choice. Do you want to use it with a variety of different media? Is it mainly for detailed work or broader areas? Airbrushes can be left- or right-handed according to where the reservoir or colour cup is mounted. Those which have a top-mounted reservoir, or one which is incorporated into the body of the airbrush, can be used by both hands. These gravity-fed models are used for detailed work as they do not require a siphon to help the liquid pigment flow to the needle. Suction-fed or bottom-fed airbrushes usually have screw-on jars underneath which act as reservoirs. These facilitate quick colour changes and allow the user to spray larger areas without the need for constant refilling.

Airbrushes are fed with air by electric compressors, refillable carbon dioxide tanks or cans of aerosol propellant. Occasional users or students may well find it more convenient and economical to use these propellants (they are in any event always useful for working outside the studio or in case of a power failure). Most manufacturers of airbrushes supply these cans, as do large graphics suppliers. The committed airbrush artist, however, really requires a good electric compressor to provide a reliable supply of pure, pulse-free air at constant pressure.

Compressors have different capacities, depending on their size. An artist spraying with very viscous fluids at pressures of up to 50 p.s.i. will need a large model while a small compact one would be sufficient for someone working with light fluids at pressures of 30 p.s.i. or less. For a studio where more than one person may be airbrushing at the same time a large compressor with several outlet taps is an economical buy. Modern compressors are much more reliable and sturdy while remaining reasonably portable. The best types have efficient filters to purify the air, a reservoir to smooth out uneven air pressures and, as a safety precaution, a minimum of exposed moving parts. A thermal cut-out is an advantage in protecting the compressor from damage if it is left switched on for extended periods of time. An optional footswitch control is also useful for completely hands-free operation. Before purchasing, remember to check that you have the appropriate couplings to connect your particular make of airbrush to the compressor. Adaptors are available to match up hoses and outlet taps of different threads. Always ensure that all connections are tight as any leakage effectively reduces air pressure. The hose between the compressor and the airbrush should be a minimum of 120cm (4 ft) in length for ease of movement. A braided hose (rubber encased in a woven fibre sleeve) reduces the risk of kinking and tangling during use.

The size of the nozzle on the airbrush affects the rate at which the air/pigment mixture is expelled. The nozzle and cap are often adjustable to give different degrees of coverage but special wide-angle ones, combined with a high flow needle, are available for particularly large areas. A spatter cap will give a coarse, uneven finish and is useful for textured effects.

In most airbrushes any liquid of a consistency that will pass through an ordinary wire tea-strainer can be used. Ensure that the pigments are properly thinned and mixed: any coarseness or inconsistency will cause an uneven coverage or clog the nozzle. Fill the reservoir carefully with an eyedropper, syringe or brush, wiping the outside of the airbrush with a clean cloth or tissue to prevent drips running down the barrel on to the artwork.

An airbrush is a delicate precision instrument and, like a drafting pen, must be treated with care and respect. The slightest damage to the air cap or needle will cause distortion and result in imperfections in the spray pattern. It is most important that all parts are kept scrupulously clean and that pigment is never allowed to dry and become encrusted inside the mechanism. The airbrush should be rinsed out thoroughly with clean water before each fresh colour is used and the colour cup and nozzle should be cleaned after each airbrushing session with a suitable solvent and soft brush. Petroleum-based solvents supplied in aerosol sprays are the most effective for this (see Adhesives, Tapes and Sprays, pp. 112-19). The needle can be removed for cleaning if necessary (in the case of severe clogging) but only with extreme care.

BADGER AIR-BRUSH COMPANY

The Badger Air-Brush Company is the largest manufacturer of airbrushes in America and is recommended by technical illustrators and commercial artists for the dependability and general all-round high quality of their products.

MODEL 250-3

An easy-to-handle, external-mix spray gun for lines from 19mm (¾ in.) to 50mm (2 in.). The spray pattern is adjusted by turning the paint tip at the head of the gun. The gun is not designed for detailed work but is effective for broad coverage, making textures and working with stencils. It will handle media of a medium to heavy viscosity.

This set contains all the basic equipment you need to start spraying – jars, hose, regulator, can of propellant and instruction book.

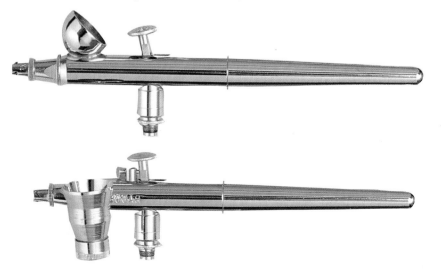

Airbrushes from the Badger range of products.

MODEL 350-2

A single action airbrush beginners' set supplied complete with jars, hose, regulator, can of propellant, spanner for changing nozzles and instruction book. The airbrush comes fitted with a medium-sized nozzle capable of spraying a line from 6.3mm (¼ in.) to 30mm (1¼ in.) but alternative fine (3.2mm/⅛ in. to 25.4mm/1 in.) or heavy nozzles (12.5mm/½ in. to 50.8mm/2 in.) are also available for this model.

Model 200-3

An inexpensive set containing a single action airbrush, three jars, hose, regulator, can of propellant and instruction book. This is an ideal purchase for a student who has not yet mastered the technique of using a dual action airbrush: the spray width can be adjusted and locked in position using a screw at the end of the handle. The airbrush is supplied with a medium nozzle (ref. IL) which will spray a line from 1.5mm (1/16 in.) to 38mm (1½ in.) but fine nozzles (ref. XF – pencil width to 25.4mm/1 in.) and heavy nozzles (ref. HD – 3.2mm/⅛ in. to 50.8mm/2 in.) can also be fitted.

MODEL 150-4 PK(W)

A professional's set in a wooden case, containing the Model 150 dual action airbrush complete with the three different nozzle assemblies and appropriate needles (XF, IL and HD), three jars, a colour cup, braided hose, compressor adaptor and instruction book. The Model 150 airbrush is bottom fed and can be adapted to take both 22ml (¾ oz.) and 60ml (2 oz.) paint jars and a 7ml (¼ oz.) colour cup.

MODEL 100-1-XF

A dual action airbrush recommended for particularly fine detailing with low viscosity media. The colour cup is side mounted to allow an uninterrupted view of the nozzle (both left- and right-handed models are available) and can be adjusted for horizontal and vertical work.

MODEL 100-5-LGXF

A gravity-fed dual action airbrush with a permanently top-mounted 14ml (½ oz.) colour cup. This feature allows the good liquid flow to the nozzle required for extremely finely detailed work. This model can be used either left- or right-handed, vertically and horizontally. It is supplied with an XF nozzle but IL and HD assemblies can also be fitted.

Note: The XF nozzle is designed to be used with media of a low viscosity (watercolours, inks, dyes, thinned acrylics and gouaches).

The IL nozzle can spray twice as much fluid as the XF and can also handle slightly thicker media, such as thinned down lacquers and enamels.

The HD nozzle has a large opening capable of spraying four times the amount of material as the XF. It is designed to be used with highly viscous media such as ceramic glazes, acrylics and automotive paints.

DE VILBISS

AEROGRAPH SUPER 63 'A' and 'E' MODELS

Highly recommended airbrushes for the professional user, these are especially suited to delicate retouching and other very detailed work. The ink reservoir is incorporated into the body of the airbrush on the 'A' model, giving a completely unobstructed view of the nozzle, while the 'E' model has a 5ml (1/6 oz.) top-mounted colour cup for continuous high-speed coverage of larger areas. Both have an adjustable cam ring behind the double action control lever which enables the user to pre-set the rate of colour flow to the needle, and both can handle a rull range of media from watercolours to acrylic paints and enamels.

AEROGRAPH SPRITE AND SPRITE MAJOR

A good choice for a student or semi-professional user who definitely wants a double action airbrush but does not require the high degree of sophistication of the Super 63 models. Although modestly priced, these models provide excellent control and permit fine detailed work as well as broader coverage. They also have an adjustable cam ring to pre-set the rate of colour flow to the needle. The top-mounted 5ml (1/6 oz.) plastic colour cup on the Sprite has a useful tight-fitting cap to prevent accidental spillage of the liquid pigment while the suction-fed Sprite Major has a 28.4ml (1 oz.) glass jar for spraying larger areas. A wide angle air cap and nozzle set and a high flow needle are also available.

AEROGRAPH IMP

An economically priced, external-mix, single action airbrush. It has an adjustable nozzle which can alter the spray pattern from 5mm (3/16 in.) to 25mm (1 in.) and a control valve incorporated into the handle to regulate air pressure.

HUMBROL

STUDIO I AIRBRUSH SET

A beginners' set specifically designed for graphic artists and modellers, complete with three spare capped jars and a standard size can of propellant. The single action airbrush has an adjustable elongated colour cup, and air/pigment control is operated by a moulded plastic sliding switch.

LETRASET

LETRAJET AIR MARKER

LetraJet consists of a light plastic housing which carries a fine nozzled air jet. A Pantone Fine marker is slotted into place and compressed air from a can or compressor, activated by a trigger mechanism, blows pigment from the marker's tip on to the work surface. It is, in essence, the equivalent of a single action, external-mix airbrush and offers much the same degree of control. Density and weight of line can be varied by altering the distance between the tip and the work, or by changing the speed of the stroke. Although it cannot offer the delicacy of an expensive airbrush, LetraJet does have several useful features: quick colour changes are possible without the need to clean any part of the air jet and there is, of course, a vast array of ready-mixed colours available. These can also be matched at further stages of a job as they are part of the standard Pantone system (see pp. 123-4).

The LetraJet Airmarker, which uses a Pantone marker in place of a colour cup.

PAASCHE

PAASCHE AB

An exceptionally high-quality airbrush, employed by artists, illustrators and photographic retouchers for the very finest detail. Its delicate mechanism is easily clogged so only use with fluids of a very low viscosity. It can draw the finest hairline dot and line, make a clean edge, or apply a fine or coarse stipple.

PAASCHE H RANGE

A popular range of single action airbrushes suitable for use with most media. Interchangeable nozzle sets are available to convert the spray pattern from fine line through to broad coverage.

PAASCHE V AND VJR RANGES

Double action airbrushes which, with the exception of the AB model, give the smallest spray pattern. In most cases, for the general user, these offer a sufficient degree of high-quality precision and have the advantage for the 'once only' purchaser of being adjustable for broader coverage and convertible to larger nozzles for heavier fluids.

PAASCHE F I

An inexpensive and durable single action airbrush ideal for the beginner. Operation using media of a relatively low viscosity is easy to master and it offers a useful small to medium scale spray range.

PAASCHE AEC AIR ERASER

A specialist airbrush for erasing permanent pigments using an aluminium oxide compound. It is also employed for etching on glass or dulling precious metals.

SIMAIR

OLYMPOS HP100 Series (A, B and C)

An economical range of dual action airbrushes suitable for use with almost all types of pigment. Model A, recommended for fine detailed work, has a 0.3ml reservoir incorporated into its body, while Model B, used for the same tasks, has a slightly larger 1ml top-mounted colour cup giving greater range but a less satisfactory view of the work in hand. Model C is adapted for broad spraying with a large capacity, capped 7ml (1/4 oz.) colour cup.

OLYMPOS SPECIAL SERIES (A, B AND C)

A finely tuned range for the professional user, offering a high degree of spray accuracy. A vernier scale adjusting screw at the end of the handle allows very precise setting of the colour flow by altering the position of the needle. Olympos Specials also incorporate an adjustable return spring in the handle with which the tension of the control lever can be altered to suit personal preference. The A, B and C models vary in similar ways to those in the HP100 Series.

All Olympos airbrushes can produce a spatter effect without the use of a special spatter cap. This is achieved by removing the nozzle cap and needle cap and reducing the air pressure. However, great care must be taken when using the airbrush in this way as the needle is exposed and very vulnerable to damage.

THAYER & CHANDLER

THAYER & CHANDLER A AND AA

Model A is a good all-purpose double action airbrush for fine line retouching and illustration work requiring shading, backgrounds or borders. The V-shaped, flat-bottomed colour cup is particularly easy to clean and has a protective cap to prevent accidental spillage of pigment. Model AA will spray twice the amount of colour as Model A and can cope with more viscous media such as lacquers and enamels.

THAYER & CHANDLER E

A modestly priced single action airbrush. It will handle all types of lacquers and enamels in industrial use without clogging and is recommended for touching up or smooth coverage of small to medium sized areas.

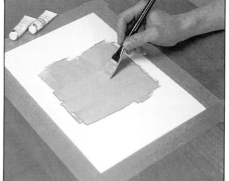

I Work on a fairly heavy cartridge (drawing) paper on artboard (bristol board). Tape down all four sides. Lay the board flat and select a thick brush. A flat wash brush is ideal. Mix up a large quantity of paint, more than you think you will need as it is almost impossible to mix the same colour twice if you run out.

2 Fill your brush with paint. Starting at the top left-hand corner and working fairly quickly, apply the colour in steady horizontal strokes from left to right, overlapping the edges of each one as you move down the page. When you have covered the area completely, brush vertically from top to bottom to eliminate any lines.

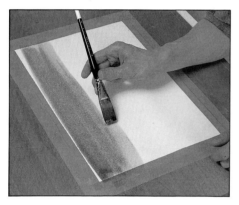

APPLYING A WASH

I Use stretched watercolour paper or a piece of artboard (bristol board), and a large thick wash brush. Prop the board up underneath the top edge so that it slopes towards you at an angle of approximately 30°. Keep some blotting paper at the ready.

2 You must work quickly to achieve an even effect before the colour dries. Dip the brush into the colour and wipe off any drips before taking it to the paper. With an even stroke, paint a line across the top of the paper. Repeat the strokes, alternating backwards and forwards. Reload the brush with paint after each stroke.

3 If the paint starts to drip down the page, there is too much on the brush. Make another stroke without refilling it. Overlaying areas with the same colour enables you to build up a density of colour.

4 When you reach the bottom of the page, soak up the excess paint with blotting paper. The paper must be left to dry completely before further applications.

SPECIAL EFFECTS WITH PAINTS AND INKS

1 Carefully mask off any area that is to remain clean. Load an old toothbrush with watercolour, gouache or ink. Draw a flat-bladed tool across the toothbrush towards you. This will produce an uneven spatter effect.

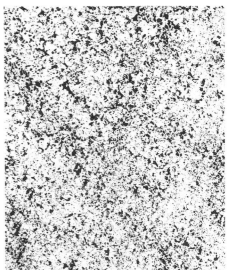

2 Mix up watercolour, gouache or ink in a saucer. Dab a sponge into the paint and then on to the drawing surface. Experiment with other materials such as cottonwool (absorbent cotton) or tissue paper to create different textural effects.

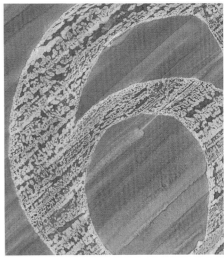

3 Candle wax and wax crayons are an effective resist. Draw a design, or rub over a texture with the wax and then paint with a fairly thin pigment.

1 A spatter cap will give a coarse, uneven finish and is useful for special textured effects.

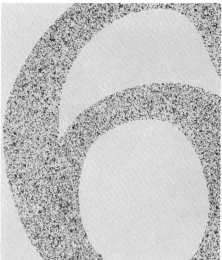

2 Background effects are achieved by using a broad, freehand technique. Move your arm smoothly backwards and forwards from the shoulder. Gradually build up the density by adding more layers.

3 Holding a piece of torn paper between the working surface and the spray will give a rough edge. The line will be softer if the mask is further from the working surface.

**USING AN AIRBRUSH
(cont.)**

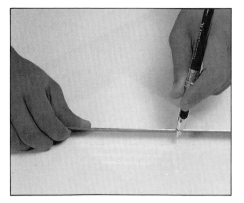

4 To spray thin straight lines, rest a steel rule on the working surface and lift the edge towards you. Hold the nozzle of the airbrush against this edge and about 10mm (⅜ in.) above the paper. Hold the rule steady and slide the nozzle along it. For broader lines hold the nozzle about 20mm (¾ in.) from the paper.

AIRBRUSH CARE

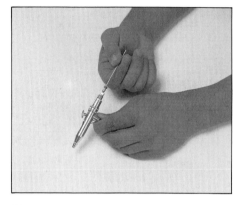

1 Every so often, blow air through the airbrush on to a piece of scrap paper. This helps prevent blockages in the nozzle.

2 Loosen the locking screw, and draw back the needle, do not remove the needle. Lock the needle in this position.

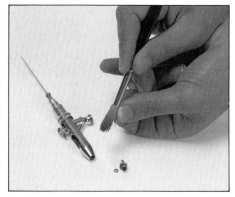

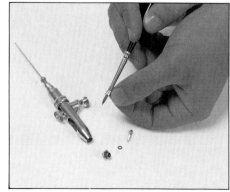

3 Separate a few hairs from a large long-haired paintbrush; use these to clear any blockage in the nozzle.

4 Use a clean dry brush to remove excess moisture from the nozzle.

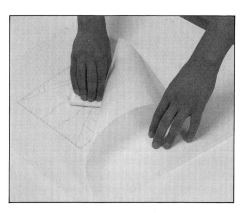

USING MASKING FILM

There are two different ways in which masking film can be used. Steps 1 and 2 are applicable if you want to apply a mask to an already outlined area, or a photograph. Steps 3 and 4 are more useful if you will be working several colours on one piece of artwork.

1 Peel away the waxed paper backing sheet, and apply mask to the artwork. The film is repositionable for perfect accuracy. For finely detailed areas of an image, it may be necessary to cut the film in position on the artwork.

2 Cut out the shape required with a very sharp knife – the sharper the blade, the cleaner and crisper the mask will be. There is no need to press deeply into the surface as the film should cut quite easily.

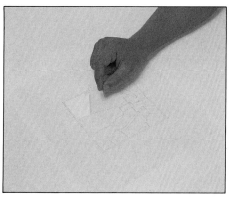

3 Stick the masking film on to the surface. Trace the image carefully in pencil or artists' tracing carbon on to the film.

4 Peel away the areas of film to be coloured one by one. The masks can be returned to their correct positions when you are ready to work on the next area.

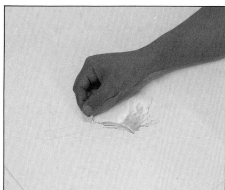

USING MASKING FLUID

Masking fluid is a solution of liquid rubber, and is ideal for protecting fine lines, and for masking irregular shapes where cutting a mask might prove difficult.

1 Paint on the fluid carefully with an old paintbrush reserved for this purpose. Allow to dry completely to a thin film.

2 To remove after masking is complete, rub the surface gently with your finger. The film will peel away easily.

MATERIALS

In this section, we consider the materials which it is necessary – and not so vital, but which are generally useful – to have around the studio in order to produce a piece of graphic design from initial rough to finished artwork. These materials include papers and boards, films and acetates, adhesives, and lettering and colour systems.

PAPER

It might seem obvious to say that paper is the most frequently used surface that graphic designers work on. What might not be at first appreciated, though, behind this glaringly simple statement, is the enormous range of papers on the market.

There is a relatively small classification list of papers and certainly manufacturers tend to offer a range that falls within the fairly simple list. But this apparent straightforwardness is complicated again by the fact that many retailers, especially the larger ones, sell these papers under their own names and not under those of the manufacturer. There are exceptions to this in that the manufacturers of expensive, high-quality, specialized materials – such as illustration board and watercolour paper – realize the advantage of having their names retained on these prestige products. But, by and large, this section of the book will concentrate on describing the characteristics and accepted uses of the different kinds of paper in general use, rather than on naming particular brands.

GENERAL PURPOSE PAPERS

LAYOUT PAPER

This is a thin, fairly transparent paper, probably the cheapest in the range commonly used by most designers. Its main use is in the preparation of first ideas, and for this reason it is often called visualizing paper. It can also be used for tracing-off type, lettering and other material in the preparation of visuals, and for this reason it is sometimes also called detail paper.

TRACING PAPER

More transparent than layout paper, this is also a harder and stronger material. Its translucency makes it suitable for tracing the finest details, its hardness means that it will accept even very thin lines consistently with very little spread, and because of its strength, mistakes in the ink line can be removed by scraping with a sharp blade. It is available in various weights.

The heavier and higher quality tracing papers are sometimes called 'tracing vellum'.

CARTRIDGE/DRAWING PAPER

Cartridge (drawing) paper is what most people use for drawing. It is fairly soft and has a finish that is neither very smooth nor particularly rough or textured. For these reasons it takes most kinds of pencil very well. Crayons, pastels, pen and ink, gouache or watercolours can also be used with confidence on this paper.

WATERCOLOUR PAPERS

The best watercolour papers are still hand made from a 100 per cent rag pulp. The rag is pounded, shredded and mixed to a fine textured pulp, which is then laid on frames of wire mesh. Water is drenched over the frame to establish an even thickness of pulp and allow the fibres of the mixture to intertwine, thus forming a properly structured sheet of paper.

This crude sheet is transferred to a layer of felt over which another felt is placed. This process is repeated, building up a pile of sheets of paper and felt. The stack of paper and felt is then put in a screw press to remove most of the water. The sheets of paper are then dried and sized, as required. Some papers are further finished by pressing through hot rollers and others through cold rollers. The first produces what is known as 'Hot-pressed', or 'HP', paper, characterized by its smooth finish. The cold-rolled paper is termed (somewhat confusingly in the UK), 'Not' paper, which simply means 'not hot-pressed'. (In the United States, this paper is called cold-pressed.) Paper which is neither hot nor cold pressed but left in its simple state is called 'Rough'. This has a richly textured surface, giving the characteristic speckled look of some watercolour work as the pigment settles in the dips in the paper and falls away from the raised parts.

These fine papers are available in various weights: 90lb, 140lb, and 200lb being the usual values. Some papers are expressed in grammes per square metre (gsm). Excellent manufacturers are Fabriano, Whatman, and Saunders.

SPECIALIST STUDIO PAPERS

With the increasing technical standard of printing has come the opportunity to expect a very high standard of fielding to the original during the reproduction process. Artists and designers need to have very high-quality drawing and painting surfaces to enable them to maximize the usefulness of high technology printing.

Bristol boards and illustration boards both provide finish and good dimensional stability.

Bristol board is a smooth-finished sheet which can be used on either side. Bonding sheets together increases the availability of thicknesses: 2 sheet, 4 sheet, 6 sheet, and so on.

Illustration boards are made by bonding high-quality drawing papers on to a stiff backing board. This enables all kinds of work to be done without buckling. The range of surfaces available enables the calligrapher, the technical draftsman and the free-wash illustrator to work with confidence and up to the highest levels.

TRANSFER PAPER

A paper that works like carbon paper. A drawing can be moved from one surface to another by interposing the transfer paper. The desired drawing is imprinted upon the new surface in a grease-free line, any traces of which can be erased after the new drawing has been completed.

COLOURED PAPERS

Some good drawing papers, such as Ingres papers, are available in a large range of colours in addition to white and are particularly suited to pencil, crayon and pastel work. They have a characteristic grooved texture which retains the loose particles of these media very well. Other papers not suited to drawing are also available in an enormous range of colours. These are useful for flat colour presentation, and for flapping over other work.

They will take airbrushed pigments with effect and also acrylic paints but are not the natural choice for gouache or watercolour.

Other coloured stock is very useful in the preparation of package designs and other three-dimensional mock-ups for display purposes. These papers will take ink, markers and dry transfer lettering.

CHROMOLUX PAPERS/COVER STOCK

A high-gloss finish in various colours coats this stock which is ideal for package presentations, dummies and signs. The extra-smooth surface on these papers and boards also makes an excellent ground for accurate ink drawing with drafting pens. Fine lines can be produced without 'feathering' occurring.

OTHER SPECIALIST PAPERS AND BOARDS

FOAM-CORE BOARD

These are extremely light and rigid polystyrene boards coated on both sides with smooth white paper. They can be cut easily to any shape and are ideal for display purposes.

PRE-PRINTED PAPERS

There is a large range of papers pre-printed, usually in non-photosensitive blue, with grids, isometric (both axes at 45° to the horizontal or vertical), axonometric (one axis at 60°, and one at 30°, to the horizontal or vertical), and other projections enabling accurate drawings to be done without the laborious necessity of drawing up the grids by hand.

TV LAYOUT PADS

These packs of paper are pre-printed, usually in grey, with TV screen-shaped masks, allowing storyboard presentations to be made.

FILMS AND ACETATES

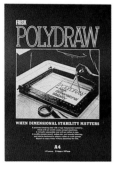

DRAFTING FILM

In recent years, drafting on film has proved such a success that these products have become more and more sophisticated and are now used extensively in numerous fields of the design industry. Plastic and polyester drafting film is tear resistant, dimensionally stable (that is, insensitive to fluctuations in temperature and humidity) and gives excellent results in reproduction, thereby providing an ideal ground for all kinds of specialist technical drawing and artwork where a high degree of accuracy is essential. Its resilience and strength make it particularly useful for mechanical plotters or use in architects' and cartographers' offices. The graphic designer uses drafting film mainly for overlays on artwork where exact registration is required between colour separations.

Drafting film comes in a range of thicknesses (usually .003 in., .004 in., and .007 in.) and surface finishes. It is important for the graphic designer to choose a film which has a specially treated matt surface capable of accepting a variety of drawing media. Any kind of pencil, for instance, needs a degree of 'tooth' in order to hold to the surface but it must be smooth enough to give fine ink lines without feathering. Most films have a highly abrasive surface (although this is microscopic) which will eventually ruin the normal drawing point of a drafting pen so it is essential to use a special tip on this material (see Drafting Pens, pp.72-5). Also, ensure that marks can be erased readily without damaging the surface unduly and that the moisture content of rubber-based adhesives will not buckle the film. For this it is often necessary to buy a slightly thicker and heavier product although a high degree of translucency is important to maintain accurate registration. If you will be doing a lot of artwork of varying sizes, buy a large roll of film which can be trimmed to shape as required. If not, a pad of ready trimmed sheets could be more convenient.

ERASA/DURE
Not available in the UK

POLYESTER DRAFTING FILM
Sizes: Available in 20 yd rolls in widths of 30 in., 32 in., 36 in., 42 in.; in 50 yd rolls in widths of 30 in., 32 in., 36 in., 42 in.; in 8½ × 11 in., 11 × 17 in. sheets
Dimensionally stable film, with a matt coating on either one or both sides. It has a high tearing strength, good visual transparency and smooth ink and pencil acceptance.

FRISK/FRISKET

FRISK K-TRACE
Sizes: Available in 5m (5½ yd) and 10m (11 yd) rolls in widths of 550mm (21 in.), 775mm (30½ in.), 1100mm (42 in.); in A2, A3, A4 pads
K-trace was the original drafting and tracing film and its name is often used as an alternative generic title for these products. It has a faintly blue non-repro tint but is exceptionally translucent and ideal for overlays and colour separations since it is dimensionally stable in normal working conditions. K-trace has one gloss and one matt surface, the latter offering a very good surface for drafting in both ink and pencil, and has the helpful characteristic of staying flat when unrolled.

FRISK POLYDRAW
Sizes: Available in 5m (5½ yd) and 10m (11 yd) rolls in widths of 594mm (23½ in.), 860mm (34 in.); in A2, A3, A4 pads
Polydraw differs from K-trace in having a double matt surface, particularly advantageous on occasions when dimensional stability really matters or in changeable working conditions where heat and humidity are fluctuating rapidly. Its strength and thickness make it exceptionally resistant to stretching, contracting or tearing providing the edge is not nicked and it will not yellow or become brittle over time, even when exposed to ultraviolet light.

FRISK DIACEL
Sizes: Available in 5m (5½ yd) and 10m (11 yd) rolls in widths of 550mm (21 in.), 775mm (30½ in.), 1100mm (42 in.); in A2, A3, A4 pads; in 15m (16¼ yd) overhead projection rolls

260mm (10¼ in.) wide; in 267 × 267mm (10½ × 10½ in.) overhead projection panels Diacel is an untreated clear diacetate film which will accept specialist water-based markers, wax-based products or film colours. It can be used as a protective covering, to give a laminated appearance to artwork or for overhead projection and animation work.

FRISK ARTCEL
Sizes: Available in 5m (5½ yd) and 10m (11 yd) rolls in width of 545mm (21 in.); in A2, A3, A4 pads; in 15m (16¼ yd) overhead projection rolls 260mm (10¼ in.) wide; in 267 × 267mm (10½ × 10½ in.) overhead projection panels Both water- and spirit-based drawing materials can be applied directly to the surface of this specially coated clear triacetate film. Watercolours, acrylic colours, gouache and inks, applied with either brushes or pens, will all adhere well and give good finished results, as will dry transfer lettering.

MECANORMA
Not available in the USA

POLYESTER
Sizes: Available in A2, A3 pads
A dimensionally stable drafting film for technical drawing and precision overlays. It has good resistance to heat and humidity.

KEUFFEL AND ESSER

HERCULENE STATIC-FREE DRAFTING FILM
Sizes: Available in 20m (22 yd) rolls in widths of 750mm (30 in.), 1000mm (40 in.), 1200mm (48 in.), 1340mm (54 in.), 1500mm (60 in.); in A0, A1, A2, A3, A4, 750 × 1000mm (30 × 40 in.) cut sheets
A popular transparent drafting film chosen for use in many design studios for its consistency and resilience. The matt surface is much less abrasive than many other products, offering excellent results with both pencil and ink with little wear on the drawing tool. Marks are very easy to erase cleanly and the surface can even be typed upon if required. It is resistant to cracking, yellowing and heat damage and will repel moisture and grease from hands.

HERCULENE HI-TRANS DRAFTING FILM
Sizes: Available in 18.2m (20 yd) and 45.7m (50 yd) rolls in widths of 750mm (30 in.), 860mm (34 in.), 900mm (36 in.), 1050mm (42 in.)

Similar in most respects to ordinary Herculene Drafting Film, this product has the particular dimensional stability and translucency required for precision overlay drafting.

ACETATE

Acetate is not often used for overlays on finished artwork as it is not as stable or strong as drafting film. It has a high gloss finish which rejects water-based media such as markers and picks up grease and dirt easily from your hands and other surfaces, making the application of some spirit (alcohol)-based media difficult. However, acetate is frequently employed in preparing presentation roughs and dummies where one-off overlays of type and/or images are required. For this, the surface must either have been specially coated by the manufacturer to accept conventional studio materials or be prepared carefully by hand. Wipe the acetate thoroughly with lighter fuel (fluid) before applying paint or inks and try to keep your hands from resting directly on the surface during use. Cover the areas you are not actually working on at present with a piece of tissue or paper.

Water-based paints such as gouache should be used at a slightly thicker consistency than normal to ensure good adhesion. Acetate is also extremely useful as a removable covering for dummies and finished roughs, keeping them clean no matter how much they are handled.

RETAILERS' BRANDS

Acetate is often purchased direct from manufacturers and sold by art suppliers under their own name or unbranded. For example, **ARTHUR BROWN** (in the USA) sell:

PREFIXED ACETATE
Sizes: Available in 11 × 14 in., 14 × 17 in., 20 × 25 in. sheets; in 9 × 12 in., 11 × 14 in., 14 × 17 in., 19 × 24 in. pads
A completely clear acetate, coated on both sides, which will accept poster paint, watercolours, inks and dyes without prior preparation.

ACETATE
Sizes: Available in 36ft rolls 40 in. wide; in 100ft rolls 40 in. wide; in 25 × 40 in. sheets

Cellulose acetate with either a translucent (frosted on one side) or completely transparent finish. Good for overlays and protective finishes.

COLORED ACETATE

Sizes: Available in 20 × 50 in. sheets
Colour range: amber, blue, green, red
Transparent uncoated acetate for overhead projection work, presentation visuals and so on.

A. I. FRIEDMAN
(also in the USA) sell:

PREPARED ACETATE

Sizes: Available in 50 yd rolls in widths of 20 in., 40 in.; in 100 yd rolls in widths of 20 in., 40 in.; in 9 × 12 in., 11 × 14 in., 14 × 17 in., 20 × 25 in. sheets; in 9 × 12 in., 11 × 14 in., 14 × 17 in., 19 × 24 in. pads
A completely clear acetate with a special coating on both sides which will accept all types of paints and inks easily. Mistakes can be erased easily with water without affecting the treated surface.

ACETATE PADS

Sizes: Available in 9 × 12 in., 11 × 14 in., 14 × 17 in., 19 × 24 in. pads
A clear film for use in presentation, packaging and display. Dry transfer products, wax- and spirit (alcohol)-based media can be used successfully on the surface.

LETRASET

LETRASET TRI-ACETATE PADS

Sizes: Available in A2, A3, A4 pads
A clear triacetate product coated to accept most conventional studio materials without the need for prior preparation. Excellent adhesion is possible with both water- and spirit (alcohol)-based media making this a generally useful tool for artwork, visuals, overlays on dummies and audiovisual work. Each pad comes with a pre-printed grid for the easy layout of artwork.

MECANORMA
Not available in the USA

ACETATE 1

Sizes: Available in A2, A3 pads
A completely clear film, coated on both sides, for working in gouache, inks and markers without the need for prior preparation of the surface.

Acetate 2, also available in A2 and A3 pads, is transparent, and has a matt surface on one side. It is particularly suited to line work in gouache, inks and markers and will also accept pencil easily.

ROSCOART
Not available in the UK

COLORED ACETATE

Size: Available in 20 × 24 in. sheets
Colour range: 35 colours
An exceptionally wide range of colours are offered in this range of optically clear acetate. They are bright and vivid and are ideal for projection work and the preparation of presentation visuals.

A 4 × 1 in. swatchbook is available giving a sample sheet of each colour.

SELF-ADHESIVE FILM

Transparent self-adhesive film provides another protective covering material although obviously it is very difficult to remove without damage to the item underneath. However, it does offer a good seal against oil, grease, water and wear and tear for charts, maps, diagrams and so on. Coloured transparent adhesive films can be used to apply areas of even colour to artwork and visuals in much the same way as Pantone colour overlays (see The Pantone System, pp. 123-4).

FRISK/FRISKET

FRISK COVERSEAL

Sizes: Available in 9.1m (10 yd) and 23m (25 yd) rolls in widths of 500mm (20 in.), 1000mm (40 in.)
Gloss colour range: black, red, blue, green, yellow, white
A gloss or matt finish self-adhesive vinyl film for covering and protecting. The coloured films can be used to apply brilliant translucent colours to artwork; black and white give an opaque look.

NORMAFRISKET NO 2

Sizes: Available in 320 × 400mm (12½ × 15¾ in.), 500 × 600mm (19¾ × 24 in.) sheets
This film should not be used for masking (unlike Normafrisket No 1, see p. 111) as it has a particularly strong adhesive backing. It is specially designed for adding amendments to artwork, with a surface which will accept typed or handwritten matter. It does not show up in reproduction.

LETRASET

LETRASET CLEARFILM

Sizes: Available in 254 × 381mm (10 × 15 in.), 381 × 508mm (15 × 20 in.) cut sheets
Self-adhesive transparent film with either a matt or gloss surface which can be used for simulating a laminated finish on visuals, protecting drawings, or as a masking medium.

LETRACOPY PF

Sizes: Available in packs of 10 and 50 A4 sheets
Like WEB Transtext (see below), this product offers the opportunity to transfer your own text or images on to self-adhesive film which can then be applied to artwork wherever necessary. By feeding Letracopy PF through a photocopier (check for suitability first) your own illustrations can be treated exactly like a Letratone sheet (see Letratone, p.122), creating a permanent bond when burnished. This offers the graphic designer many opportunities for the creative use of invented textures, tones and patterns on artwork, as well as individual symbols, captions and so on.

WESTWOOD GRAPHICS

Not available in the USA

WEB TRANSPASEAL

Sizes: Available in 10m (11 yd) and 25m (27 yd) rolls in widths of 450mm (18 in.), 620mm (24 in.), 900mm (36 in.), 1240mm (48 in.) – colours only available in 450mm (18 in.) and 900mm (36 in.) widths; gloss finish also available in packs of flat sheets for covering A3 and A4 surfaces – 330 × 470mm (13 × 19½ in., suitable for A3), 228 × 340mm (9 × 13½ in., suitable for A4)
Gloss colour range: black, red, blue, green, yellow
A matt or gloss finish self-adhesive transparent film which provides an effective method of permanently protecting all kinds of drawings, books, notices, and so on. The high-tack film comes with an easy-peel backing sheet printed with a grid for easier cutting.

WEB TRANSTEXT

Size: Available in A4 (297 × 210mm/11¾ × 8¼ in.) sheets
An extremely versatile type of self-adhesive matt film which can be written on, typed on, drawn on and even photocopied on. This means that such items as captions, symbols and numbers can be easily applied to artwork by hand. Simply type or draw the required text or image on to the sheet, cut out and stick the film on to the artwork. The film is almost invisible in reproduction. For a number of repeated items it is possible to feed Transtext through some photocopiers but it is important to check on the compatibility of the copier before attempting this procedure.

MASKING FILMS

Self-adhesive masking films are used to control more easily the broadcast application of colour or other media to a drawing surface. They are employed mainly when using an airbrush (see Airbrushes, pp. 92-5) but can also serve the same purpose when used in conjunction with other hand illustration techniques. The adhesive backing must be low tack (so ordinary self-adhesive covering films are unsuitable) to allow easy removal of the film without damage to the artwork, but it should adhere sufficiently to hold firmly in place and prevent seepage of wet media around the edges. The film must be thin enough to cut cleanly, even for fine detail, but strong enough to resist tearing and accidental damage during use.

To make a mask, trace down the image carefully in pencil or artists' tracing carbon on to the film. Cut out the shape required with a very sharp scalpel (X-Acto knife) – the sharper the blade, the cleaner and neater the mask will be. There is no need to press deeply into the surface as the film should cut quite easily. Peel away the waxed paper backing and apply the shape to the artwork. The film is repositionable for perfect accuracy. For very finely detailed areas of an image it may be necessary to cut the film while in position on the artwork. Trim off a piece of film large enough to give a margin all round the shape. Peel it from its backing sheet, lay it on to the artwork and smooth down gently. With a fresh blade cut lightly and delicately around the area to be masked – do not cut deeply as this will score the artwork underneath – and peel away the unwanted margin.

When using inks and other non-viscous wet media in conjunction with film, allow them to dry thoroughly before removing the mask as liquid patches may still bleed or drip. However, after application of heavy layers of acrylic or enamel paints the film should be peeled away before a thick coating has dried upon it as cracking could occur at the edges of the image.

Masking film makes a good temporary protective covering for presentation artwork if it has to leave the studio for any reason before final corrections and alterations are made. It can be applied in a large sheet to the entire area, then easily peeled away at a later date without damage to the surface.

Specialist photographic and lithographic masking films are used extensively in reprographic studios. These need to have good opacity to ultraviolet light to make them photographically safe, but remain sufficiently transparent for detailed cutting procedures to be carried out over a light box or table. A degree of dimensional stability is also required as this type of film is often exposed to both heat and dampness. Red film, known as 'Rubylith', is a stripping film coated on a polyester backing sheet. A special adhesive allows portions of the film to be repositioned on to the polyester if necessary or it can be used on film negatives and positives. The adhesive always stays on the Rubylith, never on the polyester. 'Amberlith' is identical, and can be cut and peeled in the same way, but is amber in colour and slightly less light-safe than Rubylith. However, it has better visual transparency and so is preferred for detailed jobs.

RETAILERS' BRANDS

Like acetate, masking film is often purchased direct from manufacturers and sold by retailers under their own name or unbranded. For example, **ARTHUR BROWN** in the USA sell:

READY STRIP MASKING FILM
Sizes: Available in 30 × 40 in., 11 × 14 in., 14 × 17 in. rolls
A polyester-backing sheet coated in a coloured plastic emulsion (either ruby or amber). The coating can be cut and stripped away to reveal the clear film underneath. It is dimensionally stable and is usually used as complete sheets for colour separations or silk screen positives.

A. I. FRIEDMAN
(also in the USA) sell:

RUBYLITH AND AMBERLITH
Sizes: Available in 20 yd rolls 25 in. wide; in 40 in. rolls × 150 in., 300 in.
Light-safe masking films for stripping on photographic positives and negatives. Supplied on a polyester backing.

PARAPAQUE
Sizes: Available in 10 × 14 in., 20 × 28 in. sheets
A transparent acetate sheet which is laminated to a protective backing sheet. It is light safe and has a matt surface. Ideal for corrections or opaquing on film negatives.

AUTOTYPE

AUTOMASK
Sizes: Available in 3m (3¼ yd), 5m (5½ yd) and 10m (11 yd) rolls in widths of 1020mm (40 in.), 1220mm (48 in.); in eight different sheet sizes from 130 × 180mm (5 × 8 in.) to 700 × 1000mm (27½ × 39 in.)
Automask is not just one product but a large range of economical masking materials for the designer to use at all stages of the artwork and printing process. Clear Automask makes a very reliable polyester masking film for artwork purposes. It will lie flat, will not curl, distort or stretch and protects well against edge bleed. Masks cut from this material have a good shelf life and can be reused at a later date with equally good results.

While possessing many of the useful qualities of Clear Automask, Automask Ruby is also a completely lightproof red masking film for all photographic and lithographic uses. It has proved very popular with both designers and printers.

Automask Amber has a narrower spectrum absorption range so can only be used with blue sensitive photographic materials. Its higher transparency makes it particularly useful for executing very detailed trace cutting work.

AUTOPAQUE
Sizes: Available in 10m (11 yd) and 25m (27 yd) rolls in widths of 340mm (13½ in.), 680mm (27 in.); in 500 × 710mm (19 × 28 in.) sheets
A high-quality, but economical, blocking out medium, offering excellent dimensional stability. It is available with either the normal waxed paper backing or a transparent film backing which allows large sheets of the material to lie flat more easily. Although coloured red to provide opacity to actinic light, Autopaque has very good visual transparency and can be used quite comfortably for detailed work. Its matt surface reduces glare and accepts pencil guidelines readily and its low-tack adhesive is pressure sensitive for good adhesion but easy removal.

BADGER AIR BRUSH CO

FOTO-FRISKET FILM
Sizes: Available in 4.5m (3¾ yd) rolls in widths of

300mm (12 in.), 600mm (24 in.); in 215 × 280mm (8½ × 11 in.) sheets

A completely transparent low-tack film which can be used on virtually any surface although the manufacturers do recommend prior testing on particularly soft or highly textured surfaces. It has a long shelf life, and is easy to cut but resistant to tearing during removal so is reusable for repeated shapes. Its transparent backing makes it good for cutting masks and stencils on a light box or table.

Rolls of Foto-Frisket Film are provided with a convenient pre-scored peeling edge for quick removal of the backing sheet.

FRISK/FRISKET

FRISKFILM FOR AIRBRUSH WORK

Sizes: Available in 3.6m (4 yd) rolls in widths of 150mm (6 in.), 300mm (12 in.), 600mm (24 in.); in 9.1m (10 yd) rolls 600mm (24 in.) wide; in 300 × 200mm (12 × 8 in.), 600 × 450mm (24 × 18 in.) sheets

A very popular masking film for airbrush work, recommended by many professionals. It is low tack, easy to cut and peel and guards against edge bleed. Friskfilm is available in both gloss and matt finishes: a matt surface is particularly good at accepting fine pencil guidelines, so is useful for detailed work.

LETRASET

CLEARFILM

Sizes: Available in 254 × 381mm (10 × 15 in.), 381 × 508mm (15 × 20 in.) sheets

A versatile transparent acetate film with either a matt or gloss finish. Its low-tack dyeline resistant adhesive makes it suitable for use as an airbrush masking medium or as a protective laminating overlay for mock-ups and artwork. Amendments or additions to artwork can be prepared on the matt sheets (which will readily accept drafting ink, typing and handwriting) and these can then be cut out and positioned precisely.

Dry transfer products can also be burnished on to Clearfilm and the low-tack adhesive allows spacing to be varied and re-alignments to be made.

LETRAPAQUE

Sizes: Available in 508 × 658mm (20 × 26 in.), 254 × 325mm (10 × 13 in.) sheets

A useful low-tack, repositionable masking film which can be used not only on film and acetate but also on art board. It is ideal for masks, colour separations and silhouettes on camera-ready artwork. Two types are available – Photo Red and Vivid Red.

Vivid Red has 20 per cent of the colour density of the Photo Red, so slightly better visual transparency when detailed cutting is necessary.

MECANORMA

Not available in the USA

PEEL OFF MASKING FILM

Sizes: Available in A3, A4 pads

A transparent red, light-safe masking film. It is not self-adhesive to other surfaces but peels from a polyester backing. It should be used as a complete sheet overlay with the areas not to be masked carefully cut and peeled away, leaving the masked areas on the backing.

NORMAPAQUE

Sizes: Available in 320 × 400mm (12½ × 15¾ in.), 500 × 600mm (19¾ × 24 in.) sheets

A matt surfaced, red, light-safe film. Transparent and self-adhesive for masking positive or negative films prior to making printing plates.

NORMAFRISKET NO 1

Sizes: Available in 320 × 400mm (9 × 15¾ in.), 500 × 600mm (19¾ × 24 in.) sheets

Low-tack, self-adhesive masking film, designed for use in airbrushing and retouching on coated papers, photographs and films.

ROYAL SOVEREIGN

Not available in the USA

SPEEDRY MAGIC MARKER MASKING FILM

Sizes: Available in 4m (4¼ yd) rolls in widths of 300mm (12 in.), 600mm (24 in.); in 10m (11 yd) rolls 500mm (20 in.) wide; in packs of ten A4 plus sheets 330 × 240mm (13 × 9½ in.)

A completely clear, low-tack masking film suitable for use with all conventional studio media. It will not allow any seepage.

SELLOTAPE

SELLOTAPE LITHOGRAPHIC 1129

Sizes: Available in 66m (72 yd) rolls in widths of 12mm (½ in.), 25mm (1 in.)

A red, transparent, self-adhesive tape developed specially for the opaquing, stripping and edging of lithographic films.

The tape is opaque to ultraviolet light and accepts retouching paint.

Mecanorma opaque marker for masking on film and acetate.

3M

SCOTCH BLACK PHOTOGRAPHIC TAPE

Sizes: Available in 25m (27 yd) and 55m (60 yd) rolls 25mm (1 in.) wide

A completely lightproof black tape for masking, cropping and blocking out unwanted portions on colour negatives. The adhesive backing will not damage the negatives and the tape can be removed easily if necessary.

SCOTCH LITHOGRAPHIC TAPE

Sizes: Available in 66m (72 yd) rolls in widths of 12mm (½ in.), 19mm (¾ in.), 25mm (1 in.)

The photo red opaque surface of this tape blocks out the ultraviolet light which could affect photosensitive films for making lithographic plates. An essential masking medium for edging and stripping work in film make-up.

SCOTCH SILVER PHOTOGRAPHIC TAPE

Sizes: Available in 66m (72 yd) rolls in widths of 12mm (½ in.), 25mm (1 in.)

This opaque silver foil tape has a perfectly straight edge for the accurate cropping, edging and masking of 35mm slides.

WESTWOOD GRAPHICS

WEB AIRBRUSH MASKING FILM

Sizes: Available in 5m (5½ yd) rolls in widths of 310mm (12 in.), 620mm (24 in.); in 10m (11 yd) rolls 620mm (24 in.) wide; in 25m (27 yd) rolls 620mm (24 in.) wide; in packs of ten A4 sheets

A highly transparent PVC film which is easy to cut and reposition, leaving no sticky residue or scuffed surfaces. It has a long shelf life with no deterioration of the adhesive backing.

WEB RED PHOTOPAQUE MASKING FILM

Sizes: Available in packs of ten 590 × 500mm (29 × 20 in.) sheets

A dimensionally stable red photographic masking medium offering excellent opacity to ultraviolet light. The film has good adhesive properties but its unplasticized PVC composition makes intricate cutting very easy.

ADHESIVES, TAPES AND SPRAYS

Although the large array of products on the market might at first appear to be a little unnecessary, it is important to keep a number of different adhesives in the studio ready to meet changing requirements at various stages of a design job. Three main types of adhesives are available for producing finished artwork. The traditional and still probably most popular adhesive for paste-up work is rubber-based cement which is cheap and economical. This comes in cans and tubes in a thick liquid form and should be applied thinly and evenly, using a spreader (one-coat products to one surface only, two-coat to both surfaces). Always lay down a larger area of adhesive on to the base board than the size of the item to be attached and rub off the excess when dry using an eraser (or a rubber cement pick-up). The best type is one made from the rubber solution itself. Apply a thin coat of solution to an even, glossy surface and allow to dry thoroughly, then roll the film into a ball using your fingers. This 'eraser' will now easily pick up excess cement without leaving any tell-tale particles behind. Stubborn marks on artwork can also be removed using this technique. Lay down a thin coat of rubber solution over the area to be cleaned, allow to dry and remove using your eraser or pick-up.

For an instantly firm bond using two-coat rubber-based adhesive, wait approximately ten minutes until the cement is dry to the touch before bringing the surfaces together. If the surfaces are brought into contact while still wet some sliding of the loose item is still possible, allowing easy repositioning for absolute accuracy. Although rubber-based cement provides a very firm bond, such items as illustrations and photographs can be peeled easily from artwork even after months in storage. If any difficulty is experienced, simply lift one corner and apply some petrol-based cleaner (rubber cement thinner) underneath to dissolve the cement.

Many designers took to using aerosol spray adhesives when these first came on to the market. They proved to be very convenient, simple to use and allowed easy repositioning when sprayed on to one surface only, making them ideal for both paste-up and layout work where the quick fixing of many small items is necessary. However, these products are both dangerous to health and messy in use. The fine spray particles are broadcast widely into the air where they can be breathed into the lungs, and settle on every surface around the studio, inevitably attracting dirt and dust. If they are to be used at all it must be in limited quantities and with a degree of discipline.

The last widely used method for paste-up is a waxing system. Waxers are electrically operated tools which deliver a thin coat of melted wax, via a roller, on to the artwork to be bonded. The wax is only slightly tacky so repositioning is possible, but a firm bond is achieved once the item has been burnished. This process produces a smooth even finish with no wrinkling and, as the bond is not solid, no damage to the artwork, even if peeled off at a later date. Wax is a very versatile adhesive medium which will not dry out, even after many months. Big table-top waxers are popular in large studios where there is a sustained output of artwork. Although small hand-held versions are also available, these are not really economical or practical for the individual unless you have to do a fairly considerable amount of paste-up. Several types of waxers are available; the lists that follow are only able to include a few.

Other types of adhesive are produced in the form of solid sticks or thin liquids. These are often convenient to use (especially if spray adhesive has been rejected) for small quick jobs on layouts as they are delivered in handy dispensers and applicators. However, they are really not suitable for high-quality accurate artwork where both repositioning and, ultimately, a firm bond are required.

A similar wide range of tapes is now available, again each type meeting a different design need. Clear, cellulose-based sticky tape was the original development in this field. It is extremely strong and difficult to tear unless the edge is nicked but its high tack quality makes it unsuitable for much work around the studio. Low tack is essential for the removal of sticky tapes from paper surfaces without damage. Masking or drafting tape is the most commonly used by designers and draftsmen. It is low tack, so easily removable, with a paper backing which can be torn easily in the fingers. It is invaluable around the studio and can be used for holding drawings in place on the drawing board, attaching overlays to artwork, masking, blocking out, cropping illustrations, and so on. In fact, it is an invaluable and essential tool.

Invisible or 'magic' tape has a lower tack than transparent tape and, as its name implies, is almost invisible once firmly pressed down. Its non-reflective matt surface makes it suitable for photographic reproduction and copying processes. It is often used to attach overlays to artwork, giving a clean, neatly finished professional look. Double-sided tape is also useful in this capacity although it is extremely high tack, making mistakes difficult to correct. This, however, makes it ideal for attaching tiny items to artwork when using an adhesive would be both difficult and messy.

Spray fixatives are used to protect drawings against smudging and abrasion. The aerosol deposits a fine transparent film of lacquer which holds any loose particles of graphite, chalk, pastel and so on in place. Some fixatives can also be used to protect dry transfer products against scratches. When using these aerosols, always hold the drawing upright and spray lightly and evenly. Too heavy a coat will only spot and stain the work and can, in some cases, change its appearance by darkening the tonal quality. As with spray adhesives, do not breathe in the mist and work in a well-ventilated room. As an alternative to aerosols, liquid fixative from a bottle can be applied using a mouth spray.

BEST-TEST

BEST-TEST RUBBER CEMENT
Sizes: Available in 28g (4 oz.), 250ml (½ pt), 550ml (1 pt), 1.13lit. (1 qt), 4.5lit. (1 gal.) cans
For mounting all types of artwork, photographs, illustrations and any other work requiring clean repositionable bonding. Thin papers can be joined without the risk of creasing or curling.

BEST-TEST ONE-COAT RUBBER CEMENT
Sizes: Available in 1.13lit. (1 qt), 4.5lit. (1 gal.) cans
A very easy-to-use pressure sensitive adhesive for temporary or permanent bonding of artwork. Ideal for quick paste-up as application to one surface only is sufficient to ensure good adhesion. The glued surface will remain tacky even if lifted and reapplied several times.

BLAIR
Not available in the UK

BLAIR SPRAY FIX
Size: Available in 16 oz. cans
A fast-drying, matt fixative spray which can be used on pencil, pastel, charcoal, tempera, ink and watercolour work. It will not affect the drawing surface and can be worked over with any media.

BLAIR SPRAY CLEAR
Size: Available in 16 oz. cans
An invisible spray which gives a durable protective coating against moisture and dirt to paper, leather, wood and metal surfaces. It is also recommended for preventing smudging on wet printers' proofs. It will not yellow with age, and is available in high gloss or non-reflective matt finish.

CASLON
Not available in the USA

SUPAWAXA 30e AND 50e
Waxing areas: 300mm (12 in.), 500mm (19 in.) wide respectively
Virtually any type of artwork can be passed through the coating rollers of these studio waxers, even resin-coated photographic papers. Items can be lifted and repositioned many times leaving no deposit of wax on the base material. For a particularly high-tack bond, Caslon produce Supawax X which is compatible with these waxers.
    Both models are fitted with a footswitch control, a particularly useful feature when feeding extra large items through the 50e version.

EDDING
Not available in the USA

EDDING C25 GLUE STICK
For accurate and detailed application of a liquid latex adhesive the oblique angled tip and extended shape of this glue stick offer a good choice. It fits comfortably in the hand like a drawing tool and can be used with as much delicacy as a fairly thick felt-tipped marker.

EDDING C30 GLUE STICK
A shorter, stumpier barrel shape and applicator head make this liquid glue stick more suitable for broader areas. It can be used as a temporary repositionable adhesive on paper, card, glass, ceramics and metal.

EDDING C50 GLUE STICK
A cellulose-based liquid glue suitable for use on paper and card. The stick is supplied with a rounded foam tip for simple, clean application.

ELMER'S
Not available in the UK

ELMER'S GLUE-ALL
Sizes: Available in 1 1/4 oz., 4 oz., 8 oz., 16 oz., 22 oz., 1 qt, 1 gal. bottles
An adhesive for all porous materials such as cloth, paper and wood. It dries fast to a clear, non-staining finish and is good for repairs, modelling or packaging work.

ELMER'S LATEX BASE CONTACT CEMENT
Sizes: Available in 1 oz., 3 oz. tubes
A heat-resistant adhesive for both porous and non-porous materials, specially recommended for joining surfaces which are difficult to get at or hard to hold together. The bond dries instantly but can be cleaned with water while still wet.

FABER-CASTELL

PENOL GLUE STICKS
Sizes: Available in 7.5g (1/4 oz.), 15g (1/2 oz.), 40g (1 1/4 oz.) sticks
A strong, non-toxic solid adhesive for bonding all types of paper and card. Its solid nature reduces the risk of rippling usually experienced when applying adhesives to thin papers such as newsprint or tissue. It makes a useful secondary adhesive for small or medium-sized items of paste-up work.

FRISK/FRISKET

FRISK/FIXATIVE LACQUER
Size: Available in 285g (10 oz.) cans
A fast-drying colourless lacquer spray for protecting dry transfer lettering and artwork from scratches, smudging and grease marks. This

can also be employed as an anti-corrosive coating for bright metal surfaces, helping to protect such things as drawing instruments which are often in contact with water. Available with a matt or gloss finish.

FRISKFIX
Size: Available in 285g (10 oz.) cans
A general-purpose aerosol spray fixative mainly used for stabilizing crayon, charcoal and pastel drawings, this is also compatible with dry transfer products as a protective coating.

GOODKIN
Not available in the UK

GOODKIN WAX COATER
Waxing areas: 12 in., 18 in. wide
A table-top waxer, supplied with burnishing roller, suitable for coating photographs, typesetting, artwork and illustrations. It can cope with any thickness from .002 in. up to ¼ in. Waxing area can be restricted to any width down to ⅛ × ¼ in.

GRUMBACHER
Not available in the UK

GRUMBACHER TUFFILM
Sizes: Available in 13 oz. cans
A permanent protective spray coating and fixative for all artwork and illustrations. It is quick drying and will repel moisture, dirt and grease effectively.

GRUMBACHER MYSTON
Size: Available in 13 oz. cans
Although this is also a clear fixative spray, it differs from Tuffilm in providing a workable surface on drawings for making amendments with watercolours. It is also particularly useful for preparing normally water-repellent surfaces (such as acetate) for painting with water-based media.

J. J. HUBER

HUBER WAXCOTE-310 WAXER
Waxing area: 310mm (12 in.) wide
This is a studio table-top waxer giving either an all-over 100 per cent coverage or a striped coating, and can handle all types of artwork, phototypesetting paper, illustrations and photographs.

A permanent bond is achieved by burnishing the item using the tools provided with the waxer.

The degree of tack between the two materials can be controlled by varying the pressure applied. A standard footswitch attachment enables convenient hands-free operation.

HUBER HAND HELD LECTRO-STIK WAXER
Waxing area: 38mm (1½ in.) wide
An economical hand-held waxer more suited to individual use, this performs in a similar way to the table-top version to give a smooth adhesive wax coating on any type of artwork. The element can be left on all day to keep the wax at the correct temperature. Replacement tablets of Hi-Tak Huberwax are available separately for both models.

HUMBROL

HUMBROL SUPERSTIK
Size: Available in 25ml (1 oz.) tubes
A very strong contact adhesive which can be accurately repositioned before final bonding takes place.

HUMBROL GLUE GUN
An accurate and controllable method of applying very strong quick-drying adhesive to virtually any material. Solid sticks of adhesive are heated in the gun and then squeezed out in a liquid stream through the nozzle. The bond formed dries in approximately one minute and is completely waterproof.

HUMBROL ALL-PURPOSE CLEAR ADHESIVE
Size: Available in 12ml (½ oz.) tubes
This adhesive will instantly bond almost any materials so repositioning is not possible. It dries to a clear, non-staining finish and is used for modelling and repair jobs.

KRYLON
Not available in the UK

KRYLON CRYSTAL CLEAR AND MATTE FINISH
Size: Available in 1 pt cans
Fast-drying acrylic coatings for all kinds of artwork, these are permanent and provide a seal against water, grease and dirt. Crystal Clear can also be used on tools, brass, leather and so on, for the same purpose.

Matte finish is particularly recommended for eliminating any unwanted glossy sheen on artwork, for example, if it is to be photographed.

KRYLON WORKABLE FIXATIVE

Size: Available in 1 pt cans

A fixative for use at intermediate stages of a job. It dries in seconds but does not affect the texture of the drawing surface or the medium being used. It is also possible to erase through the coating.

LETRASET

LETRASET TAPE SET

Sizes: Available in 33m (36 yd) rolls in widths of 12mm (½ in.), 19mm (¾ in.), 25mm (1 in.), 50mm (2 in.), 305mm (12 in.)

A strong double-sided adhesive tape suitable for use on artwork, as well as general fixing jobs. The thin film does not show through most papers or leave tell-tale raised areas.

LETRASET GUM SET

Sizes: Available in 250ml (½ pt), 500ml (1 pt) cans

The traditional liquid rubber cement adhesive for paste-up work and all bonding of papers and boards. This kind of adhesive has the advantages of economy and adaptability, and items can be removed easily at a later date. The cans are supplied with a double-headed spatula. The lid must be replaced after use to prevent evaporation and drying up.

LETRASET SPRAY SET

Size: Available in 397g (14 oz.) cans

A repositionable spray adhesive for paste-up and mounting work, this will give a strong bond if applied to both surfaces.

LETRASET 101 SPRAY

Size: Available in 134g (4½ oz.) cans

This was specially developed to provide a protective coating for dry transfer products after burnishing and will help to prevent the damage from scratches and rubbing which are inevitable during further work and storage. It gives a slightly glossy appearance when dry and can be applied to most drawing surfaces. One coat will fix the transfer firmly but a further coat will provide an even better shield.

LETRACOTE GLOSS 102 AND LETRACOTE MATT 103

Size: Available in 227g (8 oz.) cans

Like Letraset 101 Spray these, too, can be used to protect dry transfer products but also have a more wide-ranging application as general fixatives for artwork and drawings. The first coating is often sufficient, especially for work in progress, but a final respray is advised for maximum protection. The lacquer comes in a gloss or matt finish and will dry completely in about 12 hours.

Do not use either of these sprays if dyeline copying of the item is to be carried out after spraying.

LETRASET STICK SET

Sizes: Available in 90mm (3½ in.), 105mm (4 in.) sticks

This is solid adhesive supplied in a twist-up stick for convenient application. It is most useful for small items of paste-up or as a handy tool for quick last-minute jobs.

LETRAFILM SOLVENT

A specially developed solvent spray for use with dry transfer lettering and Letrafilm Matt sheets (see The Pantone System, pp. 123 - 4) to create coloured lettering instantly. The transfer is applied to the Letrafilm sheet which is then sprayed with Solvent. This dissolves the coloured area around the letters which have acted as a mask. When dry, the black transfer letters can be removed with adhesive tape to reveal the coloured letters underneath. The clear area of the Letrafilm sheet, carrying these new letters, is then applied in the normal way to the artwork.

MECANORMA

Not available in the USA

LIGHT FAST NORMATAPE

Sizes: Available in 12m (13⅓ yd) rolls in widths of 0.40mm (1/64 in.), 0.79mm (1/32 in.), 1.59mm (1/16 in.), 3.17mm (1/8 in.), 6.35mm (1/4 in.), 12.70mm (1/2 in.)

Light-safe, transparent, red self-adhesive tapes for masking and edging negatives. The smallest widths are particularly convenient for very detailed jobs.

KLEER TAK RUBBER CEMENT

Sizes: Available in 1 lit. (1¾ pt), 5 lit. (8¾ pt) cans; in 250ml (½ pt) bottles with brush; in 100g (3½ oz.) tubes.

A traditional rubber-based adhesive for paste-up work. This product is particularly recommended for its ease of application. It is slightly thinner than similar adhesives from other manufacturers and can be applied conveniently with a brush. It becomes tacky within a few seconds and forms a good firm bond, but items can be lifted easily for repositioning if necessary. It is completely transparent and does not wrinkle delicate surfaces or stain coloured areas.

Kleer Tak Thinner is available in 1 lit. (1¾ pt) cans in case the liquid thickens up.

KLEER TAK PERMANENT RUBBER CEMENT TAK 01

Sizes: Available in 1 lit. (1¾ pt) cans; in 250ml (½ pt) bottles with brush

Similar to ordinary Kleer Tak, this need be applied only to one surface to give excellent adhesion. Items remain tacky even if repositioned several times.

ARTWORK SPRAY
A repositionable aerosol adhesive ideal for mounting lightweight papers and fabrics as it will not stain, wrinkle or soak through. It is guaranteed non-toxic by the manufacturer.

DISPLAY SPRAY
A permanent aerosol adhesive giving a very strong bond when applied to both surfaces. Can be used on most materials – paper, card, photographs, film, glass, wood, metal, fabrics, rubber and polystyrene – making it especially useful for exhibition and display work. It is guaranteed non-toxic.

FILM SPRAY
A repositionable aerosol adhesive which can be used without damage or wrinkling on films, acetate and polyester. It is guaranteed non-toxic.

MECANORMA TRANSFER ADHESIVE
Sizes: Available in A4 sheets; in 220mm (8⅝ in.) strips in widths of 15mm (⅝ in.), 45mm (1¾ in.)
A new concept in repositionable adhesives for pasting photographic papers and card to most surfaces. The trimmed document is placed on the transfer sheet, lightly rubbed with a finger to pick up the adhesive and then removed to be fixed to the artwork. This process is extremely neat, clean, non-toxic and odour-free and is ideal for precision mounting. The adhesive can be removed with a Kleer Tak eraser if the item needs to be reused in another context.

SOLVENT THINNER
A useful non-toxic thinner in the form of an aerosol spray. Apart from dissolving rubber adhesives and grease marks, it can be used to rejuvenate spirit-based markers, by using a pipette fitted to the valve, and to create special blending effects when working with these markers. The pipette is also useful for applying solvent accurately to small areas, for example ungumming a line of typesetting.

LET-FIX CRYSTAL, LET-FIX MATT AND LET-FIX GLOSS
A versatile range of all-purpose aerosol sprays for fixing and protecting drawings and dry transfer products. A single coat of Let-Fix Crystal or Let-Fix Matt protects artwork but allows for subsequent reworking of the surface with most media, if necessary. Further applications of Let-Fix Crystal produce a resistant satin finish while Let-Fix Matt deposits a matt coat. This is recommended for documents which are going to be copied, where reduction of glare is important, and for matting glossy photographs. Let-Fix Gloss gives a deep, glossy, colourless coating with one application only.

PELIKAN

PELI-FIX GLUE STICK
A solid stick of wax-like adhesive, convenient for general office use or for bonding small areas of paper, light card and so on.

PENTEL

PENTEL ROLL 'N' GLUE AND ROLL 'N' GLUE EXTRA STRONG
Sizes: Available in 30ml (1 oz.) and 20ml (⅔ oz.) bottles respectively
Surprisingly strong thin liquid adhesive for bonding paper and card. The plastic bottles are supplied with a convenient roller head for quick, non-messy application.

PRESTO
Not available in the UK

PRESTO ONE-COAT RUBBER CEMENT
Sizes: Available in 1 pt, 1 qt, 1 gal. cans
A pressure-sensitive adhesive that need be applied to one surface only. It remains tacky indefinitely and items can be lifted and repositioned as many times as is necessary. Non-wrinkling, curl-proof, transparent and non-staining.

ROYAL SOVEREIGN
Not available in the USA

COW GUM/RUBBER CEMENT
Sizes: Available in 250ml (½ pt), 500ml (1 pt) cans; 500ml (1 pt) tubes
The original rubber cement, popular throughout the world, which gave its name to this kind of adhesive in the UK. All types of paper, board and even photographs are easily repositioned at any time during or after bonding. To avoid evaporation always replace the lid after use.

MARABU KLARPAUS
Size: Available in 300ml (11 oz.) cans
An invaluable aid to dyeline and other copying.

processes, this aerosol spray transforms opaque paper into transparent documents without damaging the paper surface or the drawing and evaporates to leave no visible mark.

MARABU MATTLACK
Size: Available in 300ml (11 oz.) cans
A versatile transparent matt lacquer, good for applying a protective weatherproof coating to paper, board, metal, plastics and even glass. Useful for protecting product dummies after the application of graphics.

MARABU UV-SCHUTZ
Size: Available in 300ml (11 oz.) cans
The UV-filter in this matt spray absorbs the harmful ultraviolet radiation in sunlight, thereby protecting any vulnerable surfaces (including clear varnishes) from the yellowing and decaying effects associated with ageing.

SELLOTAPE
Not available in the USA

SELLOTAPE STANDARD MASKING 2551
Sizes: Available in 50m (55 yd) rolls in widths of 19mm (¾ in.), 25mm (1 in.), 38mm (1½ in.), 50mm (2 in.), 75mm (3 in.), 100mm (4 in.)
A medium-tack paper tape for general use around the studio. It is solid enough for wet media masking, and for packaging.

SELLOTAPE LOW TACK MASKING 2552
Sizes: Available in 50m (55 yd), rolls in widths of 25mm (1 in.), 50mm (2 in.)
Similar to Standard Masking, this tape also has a special low-tack adhesive for easier removal.

SELLOTAPE DRAFTING 2554
Sizes: Available in 50m (55 yd) rolls 25mm (1 in.) wide
A tape for holding tracings and drawings in place with minimal damage to the drawing surface.

SELLOTAPE DOUBLE SIDED 4405
Sizes: Available in 33m (36 yd) rolls in widths of 12mm (½ in.), 15mm (⅝ in.), 19mm (¾ in.), 25mm (1 in.), 50mm (2 in.), 300mm (11¾ in.), 305mm (12 in.)
A very strong tape consisting of vinyl film coated on both sides with high-tack adhesive and with a waxed paper interleaf.

SELLOTAPE INVISIBLE 1319
Sizes: Available in 33m (36 yd) rolls 19mm (¾ in.) wide; in 66m (72 yd) rolls 25mm (1 in.) wide

This tape has a slightly white opaque appearance on the roll but is actually almost invisible in use and copies very well. It will not embrittle or yellow with age and its matt surface can be typed or written upon with pencil and ballpoint.

SELLOTAPE CLEAR 1109
Sizes: Available in 33m (36 yd) and 66m (72 yd) rolls in widths of 12mm (½ in.), 15mm (⅝ in.), 19mm (¾ in.), 25mm (1 in.)
This is the product whose brand name has become a generic title for this kind of tape in the UK. It is cellulose based with a transparent gloss surface which is difficult to mark but is remarkably tough and strong.

SELLOTAPE BUFF CASE SEALING 1554 AND COLOURED VINYL
Sizes: Available in 66m (72 yd) rolls in widths of 9mm (⅜ in.), 12mm (½ in.), 25mm (1 in.), 38mm (1½ in.), 50mm (2 in.)
Colour range: buff, black, blue, red, green, yellow, white
Particularly strong high-tack vinyl-backed tapes for packing and sealing. The Buff Case Sealing tape is adapted to withstand exposure to dampness and sunlight while the coloured versions are good for decorative work or any job where colour coding is necessary.

SELLOTAPE STICKY FIXERS
Sizes: Available in boxes of 40 or 100 pads
Sticky Fixers consist of small pieces of foam, 25 × 12mm (1 × ½ in.), coated on both sides with a very strong adhesive. They are ideal for any kind of mounting, including exhibition work, but their extremely high tack makes them very difficult to remove without damaging both surfaces. They should, therefore, be regarded as a fairly permanent fixing method.

3M

SCOTCH DRAFTING TAPE
Sizes: Available in 7.5m (8¼ yd) rolls 19mm (¾ in.) wide; in 50m (55 yd) rolls 25mm (1 in.) wide
A low-tack easy release paper tape for holding tracings and drawings in place. It will not scuff paper surfaces when removed and can also be used as a general masking medium.

SCOTCH WHITE ARTISTS' TAPE
Sizes: Available in 55m (60 yd) rolls 25mm (1 in.) wide
This tape is similar to ordinary low-tack drafting tape but its pure white paper backing gives a clean professional appearance to artwork when it is used to attach overlays and flaps.

SCOTCH MASKING TAPE

Sizes: Available in 50m (55 yd) rolls in widths of 12mm (½ in.), 19mm (¾ in.), 25mm (1 in.), 38mm (1½ in.), 50mm (2 in.)
A general-purpose medium-tack studio tape with a hard-wearing paper backing.

SCOTCH DOUBLE SIDED TAPE

Sizes: Available in 33m (36 yd) rolls in widths of 12mm (½ in.), 19mm (¾ in.), 25mm (1 in.), 50mm (2 in.), 75mm (3 in.), 150mm (6 in.)
A useful high-tack double-sided tape for mounting, attaching overlays and fixing small items to artwork. Double-sided tape is often more convenient than liquid adhesives.

3M also produce a refillable Scotch ATC Double Sided Dispenser which lays tape, automatically peeled on both sides, cleanly on to the paper ready for immediate fixing – a useful gadget if this kind of tape is frequently used.

SCOTCH MAGIC TAPE

Sizes: Available in 33m (36 yd) and 66m (72 yd) rolls in widths of 12mm (½ in.), 19mm (¾ in.), 25mm (1 in.)
A matt surfaced slightly opaque tape which is invisible in use and can be written upon with most media. It is dimensionally stable, copies well and will not discolour with age so is ideal for attaching drafting film overlays to artwork or repairing torn items which need to be recopied.

SCOTCH REMOVABLE TRANSPARENT TAPE

Sizes: Available in 55m (60 yd) rolls in widths of 12mm (½ in.), 19mm (¾ in.), 25mm (1 in.)
This tape combines the useful transparency of a cellulose-based tape with the low tack of a paper-backed masking tape. It is good for the temporary and repositionable attachment of items to visuals and mock-ups since it can be removed cleanly without scuffing or leaving a sticky mark.

SCOTCH CLEAR TAPE

Sizes: Available in 33m (36 yd) and 66m (72 yd) rolls in widths of 12mm (½ in.), 15mm (⅝ in.), 19mm (¾ in.), 25mm (1 in.), 50mm (2 in.)
A very strong cellulose-based transparent tape. Its high tack makes it unsuitable for drawing board use but it is invaluable for permanent fixing.

SCOTCH POST-IT NOTES

These self-adhesive notes are easy to remove and reposition without leaving a mark, will adhere to almost anything and are ideal for communicating instructions on artwork, photographic negatives and so on.

SCOTCH FIXING PADS

Sizes: Available in boxes of 100 or 200 pads
These are heavy-duty adhesive foam pads (12 × 25mm/½ × 1 in. or 25 × 25mm/1 × 1 in.) for mounting and display work. They are extremely durable and adhere to almost anything, indoors and outdoors, but have such a high tack that removal can be difficult without damage to perishable items. Try using a petroleum-based solvent or lighter fuel (fluid) if relocation is required.

SCOTCH PEN

Size: Available in 18g (⅔ oz.) bottles
A liquid glue stick with a large ballpoint pen type rolling head for dispensing adhesive accurately. It has a flat, anti-roll marker-sized body which is comfortable and easy to hold.

SCOTCH SPRAYMOUNT ADHESIVE

Sizes: Available in 391g (14 oz.), 161g (6 oz.) cans
One of the most widely used brands of spray adhesive among professionals. It will not stain, soak or wrinkle even quite thin papers and is convenient to use for any paste-up or mounting work. If one surface only is sprayed the item can be repositioned before final bonding. Items pasted down using Spraymount can be peeled away, with some care, at a later date although the use of a petroleum-based solvent may be necessary.

SCOTCH PHOTOMOUNT ADHESIVE

Sizes: Available in 268g (9½ oz.), 111g (4 oz.) cans
Although there is a little time to reposition items before final bonding takes place, this colourless adhesive is intended for the strong, permanent mounting of photographs, prints and illustrations on heavy quality papers. It is particularly recommended for resin-coated photographic papers which are often difficult to mount flat.

SCOTCH DISPLAYMOUNT ADHESIVE

Size: Available in 288g (10 oz.) cans
An extra strong adhesive for particularly heavy-duty applications. It can be used on porous materials such as fabrics, wood and polystyrene as well as thick papers and boards. Particularly useful for exhibition and display work where adhesives are put under some stress.

SCOTCH SPRAYFIX COATING AND FIXATIVE

Size: Available in 206g (7 oz.) cans
A quick-drying colourless and waterproof spray used for protecting artwork, dry transfer products and drawings against smudging, grease and general handling. A good general-purpose spray to have in the studio.

SCOTCH CLEAN ART CLEANING FLUID

An efficient petroleum-based cleaning fluid for most items in the studio, developed after the success of ordinary lighter fuel (fluid) which many designers have found essential for cleaning grease and dirt from drawing equipment.
Recommended for unmounting typesetting and illustrations from artwork and cleaning stubborn marks from high-quality artboard. It evaporates quickly to leave no stain on paper surfaces.

SCOTCH SPRAYSHIELD STUDIO SYSTEM

A system of interconnecting trays with which to build your own containment area for spray adhesives. The trays can be fitted together to form a booth of any size and shape or be used individually to help trap particles of adhesive.

SCOTCH PMA (POSITIONABLE MOUNTING ADHESIVE) SYSTEM

A very useful alternative to traditional dry mounting, this requires no heat or electrical supply but works instead by using pressure sensitive adhesive. Simply apply a roughly trimmed piece of PMA to your artwork and pass it through the machine for the first time. After careful trimming, it can be repositioned as many times as is necessary on to the mounting board (matboard). For a permanent bond, run the mount (mat) plus artwork through the machine for a second time. The system can be used with all kinds of photographic materials, including high-quality colour printing papers, to give a completely smooth, strong and long-lasting finish. PMA can even be applied manually using a roller or squeegee.

LETTERING AND COLOUR SYSTEMS

DRY TRANSFER PRODUCTS

Dry transfer products offer the graphic designer a simple, quick alternative to laborious hand lettering and expensive display typesetting. Self-adhesive letters and symbols, carried on a transparent plastic film, are available in a huge range of typestyles and sizes and are useful for producing clean artwork and professional-looking visuals, or even correcting mistakes in typesetting. Bodytype sheets are good for giving the impression of printed text on book or magazine visuals, adhesive tapes are designed for laying down repetitive matter on charts and diagrams, while pre-drawn corners, boxes and rules make accurate artwork much simpler, even for the beginner.

The most popular typefaces are available in a range of colours but black is still the most widely used as it provides sufficient opacity and definition for enlargement or reproduction.

Dry transfer lettering must be used with a certain amount of care to produce a well-spaced, even effect. Some manufacturers provide space marks under each letter to make positioning easier but with a little practice this can be achieved by eye. If applying lettering to finished artwork it is advisable to rub down the wording on to a sheet of cartridge (drawing) or smooth art paper, correct the mistakes and then stick the whole thing down like a piece of typesetting.

If the surface to be lettered is particularly soft, hard or awkwardly shaped, a pre-release technique should be adopted. Lift the transfer sheet away from the working surface and pull it taut. Gently rub over the selected letter until it turns grey, indicating release. Now transfer it to the work surface using light finger pressure and burnish well.

Dry transfer sheets should be stored flat with their protective backing to prevent damage or accidental adhesion. Most manufacturers produce storage cabinets or trays for sheets; these are useful for filing and retrieval. Remember to save any half-used sheets – they might come in useful for other jobs.

THE LETRASET SYSTEM

LETRASET INSTANT LETTERING

Sheet size: 254 × 381mm (10 × 15 in.)
Colour range: black, white, red, blue, green, yellow, gold, silver

Letraset, the most famous of all dry transfer manufacturers, produce perhaps the most popular and comprehensive range of instant lettering: over 550 typefaces (with more added on a regular basis) in 25 different point sizes from 6pt to 288pt. All are available in black, over 100 in white and seven in red, blue, green, yellow, gold and silver. In addition, there are 30 typestyles in Greek, Cyrillic (Russian), Arabic and Hebrew alphabets and 28 ranges of numerals in a selection of sizes and colours. The Letragraphica range provides more than 216 modern headline and display faces for specialist use. The Letraset catalogue gives a complete fount of each typeface, showing all characters, numerals and incidentals.

Letraset sheets have a thick carrier film and a differential tack adhesive, making them easy to handle and rub down. The 'Spacematic' optical spacing system ensures good letter positioning and is especially helpful to the novice user. For positioning complete words and phrases on artwork use the Letraset Word Positioning System. This consists of a moistening pad and two-part transfer sheet. Rub down the word or phrase on to the paper backing strip, then lay this, face downwards, on to the transparent film of the transfer sheet. Moisten the back of the paper strip using the pad and peel it away – this transfers the lettering on to the film. This can then be moved around to see how it looks in different positions before it is finally rubbed down in the usual way. Once fixed to the paper strip, letters can be sprayed with any colour of your choice using a LetraJet Air Marker before transfer to the transparent film. This is a very useful system which both the professional and student will find helpful for manipulating type creatively and accurately. The transfer sheets are 30 × 210mm (1¼ × 8¼ in.) in size and will carry type of up to about 20mm (¾ in.) in cap height.

BODYTYPE I AND BODYTYPE 2

Sheet size: 254 × 381mm (10 × 15 in.)
Colour range: black, white

A quick, simple method for simulating text setting on visuals and layouts, available in six different typefaces and a variety of sizes. Bodytype 1 is printed on self-adhesive film and is cut and positioned on to artwork in the same way as Pantone Films (see The Pantone System, pp.128-9). Bodytype 2, better suited to packaging and mock-ups, is identical to standard dry transfer lettering and is applied using a similar rub-down

technique without the need for cutting out. It moulds itself well around three-dimensional objects and is easy to apply in intricate or awkwardly shaped areas.

LETRASIGN AND PICTOGRAMS

Letrasign sizes: 15mm (⅝ in.), 25mm (1 in.), 38mm (1½ in.), 50mm (2 in.), 75mm (3 in.), 100mm (4 in.), 150mm (6 in.)
Colour range: black, white, red

Letrasign offers a range of self-adhesive matt vinyl sign lettering for creating low cost, professional-looking signs. The individual letters are backed with a high-tack, permanent adhesive which will stick to most smooth, dust-free, dry surfaces such as glass, metal, plastic, and so on. When properly burnished they are very hard-wearing and will resist damage, making them ideal for notices and signs outside, and for exhibition and display work.

Pictograms, manufactured to the same standard, are available in two sizes – 125mm (5 in.) square and 200mm (8 in.) square – and offer a range of universally understood warning and information symbols.

LETRASET RULES, BORDERS AND SYMBOLS

Sheet size: 254 × 381mm (10 × 15 in.); Architectural and Science ranges in half sheets 184 × 241mm (7¼ × 9½ in.)
Colour range: Line rule sheets available in black and white with 12 colour sheets to complement the range; Borders and corners available in black and white; Symbols available in black, white and multicolour

Like Bodytype 1 and 2, rules, borders and symbols are available as either rub-down dry transfer sheets or self-adhesive film laminate sheets which need to be cut out before positioning on the artwork. The range is vast and offers a whole library of corners, decorative borders, dotted lines, arrows, brackets, geometric shapes, technical and architectural symbols, musical notation and many more. Use on artwork to maintain image quality and consistency, especially on repetitive work. Rules are given in point or millimetre line weights, useful for matching to corners or other hand-drawn lines on artwork. The Science range is aimed specifically at scientific and medical illustrators and is ideal for preparing high-quality artwork for scientific publications.

LETRALINE TAPES AND LETRATAPES

Sizes: Available in 16.5m (19 yd) and 8.23m (9½ yd) lengths and in various widths

Letraline self-adhesive tapes are available in a wide range of patterns, widths and colours and are designed as an accurate, fast method of laying

down repetitive material on charts and diagrams. There are over 1,000 references to choose from, including borders, corners and point rules (an alternative to those on dry transfer sheets), printed patterns, metallic, opaque and transparent coloured lines. A finished job will always look consistent even if it has been produced by a number of different people.

Letratapes are dry transfer lettering in tape format and are printed throughout their length with the same letter or numeral. Two typefaces are available in six different sizes and each tape carries between 300 and 900 characters, depending on size.

LETRASET SPECIALS
Letraset offer a useful personal service and are willing to print (from camera-ready artwork) any individual symbol or type design on to a Letraset sheet or tape. These can be in the form of rub-down transfer sheets or self-adhesive film laminate sheets and are a particularly convenient method of applying company logos or other frequently used material.

THE LETRATONE SYSTEM
Sheet sizes: Standard 254 × 381mm (10 × 15 in.) in all patterns; Large format 508 × 381mm (20 × 15 in.) in a smaller range of 85 references
As its name implies, the Letratone system was originally developed to provide a convenient, easy-to-use, consistent source of tones and mechanical tints for use on all kinds of artwork and illustration. This has now extended into a range of over 600 different references covering not only percentage dot screen tints but also line tints, grids, line and dot patterns, cartographic and geological patterns, special effect textures, architectural patterns and special symbols. The system consists of pre-printed sheets of low-tack self-adhesive acetate film which can be cut to any size or shape and repositioned if necessary but will hold firmly to most surfaces when burnished. The method of use is identical to that for Pantone Colour Overlays (see pp.128-9).

The range is especially useful to the graphic designer as a reliable, versatile and quick method of laying down reproducible tones and textures on artwork where neatness and accuracy are essential. Letratone's matt surface is printed with photo-opaque ink which gives dense, sharply defined edges without the risk of glare. The surface can be scraped with a knife to form highlights or correct mistakes. The film is heat resistant and stable to facilitate diazo/dyeline and other copying processes. Letratone also offers potential for the creative use of texture and pattern in design as well as for artwork purposes; for example, interesting moiré effects can be achieved by overlapping different sheets.

Never throw away any small unused portions

of a sheet that you might have left over at the end of a particular job – you never know when something might come in handy at some later date. Get into the habit of keeping a box or file to collect such items.

Twelve of the most popular sheets of Letratone are now available in a range of seven colours, which can be ideal for visuals and mock-ups. Letraset also undertake to reproduce any symbol or pattern from individual artwork.

INSTANTEX
Sheet size: 254 × 381mm (10 × 15 in.)
Colour range: black, yellow, orange, blue, red, green, grey, brown, beige, gold, silver
Instantex sheets are used for applying colour and texture to artwork and illustrations, enabling the designer to apply tone exactly where it is required. The method of application is the same as for instant lettering: lay the sheet over the artwork, and rub down the texture, or colour, with a burnisher. Unwanted areas can be removed with a scalpel (X-Acto knife).

Interesting effects can be achieved by overlaying different colours and tones.

ALFAC

ALFAC
Sheet sizes: 105 × 115mm (4 × 4½ in.) for letters below 8pt; 210 × 297mm (8¼ × 11¾ in.) 8 to 48pt; 297 × 420mm (11⅜ × 16½ in.) over 48pt; 120 × 250mm (4¾ × 9¾ in.) Decadry coloured letters
Colour range: black, white, red, blue, green, gold
Over 200 different typestyles are available in the Alfac range, including 50 which are exclusive to the company. Sheets are supplied in well designed re-sealable envelopes which help to protect and store them in good condition. The small format sheets make positioning of characters below 8pt in size much less difficult, and are supplied in useful sturdy blister packs containing five identical sheets. The Decadry range offers 12 typefaces, plus a selection of graphic symbols, printed in bright opaque colours. Alfac also produce bodytype, miscellaneous symbols, rules, decorative borders, geometric shapes and so on, and will undertake to print special, customized sheets if required.

EDDING

Sheet sizes: 88 × 218mm (3½ × 8½ in.); ten references also available in large sheets 250 × 350mm (9¾ × 13¾ in.)

This useful range of dry transfer sheets includes 50 international typefaces, architectural and graphic symbols, geometric shapes, arrows, brackets (parentheses) and mathematical signs. The smaller sheet size is easy to handle and often a more economical buy for a job where only a limited number of characters is required. The transfers have a good resistance to erasure.

KROY

LETTERING MACHINE

Kroy is a unique, low cost lettering system for producing your own professional-looking type on self-adhesive tape. The machine holds a moulded typedisc and a snap-in cartridge of Kroytape consisting of a dry ink ribbon to make the image and the adhesive tape to carry it. Characters from the disc are impressed on to the tape, giving sufficient definition for photographic or diazo reproduction. The carrier tape is transparent, repositionable, will not fade, yellow or curl and will not show up in reproduction. The system is faster (and often more accurate) than dry transfer lettering and less expensive than commercial typesetting. Characters are locked into perfect alignment and letters and words are automatically spaced although this can be manually adjusted if necessary. Typediscs are available in a selection of styles and sizes from 8pt to 192pt (48pt to 192pt can only be produced with the XL Kroy Machine).

MECANORMA

MECANORMA

Sheet sizes: 320 × 400mm (13½ × 16 in.) Letter-Press sheets; 120 × 230mm (4¾ × 9 in.) Transfer Card
Colour range: black, white, red, blue, green, yellow, gold, silver
Mecanorma, like Letraset, are a major manufacturer of dry transfer products and their catalogue gives an excellent overview of the graphic needs they cater for. The range offers 330 typestyles, including founts of Arabic, Cyrillic, Hebrew, Greek and Thai characters and 16 different styles of numerals. Their sheets have several innovative features which make them convenient to handle and easy to rub down cleanly. Large format Letter-Press sheets are perforated down the middle, enabling separation into two more manageable halves, and have a permanently attached backing sheet for better protection during storage. The Transfer Cards, ideally sized and shaped for positioning small characters, come with a sealed pushout protective cardboard cover which is removed

and discarded before use. The thickness of the rigid cardboard frame protects the characters from subsequent damage and accidental transfer as they are held suspended away from the work surface until pressed down individually. The cards are easy to store upright.

Mecanorma transfers come on a dimensionally stable, polyester carrier film which helps to prevent distortion of the letters, especially in unstable or changeable environments. A selection of symbols of all kinds, borders, corners, brackets, pictograms, geometric shapes, and so on, completes the dry transfer range. Mecanorma also supply self-adhesive Copytext (bodytype), texture sheets and tapes of all kinds.

THE PANTONE SYSTEM

The Pantone Matching System is a complete range of products developed by Letraset for the precise identification and communication of colour requirements at all stages of the design process from initial roughs to final printed result. As such it constitutes an internationally recognized colour language, invaluable for eliminating the ambiguities and inaccuracies which inevitably creep in when attempting to describe colours verbally. The system consists of 568 individual colours (including 56 high intensity colours and seven metallics) each with its own Pantone reference number which serves to identify it to the printer who can then mix the inks to a specific formula for perfect matching.

The range of products available also allows particular colours to be used consistently at various stages and for various applications of any design and by a team of people working on one job, without fear of variation occurring. Pantone Colour Markers (see Markers, p. 63) can be used for visualizing quickly the range of colour scheme alternatives for a design. The chosen rough can then be translated into a matching dummy or client visual using Pantone Colour Papers and Overlays bearing identical reference numbers to the markers used. The same numbers are then given to the printer with the artwork to ensure the correct reproduced result.

COLOUR PAPER

Colour range: 505 colours
Sheet size: 508 × 660mm (20 × 26 in.)

This is an extremely versatile product providing a matt coloured ground for most media such as pencils, ink, pastels, paints and dry transfer lettering. The surface is specially treated to resist staining from rubber-based adhesives and fingermarks. The large area of dense flat colour makes this an ideal background for airbrush work, posters and displays, as well as a useful material for making three-dimensional models and dummies. The top edge of each sheet is provided with a printing guide showing the effect of black overprints, white reversals and various tint strengths of that particular colour. The back of the sheet is printed with a repeated Pantone reference number, useful for identifying cut pieces at a later date. A Colour Paper Selector, showing each colour as a 51 × 102mm (2 × 4 in.) swatch, is also available.

COATED COLOUR PAPER

Colour range: 135 colours
Sheet size: 508 × 660mm (20 × 26in.)

This range is similar in most respects to the ordinary Colour Paper and will accept a variety of art media. However, its special surface gives a gloss finish without the use of spray varnish, acetate or film, simulating the final product when printed on coated stock. It is easy to cut and fold and can be overprinted. The sheet is self-adhesive with a light tack which allows repositioning but will adhere well once burnished, even around corners and angles. A Pantone Coated Colour Paper Selector is available, showing 51 × 102mm (2 × 4 in.) swatches of each colour. Graduated sheets, giving a large area of graduated colour from 100 to 5 per cent, are produced in a smaller range of colours with both coated and uncoated surfaces. These eliminate the need for expensive airbrushing of backgrounds for dummies and visuals.

COLOUR OVERLAYS

Colour range: 217 colours, plus 58 sheets divided into four screen values
Sheet size: 508 × 660mm (20 × 26 in.)

A very popular, widely used and versatile product, this is invaluable for laying down large areas of flat colour quickly and easily, making it particularly useful for charts, maps and all forms of display work. Like Coated Paper, these sheets are self-adhesive but are actually made from thin translucent film with a semi-gloss surface which will accept most types of pen and pencil and even allow erasing without damage. Their translucency makes them ideal for overlapping images or laying colour over areas of black line work; special effects can be achieved by combining various sheets one over another. The film is even flexible enough to be used around the curves and corners of three-dimensional models.

The 58 sheets giving 10, 30, 50 and 70 per cent screen values (black, white, yellow, cyan and magenta are also available as 20, 40, 60 and 80 per cent tints) are particularly useful for making maximum creative use of tones in jobs with a limited number of printing colours. Graduated sheets are also available.

A Pantone Colour Overlay Selector shows the complete range in 19 × 51mm (¾ × 2 in.) swatches.

COLOUR LETRAFILM MATT

Colour range: 96 Pantone colours, plus 14 special Letrafilm colours
Sheet size: 254 × 381mm (10 × 15 in.)

Similar in application and uses to Colour Overlay, this range has a matt surface which can be scraped with a knife or treated with Letrafilm solvent to produce special effects. The film is dimensionally stable, allowing the use of most wet media such as inks and markers, as well as pencils and dry transfer lettering. The Letrafilm Matt Selector consists of 50 × 120mm (2 × 4¾ in.) swatches of the product itself, giving a good idea of the texture and translucency of each sheet and the intermixing possible with this range.

COLOUR SPECIFIER

This looseleaf manual is one of the designer's most valuable design aids. It gives samples of every one of the 568 Pantone colours on both coated and uncoated stock in the form of perforated swatches which can be torn off and attached to the artwork, thus ensuring accurate colour communication between designer and printer.

COLOUR FORMULA GUIDE

A useful reference guide for the designer, this is the printer's 'recipe book' for mixing the colours specified by the designer, showing the exact percentages of basic colours which combine to make each shade.

COLOUR TINT SELECTOR

In this looseleaf selector 515 colours are shown in a range of tint values from 10 to 80 per cent. Each page also demonstrates the effect of colour halftones, black overprinted type, colour type and reversed out type.

COLOUR AND BLACK SELECTOR

This is a particularly useful tool for getting the most out of two-colour printing. It shows colours in combination with black in a matrix of 10 to 70 per cent for each, giving over 60 different samples on every page. A colour halftone, duotone and various treatments of type are also shown.

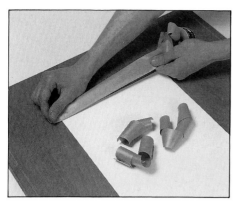

I Place the paper to be stretched on a drawing board or table larger than the size of the paper. Cut a strip of gummed paper tape for each side, but longer.

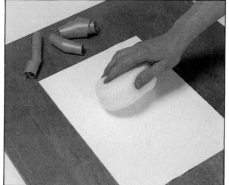

2 Dampen the sheet of paper thoroughly with a clean, wet sponge. Make sure you cover the entire surface evenly. You can dip the sheet into the bath of water if you have a large enough container.

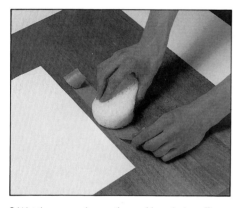

3 Wet the gummed paper thoroughly and wipe off any excess water with tissue paper or a sponge. Lay them, sticky side up, to one side.

4 Now stick the paper to the board using the strips of gummed tape. Do the two long edges first and then the two short edges. Allow the sheet to dry completely before applying paint. Although it may well look crumpled and buckled when wet, the paper will dry flat and taut.

I Trim a piece of heavy card to the required size. Mark the width of the margins, using a pencil, T-square and set square (triangle). Cut against a steel rule into the centre of the card (the waste), making several light cuts, rather than one heavy one.

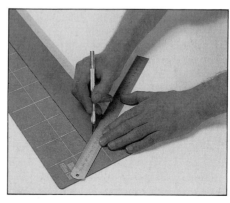

2 Cut a piece of tracing paper 5cm (2 in.) larger all round than the artwork. Place the artwork face down on the paper, fold over the top edge, and secure it with masking tape. Repeat the process with heavy coloured paper.

PRESENTATION TECHNIQUES
A heavy cardboard frame around a piece of artwork gives a truly professional appearance to a finished piece of work, and overlays and dust covers will both protect the piece during transportation and storage, and enable you to write instructions direct to the printer.

USING
LAMINATION FILM

1 Cut a piece of film from the roll, large enough to give at least 13mm (½ in.) overlap all round the artwork. Peel away about 100mm (4 in.) of the backing sheet and fold it back firmly. Carefully lower the strip of exposed film on to the artwork and smooth down evenly.

2 Place a plastic ruler on to the artwork and hold down with your left hand. Now work from left to right, releasing the backing sheet gradually with your right hand while pushing the ruler along with your left. The secret is to work slowly and patiently so that air bubbles do not develop under the film.

3 When the whole surface is covered, smooth the film down again with cottonwool.

4 Air bubbles trapped under the surface can be pricked with a pin or scalpel (X-Acto) blade point. Smooth the air towards the pin hole with your finger.

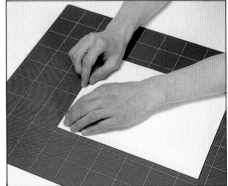

5 Trim an even border all round, and cut off the corners at 45°.

6 Turn the artwork over, fold the film down and mitre the corners.

REPROGRAPHICS

Overhead projection is ideal for the presentation of visual material to a large group of people. This section looks at the products available in this area, and also considers the advances in visualizers – probably the single most important and useful piece of studio equipment.

VISUALIZERS/ CAMERA LUCIDAS AND COPYING MACHINES

The best-known manufacturers of visualizers are Grant in the UK, and Goodkin in the USA. The Standard Grant projector (left) and Goodkin Model A Viewer (centre) both offer a large range of magnification, bright and even illumination of copy, and high-quality counterbalance mechanism. The Halco Copiscanner (right) is a smaller, less expensive, visualizer, offering a more limited range of magnification.

A visualizer (camera lucida) is probably the single most important item of technical equipment in any studio. It is essential for cutting down the time spent on tracing enlargements and reductions, scaling photographs and illustrations and preparing layouts, visuals and finished artwork. In fact, it can become a creative tool in itself.

The machine works on a very straightforward principle. The original – either a piece of flat artwork or a three-dimensional object – is placed on a movable copyboard which is brightly lit from above or from the sides. The lens is

carried by a bellows mechanism suspended above the copyboard. The user stands with his head inside the hood arrangement to see the image projected up on to the horizontal glass screen. Two handles on either side of the machine move the bellows and the copyboard up and down to change the image size and focusing.

Although basically simple mechanisms, visualizers (camera lucidas) are precision-engineered optical instruments and are therefore very expensive to buy. Check carefully on the specifications and capabilities of the model you are

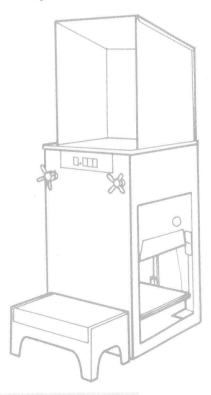

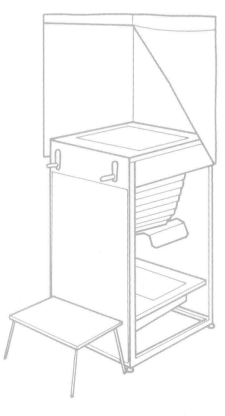

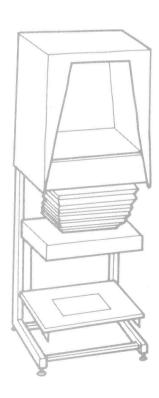

interested in. It must fulfil all your requirements as you are very unlikely to purchase such an item again. Access to the copyboard should be easy and unobstructed and both this and the bellows should move smoothly without jerking. It is very useful to be able to change the lens quickly during operation in order to increase the available range of reduction and enlargement. A lens supplied as standard with a visualizer (camera lucida) might give a range from a maximum reduction of 25 per cent to a maximum enlargement of 425 per cent but a special close-up lens could increase this from 15 to 675 per cent, which may save having to make more than one tracing (and thereby increasing the inaccuracy) if the difference in size between the original and the copy is very great. The illumination of the copyboard should be bright and even to get an intense, crisp image on the screen. The cheapest models have a completely solid copyboard but it may well be worth spending a little extra to obtain one which incorporates a light box or table panel, lit from below, which facilitates the tracing of transparencies and films.

When changing the position of the original during use, always keep your hands and arms well away from the bulbs in the machine as they get very hot and can inflict nasty burns. Remember to switch the machine off after you have finished to prevent unnecessary wear and tear on the bulbs. When making a tracing, use the hood to block out as much light as possible and fix the sheet firmly to the screen using masking tape. The best kinds of media to use are tracing, detail or thin layout paper with a hard pencil (2H to 4H) which will not smudge but can be erased to correct mistakes if necessary. Any thicker types of paper will not provide enough optical clarity for an accurate tracing.

Probably the best-known manufacturers of visualizers are Grant in the UK and Goodkin in the USA. The Grant Standard Projector gives a maximum reduction of 29 per cent and a maximum enlargement of 800 per cent. A cheaper model, the Grant Super Mini Projector, works within the range of 40 to 250 per cent, although this is increased with the addition of special lenses. The Goodkin Model A Viewer gives a range of 25 to 400 per cent with the standard lens, while the low-priced model 5B actually gives a larger range of 20 to 500 per cent,

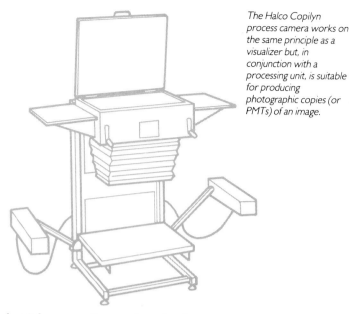

The Halco Copilyn process camera works on the same principle as a visualizer but, in conjunction with a processing unit, is suitable for producing photographic copies (or PMTs) of an image.

but it has a smaller copyboard and viewing area, and the copyboard is solid, except for an opening for viewing transparencies.

It is vital for the designer to have some kind of reprographic equipment to produce high-quality prints to any given size for artwork purposes. The most popular, widely used and versatile instrument is the Photomechanical Transfer (PMT) machine (also called a vertical camera or process camera), which works on exactly the same principle as the visualizer (camera lucida). A paper or transparent negative is employed to produce a photographic copy of the original on paper or film. This can be a direct image, or reversed right to left, or converted from black to white. Halftones can also be produced and screens used to convert continuous tones to a pattern of thousands of variously sized and shaped dots. These are designated by specifying the number of lines (of dots) per inch or centimetre. Screens are available in a wide range of sizes from 20 lines per centimetre (50 lines per inch) to 80 lines per centimetre (200 lines per inch). The one chosen differs according to the printing process and paper surface to be used in producing the finished result. The finer the screen, the finer the detail of the printed image will be. Special effects can be achieved, too, by using patterned screens.

The simplest PMT machines are combined visualizer (camera lucida)/ cameras and can be used easily by non-

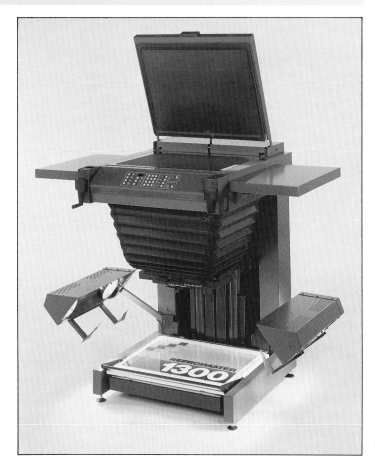

Agfa-Gevaert Repromaster 1300, a high-quality studio camera, which has an easy to read LED display panel for extremely accurate sizing, from reductions of 20 per cent to enlargements of 500 per cent. It also features a vacuum back.

now incorporate fully automatic exposure and developing controlled by computer and there is often no need for darkroom facilities.

PMT machines can even be used to simulate coloured elements for mock-ups or presentation visuals. The original is printed on to a transparent film sheet and processed to give a 'colour key' – a kind of chemical code as to where the colour should go. Any colour transparent dye can then be applied to develop the image and colours superimposed to mimic two or more printed over one another. Using the same process it is also possible to make coloured self-adhesive transfers for individual application to three-dimensional items such as packaging. Agfa-Gevaert, one of the largest and most popular manufacturers of reprographic equipment, now produce an even quicker and simpler system of colour copying. Called 'Copycolour' – it will make full-colour copies using special negative and positive film and a simple processing unit with only the steps required to produce an ordinary black and white PMT.

An older type of copying system is the dyeline process which is used mostly for reproducing large engineering and architectural drawings. This uses ultraviolet light to expose a transparent original (drawn on drafting film or tracing paper) to specially sensitized paper.

Photocopiers are now more widely used than ever before in the design studio as they become capable of higher quality reproduction and incorporate many special features. The results from most low to medium priced models are still relatively crude and are not really suitable for artwork purposes but higher priced models can produce astonishingly sharp images. Their real limitation lies in only being able to reproduce to set sizes. Two basic types of photocopier are available: a thermal copier has to be fed with special paper negatives and positives while an electrostatic copier uses no negative and can print on to any paper, and even on to transparent acetate film for making overhead transparencies (see Overhead Projection, p.141). The most useful photocopier should be able to cope with a range of paper sizes and offer enlargement and reduction facilities. Designers are beginning to discover the creative potential of these machines and are using them both to produce strange experimental images and as a general aid to the design process.

specialists. The image is first sized and focused in the normal way, then a negative placed, emulsion side down, on to the glass screen. A cover is pulled down to block out stray light from the screen and hold the negative firmly in place. Exposure is calculated according to the degree of reduction or enlargement required. After exposure, the negative is removed from the camera and matched with a positive sheet, emulsion sides together. This sandwich is then fed through a single bath table-top processor, allowed to rest for a few minutes and peeled apart to reveal a crisp black and white image. The most expensive, high technology machines on the market today

Agfa-Gevaert single bath PMT processor with footswitch.

OVERHEAD PROJECTION

The overhead projector (OHP) was originally developed as an alternative to traditional blackboard and chalk for the presentation of visual material to a group of people. The system has several inherent advantages: the presenter can face the audience at all times, the room need only be in semi-darkness, allowing the audience to take notes or refer to written material, and professional-looking coloured images can be used to add impact, clarity and authority to any presentation. OHP transparencies can be simply prepared in advance, used repeatedly with different groups, and either singly or in sequence to explain complex information step by step.

The glass-topped body of the projector contains a reflector, lamp, heat filter and lens. Light from the bulb is passed through the lens to the image lying on the glass to be projected up to the movable head. This contains a system of lenses and a 45° angled mirror which throws the image on to a vertical screen. To focus the image, move this head up and down its support and to change the image size, move the projector towards or away from the screen. To obtain an undistorted image the screen must be exactly parallel to the head. Sometimes it is necessary to tilt the head in order that the presentation can be clearly seen at the right height by the audience. If this is necessary remember that the screen must be tilted too to prevent 'keystone' distortion.

Images are prepared on rolls or sheets of transparent acetate film. Rolls can be attached to the projector and advanced during the presentation; placing them vertically over the glass allows scrolling of continuous text, and placing them horizontally gives a frame-by-frame presentation. Separate sheets can be mounted in cardboard frames to give extra rigidity – this is a good idea for images which are to be stored and re-used several times. Acetate is available in several different thicknesses: the thinnest gauges (about 0.08mm/$\frac{1}{300}$ in. thick) are suitable for one-off transparencies which are to be discarded after the presentation. Thick gauge acetate (about 0.12mm/$\frac{1}{200}$ in. thick) should be used for making transparencies with registered overlays as it is more resistant to distortion caused by moisture and heat from the projector. Always use the same gauge for all layers – different gauges stretch and contract at a different rate.

Casually produced transparencies reflect badly upon the material being presented but there are many easy and relatively quick techniques for achieving excellent results. The simplest method is to use special OHP markers directly on to the acetate. These can be either spirit (alcohol)-based, giving a permanent line, or water-based, which give a removable

ITM Astrolux portable overhead projector.

line. (Note that non-specialist water-based markers will not write on acetate.) The simpler each transparency is, the easier your audience will find it to understand and commit to memory. Therefore, reduce the amount of information given at each stage and restrict it to essential statements only – a maximum of three major details per transparency.

Lettering can be added by hand using a marker but your handwriting must be neat and legible if you employ this method. Special OHP dry transfers are available for really professional-looking lettering. These too are translucent and heat resistant. For good legibility,

especially from the back of a large room, letters of any kind should be no less than 6mm (¼ in.) high.

A simple way to produce high-quality, detailed, black and white transparencies is to copy artwork on to special sheets of acetate using an ordinary photocopier. It is important to check that the type of film chosen is compatible with your photocopier before use. These images can have colour added afterwards if desired using any of the techniques outlined above. Always store your acetate and prepared transparencies in dry conditions and at as even a temperature as possible to prevent them from stretching and contracting.

ALFAC
Not available in the USA

DECADRY OHP
Sheet sizes: 120 × 250mm (4¾ × 9¾ in.) lettering sheets; 118 × 215mm (4⅝ × 8½ in.) cutting film
Colour range: black, red, blue, green, yellow
Like Letraset, Alfac offer a comprehensive range of translucent, heat-resistant dry transfer and self-adhesive products for overhead projection work. Rub-down lettering is available in three popular typefaces (Helvetica Medium, Franklin Gothic Extra Condensed, Observer) in sizes from 12pt to 54pt and the references also include numerals, geometric shapes, graphic symbols and pictograms. Self-adhesive cutting film is available in five different tonal patterns, the five flat colours and a selection of circles and bars for preparing charts. The small format sheets are easy to handle and economical for the occasional user.

APOLLO
Not available in the UK

APOLLO A1-1000 OVERHEAD PROJECTOR
Although at the lower end of the price range for projectors, and compact in size, this machine offers high resolution, consistently vivid images and a particularly quiet and cool operation. It packs into a conveniently compact shape (the focusing column folds flush to the body of the projector) and has a thermal cut-off switch to protect the mechanism from overheating. A continuous roll attachment can be fitted which also folds away for easy storage.

Apollo also supply tough cardboard transparency mounts with a hardwearing glazed

surface which is not damaged by any pressure-sensitive tape. There is ample space for writing any notes necessary for the presentation.

FABER-CASTELL

OH-LUX DRAWING BOARD
An A4 capacity drawing board, with a transparent acrylic drafting area, which will fit neatly over the light table of an overhead projector. It is ideal for the preparation of accurate transparencies or for demonstrating drafting techniques and drawing board skills to an audience. Clamp bars hold the acetate sheet firmly in place and a transparent parallel motion (straight-edge) can be fitted to any side using guide grooves.

OH-LUX COMPASS
A very useful tool for the difficult task of rendering circles and curved lines accurately on to acetate. It is fitted with a transparent suction foot to grip the smooth surface firmly and a universal adaptor which will accept all types of overhead projection pens and markers. Without the suction foot, the compass can be used in the ordinary way on paper.

OVERHEAD PROJECTION MARKERS
Line widths: broad (wedge tip), medium, superfine
Colour range: black, blue, red, green, yellow, orange, violet, brown
Intense, translucent markers in a choice of either permanent or water-soluble inks. The fine width has a steel-encased resilient tip which is particularly good for working with straight-edges or templates. Permanent pens have black barrels and water-soluble ones have grey barrels, and both types will write on most non-porous

materials such as plastics and glass, as well as acetate. Available in plastic wallets of four, six and eight pens or plastic work boxes of eight pens complete with eraser (for permanent) or sponge (for water-soluble).

OHP ERASER
A double-ended eraser for removing both permanent marker inks and pencil lines from film. One end, impregnated with solvent, removes the ink marks while the other erases any residual traces of solvent from the surface to prevent bleeding or feathering of subsequent lines.

FILM SALES LTD
Not available in the USA

OHP FILM
Sheet sizes: A4, 267 × 216mm (10½ × 8½ in.)
Crystal-clear Acetate or Write-On-Film, both available in a variety of thicknesses and supplied in sheets or rolls. Acetate offers exceptional optical clarity (so choose this for fine detailed work) while Write-On-Film has better resistance to tearing and warping. This type is available in 50-leaf pads with 5mm (³/₁₆ in.) grid interleaving. All Film Sales sheets are supplied in useful easy-access storage boxes.

OHP MOUNTS
Frame sizes: A4, 254 × 302mm (10 × 11¾ in.), 254 × 254mm (10 × 10 in.)
Cardboard frames giving good rigidity to individual transparencies. The surface of the board will accept written notes in most media.

VELTINT COLOURED PVC FILM
Sheet sizes: A3, A4
Colour range: black, red, blue, green, yellow, orange
Although this film does not have a sticky backing it will adhere to any shiny surface without the application of glue. This makes it very economical and easy to use more than once when laying coloured areas on to transparencies.

ITM
Not available in the USA

ITM OVERHEAD PROJECTOR STARTER KIT
A compact and economical way of purchasing all the basic equipment needed for preparing transparencies. The robust carrying case contains a set of 20 markers (both water- and spirit/alcohol-based), compass, eraser, clear acetate

sheets, heavy-duty mounts, roll of masking tape and a handbook giving useful tips on preparing transparencies.

LETRASET

LETRAVISION
The LetrAVision range of co-ordinated projectable art materials comes from Letraset's vast selection of graphic products but is specially developed for use in overhead transparency work. All products are available separately or in the form of a LetrAVision Kit – a convenient plastic carrying case containing a useful selection of all the different items, including a layout board and a knife. The system is exceptionally helpful for producing high-quality transparencies quickly and easily but with little need for skill or effort.

ACETATE PADS
Each pad contains a printed millimetre grid to help with preparing transparencies (see Drafting Films, pp. 106–7). Loose A4 acetate sheets are also available in flip-top boxes of 50 sheets.

LETRAVISION LAYOUT BOARD
A sturdy working surface for preparing transparencies. The sheet of acetate, which tends to be slippery and difficult to handle, is held firmly in position by means of plastic clips and a printed millimetre grid helps in planning space and organizing the layout neatly.

LETRAVISION PROJECTABLE FILM AND TONE
Sheet size: 245 × 381mm (10 × 15 in.)
Colour range: black, blue, red, green, yellow, orange, brown, pink, purple, brick red, maroon, wine
Self-adhesive film for laying down areas of colour and texture on to a transparency once the basic shapes have been established. It is simple to smooth down, trim and peel away, and any excess can be returned to the backing sheet and reused another time. An infinite variety of effects can be achieved by overlaying different films. Nine textures are available in black, blue, red and green while all colours are available as flat sheets.

LETRAVISION PRE-PRINTED FILMS
A useful range of acetate sheets providing ready-drawn circles and boxes for charts, grids and axes for graphs, flow diagrams and information modules. The shapes are white on a pale blue background, surrounded by a white frame which does not appear during projection but allows space for writing notes about what you are going to say. Details on the charts can be filled in using markers or any of the self-adhesive products.

Circles, for instance, present particular problems. These pre-printed circles are marked out around the circumference allowing quick calculation of the divisions necessary for pie charts.

LETRAVISION PROJECTABLE LETTERING AND SYMBOLS

Sheet size: 184 × 242mm (7¼ × 9½ in.)
Colour range: black, blue, red, green, yellow
Translucent, heat-resistant dry transfer sheets for rub-down application to acetate or pre-printed films. The typeface used is Helvetica Medium which is clear, legible and compatible with most diagrammatic subjects. The lettering is available in a range of sizes from 12pt (3mm/⅛ in.) to 60pt (16.6mm/¹¹/₁₆ in.), and a selection of lines, arrows, brackets (parentheses), geometric shapes and pictograms are ideal for the creative design of charts and diagrams.

LETRAVISION SELF-ADHESIVE SYMBOLS

Colour range: blue, green, red, yellow
These differ from dry transfer symbols in that they are pre-cut from coloured self-adhesive Projectable Film. Professional-looking charts and diagrams are easy to produce with little technical skill or drawing ability as the shapes correspond exactly with those on the Pre-Printed Films. Simply lift them off their backing sheet and apply where required. The dimensions of bars, squares and circles can be altered by cutting, if required.

LETRAVISION HISTOGRAMS

Colour range: blue, green, red, yellow
Another way to make bar charts. These self-adhesive histogram sheets are printed with a pattern of 4mm (³/₁₆ in.), 6mm (¼ in.), 8mm (⁵/₁₆ in.) or 10mm (⁷/₁₆ in.) width bars which can be cut individually to the right length, then laid as a completed diagram on to an acetate sheet.

LETRAVISION PHOTOCOPIER FILM

Sheet size: A4 (297 × 210mm/11¾ × 8¼ in.)
Colour range: clear, blue, green, red, yellow
A specially treated acetate for use through a standard photocopier. Simply load the film into the paper feed and photocopy the original in the normal way. The range of colours is unusual for this type of film and is ideal for the preparation of colour-with-black line transparencies.

LETRAVISION PROJECTABLE MARKERS

Line widths: superfine, medium
Colour range: black, blue, red, green, yellow, purple
Spirit (alcohol)-based permanent markers for writing and drawing on acetate. Though suitably translucent for projection, the inks give good

density and lines do not break up. Markers are available in assorted packs of six colours.

Mistakes can be removed using a special wedge-tipped LetrAVision Correcting Marker which dissolves the ink. This is more accurate and convenient than using liquid solvents and cloths.

NOBO

Not available in the USA

Nobo manufacture two overhead projectors (a sturdy and a slimline model) and a variety of overhead projection accessories. Nobo Card Frames provide protective mounts for transparencies and can be filed in their own box which has a numbered index printed on it for easy reference and retrieval.

Nobo Plain Paper Copier Film can be fed through photocopiers to produce complex material quickly, while their ordinary acetate sheets are supplied usefully interleaved with 5mm (³/₁₆ in.) grid paper.

Permanent or water-soluble Nobo Overhead Projection Markers are available in black, blue, green, orange, yellow, purple and brown.

PILOT

PILOT MARKER FOR PROJECTION

Line widths: medium, extra fine
Colour range: black, red, blue, green, purple, brown, yellow, orange
Water-soluble or permanent ink markers giving bright, translucent lines. The medium width version has a fibre tip while the extra fine version has a durable plastic tip to prevent spreading.

ROTRING

ROTRING RAPID OVERHEAD DRAWING BOARD

An A4 board designed for drawing accurate smudge-proof lines on acetate using Isograph P drafting pens with etching ink (see Drafting Pens, pp. 72-5) or overhead markers. The acetate is held on a transparent drafting area which allows light to pass through easily when the board is fitted over a projector. A stop-and-go parallel motion (parallel straight-edge) and T-square mechanism will fit on to any side of the board.

ROTRING VISULINER AV PENS

Line widths: medium, fine
Colour range: black, blue, red, green, violet, yellow, orange, brown

A range of fibre-tipped pens with either permanent or water-soluble inks. The colours are intense and sharp but translucent when projected on to the screen and can also be used on glass, metal, plastics and so on. Mistakes made with a permanent marker can be easily erased using a Rotring AV Correcting Pen. Markers are available in plastic wallets of four, six and eight colours.

PORTA-SCRIBE
Not available in the UK

PORTA-SCRIBE OVERHEAD PROJECTOR
A high-power overhead projector which uses a 600 watt lamp to project a screen image of up to 9 ft square if needed. It gives a bright, clear image and has a thermal switch to keep the mechanism well cooled at all times. An acetate roll attachment can be fitted if necessary.

PORTA-SCRIBE 360-14
A well-designed machine, with particularly cool and quiet operation. The image produced is consistently sharp and clear and brightness can be altered between two different settings. Spare lamps are incorporated into the mechanism in case of failure during presentation.

SCHWAN-STABILO

STABILO-OHPEN
Line widths: broad (wedge tip), medium, fine, superfine
Colour range: black, blue, red, green, orange, yellow, brown, purple
A popular range of pens giving the user a tip width to suit every application. The superfine version is recommended for drawing with templates and stencils. The range is complemented by an unusual specialist overhead projection marker with an extra broad wedge tip – similar in design to Schwan-Stabilo's ordinary layout marker (see Markers, pp. 65-6) – which is particularly useful for laying down large areas of colour. It is available in the same selection of both permanent and water-soluble colours and includes a special OHP Correction Marker which contains a solvent. The inks in the pens adhere well, do not smudge or run, dry in seconds and are brilliant when projected. Water-based and permanent pens have grey or black barrel clips respectively and widths are easily identified on the end cap and barrel.

STABILO-OHP ERASER
Solvent-impregnated eraser for removing both types of ink from film. It will not damage the surface which can be written upon again immediately.

STABILO-OHP CLEANING TISSUE
Convenient, individually wrapped tissues for large-scale wiping of acetate. They will remove both permanent and water-soluble ink quickly and cleanly.

STABILO-OHP COMPASS
A special compass for carrying a Stabilo-OHPen. It has a transparent suction foot equipped with crossed guidelines for firm, accurate centring on acetate.

STABILO-OHP WORK KIT
A convenient package carrying a comprehensive selection of materials required for the preparation of overhead transparencies. The moulded vinyl wallet contains pens and markers, eraser, compass, cleaning tissues, correction marker and a pointer. It is ideal for a frequent user of the overhead projector system and keeps all his equipment within easy reach and well organized during both preparation and presentation in darkened rooms.

STABILO-OHP ACCESSORIES
Schwan-Stabilo overhead projection accessories include Helvetica rub-down lettering in three sizes and four colours (black, red, blue and green), self-adhesive translucent film in green, blue, brown, red and yellow, OHP mounting frames and two thicknesses of acetate in both sheets and rolls. An unusual addition to the range are pre-printed sheets in millimetre grid, square, line or music-ruled patterns. The print is on the reverse side so mistakes can be corrected without damage.

STAEDTLER

MARS LUMOCOLOR 660 AV DRAWING BOARD
Designed to be used with an overhead projector, this A4 board has a clear screen to allow light to pass through the transparency being prepared. A stop-and-go parallel motion (parallel straight-edge) can be fitted to any side for accurate rendering of detailed work. Good for class demonstrations too.

LUMOCOLOR MARKERS
Line widths: broad (wedge tip), medium, fine, superfine
Colour range: black, blue, red, green, yellow, orange, violet, brown
Lumocolor are popular among users of overhead projection markers for the selection of widths

available, clearly identified on both the barrel and cap. The broad width pens have wedge tips for laying down larger areas of colour. Permanent and water-soluble pens are conveniently colour coded with either black or grey barrels respectively, and the inks are translucent, crisp and instant drying to prevent smudging. Markers are available in plastic wallets of four, six and eight colours.

Marks made with permanent pens can be removed using a Lumocolor X 356 Correction Pen which contains a solvent.

LUMOPLAST ERASER

A special eraser for removing both permanent and non-permanent marks from acetate without damaging the surface. The vinyl contains a solvent which will dissolve pinpoint areas of ink.

3M

MODEL 223 TURBO OVERHEAD PROJECTOR

A high-quality projector suitable for larger room presentations as well as office use, this model is popular for the exceptionally brilliant and clear image it produces. It comes ready fitted with an acetate roll, which is advanced by turning a crank handle, but it can also be used with individual transparencies.

MODEL 589 PORTABLE OVERHEAD PROJECTOR

A remarkable slim lightweight projector for carrying between lecture venues. It weighs less than 9kg (20 lb) and is supplied with a carrying case for extra convenience. The image produced is bright and crisp and the projector is silent in operation. A good choice for frequent small-scale presentations.

SCOTCH PLAIN PAPER COPIER FILM

Sheet size: A4
Colour range: clear, blue, red, yellow, green
Special film for reproducing artwork through a photocopier. Three different types are available to suit most plain paper copiers so check which one is compatible before you buy. Maps, diagrams and even halftones can be copied successfully to give crisp, accurate transparencies.

SCOTCH FLIP FRAMES

Frame size: A4
A frame which both mounts and protects an overhead transparency. A clear plastic sleeve holds the sheet of acetate in place and preserves it from fingermarks and scratches, while fold-out flaps provide space for relevant written notes.

Flip Frames come ready punched for easy filing in standard ring binders. A good choice for particularly valuable or frequently used transparencies.

SCOTCH TRANSPARENCY MOUNTING FRAMES

Frame sizes: A4, quarto
Simple, rigid cardboard frames for mounting individual transparencies, these make storage and handling easier. Notes can be written on the frame.

SCOTCH COLOUR ADHESIVE FILM

Sheet size: A4
Colour range: blue, red, yellow, green
A 'cut-and-peel' self-adhesive film for laying areas of flat colour on to transparencies. Particularly useful for charts and diagrams.

SCOTCH TRANSPARENCY MARKING PENS

Line width: medium
Colour range: black, blue, red, green, purple
Translucent, spirit (alcohol)-based pens for all drawing and writing needs on acetate. Available in sets of five colours.

VUGRAPH

Not available in the UK

VUGRAPH III OVERHEAD PROJECTOR

This gives a bright, well-focused image and is easy to operate even for the novice user. A specially designed ventilation system cools the mechanism even after the machine has been in use for several hours.

Vugraph also supply Economy, Self-adhesive and Plastic mounting frames for preparing transparencies.

ZENITH

NEGATIVE OVERHEAD FILM

Sheet size: A4
An unusual type of opaque white acetate which projects a completely black background on to the screen. However, when special Po-Ne-Pens are used on the surface a substance in the ink dissolves the coating to give a brilliant transparent coloured image. This effect is excellent for adding particular impact and contrast to a presentation and is often restful to the eyes after looking at a white screen for some time. Po-Ne-Pens are available in fine and medium widths in clear, blue, red, green and yellow.

I Construct a diagram of what you intend to show on paper in pencil.

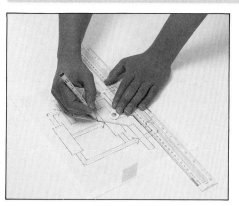

2 Lay a sheet of acetate over your pencil diagram and ink in the main features with a permanent marker.

PREPARING OVERHEAD TRANSPARENCIES

The simplest way to create overhead transparencies is to use special OHP markers directly on to the acetate. These can be either spirit(alcohol)-based, giving a permanent line, or water-based, giving a removable line.

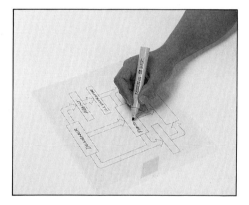

3 As you speak, fill in the details with a water-based marker. These can later be removed and your base transparency reused.

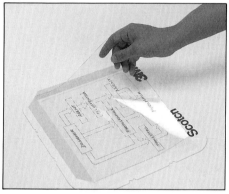

4 Overlays can be used to add information during a presentation and are ideal for explaining stages in complex processes. Stick one edge firmly to the cardboard mount with adhesive tape so that it can be folded over into exactly the right position when needed.

5 Colour can be applied using self-adhesive OHP film. It is translucent to allow light to pass through it effectively.

6 Special OHP dry transfers are available for really professional-looking lettering.

STORAGE SYSTEMS

An adequate system of storage is essential to a designer. He or she needs to transport equipment and artwork from place to place, and to protect completed work and work in progress. In this chapter, we look at the various storage systems on the market, and consider their suitability for different needs.

PLANCHESTS

Traditional wooden planchests still provide the ideal horizontal storage facility for artwork and materials. Steel ones, too, are equally useful and hardwearing. Nowadays these are unfortunately too expensive for all but the large established studio – unless you are lucky enough to pick one up secondhand – but one or two alternatives are available. Relatively new on the market in the UK are very light but remarkably strong portfolios made from rigid corrugated plastic sheets. These make excellent durable general-purpose carrying cases but can now also be collected into modular horizontal storage units to form useful

and inexpensive planchests. If necessary, any portfolio can be used to store artwork in a dust-free environment. Always try to keep any such items horizontal to prevent buckling or warping of the contents. If it is necessary to store display portfolios upright, remember to place them so that the polythene pockets hang suspended downwards from the ring binder so that the force of gravity will keep them flat. Vertical filing systems are now used increasingly in drawing offices as compact and mobile storage facilities for plans, blueprints, illustrations and finished artwork.

FILING

It is important for any designer to be methodical both in his working method and the organization of the environment around him. Although an unglamorous piece of equipment, a filing cabinet is a necessary aid, especially for the independent freelance designer, for ordering his affairs efficiently and keeping the office tidy. A simple two- or three-drawer cabinet with internal cardboard folders is quite sufficient for an

individual. For work in progress, especially over an extended period of time, job bags are invaluable for collating and organizing all the various items of artwork, typesetting, illustrations and so on related to each particular job. These can be purchased from shops in tough paper or polythene finishes but can be simply made by hand from heavy paper or thin card folded and sealed on three sides with paper tape or staples.

PORTFOLIOS

A portfolio is an essential item for any designer who is required to carry his work about, for whatever reason, outside his own studio or working area. If possible, it is best to have at least two different kinds to fulfil various different needs. The first should be a stiffened display portfolio with a ring binder spine capable of accepting transparent polythene sleeves. These will protect valuable presentation work from grease, dirt and the effects of constant handling and should have a matt or semi-

matt surface to reduce glare. The ring binding system is useful for quick and easy rearrangement of items at any time. This kind of portfolio should have an all-round zipper which will allow the opened portfolio to lie flat like a book. Popular makes are Faber-Castell, Daler and Artcare in the UK and Boyt, Arthur Brown and A.I. Friedman (graphics' suppliers, not manufacturers) in the USA.

The second portfolio should act as a kind of briefcase and be used to carry about work in progress, artwork, tools, papers and so on. A rigid type of construction is not as important here and in fact a more flexible portfolio is often an advantage for carrying bulky items to and fro. Those such as Monzac, Boyt, and Faber-Castell canvas portfolios are ideal, especially if they have a light metal frame inside to give a certain amount of rigidity. Some good sized pockets on either the inside or the outside are convenient for containing odd loose articles. This type of case could have either an opening at the top with a flap fastening or two zippers which start at either end of the spine and can meet at any point along the three open sides. This is helpful for carrying oversize or awkwardly shaped items which may have to project from the case but still need to be contained and weatherproofed as well as possible.

In the UK, portfolios are usually manufactured in four different sizes corresponding to the international 'A' sizes – A4 to A1 – although, obviously, providing a generous margin allowance all round. The most generally useful size for both display and all-purpose portfolios is A2. An A1 display portfolio is really only necessary if you are going to do a great deal of work at this size. Apart from any other considerations they are extremely bulky and difficult to carry for the individual. Generally, such things as A1 posters and broadsheets are split in

half and filed in two pockets of an A2 portfolio. An A3 case makes a useful addition for displaying smaller finished work which could look rather lost in larger pockets. In the USA the sizes are approximately $8\frac{1}{2} \times 11$ in., 11×14 in., 14×18 in., 18×24 in., 20×26 in., 23×31 in., 24×36 in., and 31×42 in.

Apart from portfolios, storage containers for drawing, painting and graphic materials are useful. Inscribe manufacture a particularly good range of Artbins, based on anglers' tackle boxes, which have cantilever shelves conveniently arranged to unfold, revealing everything you need neatly sorted into compartments. The cases can be easily carried by means of an inset plastic handle in the lid, and are ideal for students or anyone who has to transport their tools between different venues.

Tubular portfolios are also available – and prove less cumbersome – for carrying larger, rollable items, although simple rigid cardboard tubes do the same job just as well. If folded and sealed at both ends with tape these are also ideal for sending work through the post. Remember to save any for future use if they appear through your own letterbox. The traditional artists' portfolio, made from rigid cardboard covered in book cloth and with gussetted retaining flaps, is good for carrying and storing drawings, sketches, layouts and so on but is not really durable enough for sustained use.

ARTCARE
Not available in the USA

'A' RANGE PORTFOLIOS
Sizes: 890 × 665 × 40mm (35 × 26¼ × 1½ in.); 640 × 490 × 40mm (25¼ × 19¼ × 1½ in.); 465 × 360 × 40mm (18¼ × 14 × 1½ in.); 465 × 490 × 40mm (18¼ × 19¼ × 1½ in.); 350 × 280 × 40mm (13¾ × 11 × 1½ in.); 350 × 370 × 40mm (13¾ × 14½ × 1½ in.); 390 × 305 × 70mm (15¼ × 12 × 2¾ in.)

Colour range: black, brown, burgundy, sand
Professional designers and photographers who look for both practicality and durability often recommend these well-designed portfolios for the flat presentation and protection of finished work. The stiffened exterior is covered with a weatherproof PVC material and the corners are protected with brassed metal fittings. A strong handle is provided on the spine, allowing plastic display sleeves to hang vertically downwards from the ring binder inside when the portfolio is

being carried. The largest size has an additional handle on the side for easier underarm carrying. The all-round zipper and hinged spine allow the portfolio to lie completely flat for presentation. Two models are squarer, enabling both landscape and portrait items to be viewed without having to turn the case.

Five display sleeves are supplied with each case and extra are available individually.

'A' RANGE ZIP CASES
Sizes: 1275 × 875 × 40mm (50 × 34¼ × 1½ in.); 1075 × 815 × 40mm (42½ × 32½ × 1½ in.); 880 × 610 × 40mm (34½ × 23½ × 1½ in.); 645 × 565 × 40mm (25¼ × 22¼ × 1½ in.); 645 × 450 × 40mm (25¼ × 17¾ × 1½ in.); 470 × 340 × 40mm (18½ × 13½ × 1½ in.)

Colour range: black, brown
Similar to the Flap cases, these are also flexible PVC portfolios with a full-width internal pocket, useful as general-purpose carrying cases. They have the normal 40mm (1½ in.) spine but the

zipper allows the front to fold forward for easier access to, and visibility of, the contents. The reinforced base is fitted with protective rubber feet and the case has a lock fastening.

'A' RANGE FLAP MODELS

Sizes: 915 × 650 × 58mm (36½ × 23¼ × 2¼ in.); 660 × 540 × 58mm (26 × 21¼ × 2¼ in.); 660 × 440 × 58mm (26 × 17⅜ × 2¼ in.); 480 × 350 × 58mm (19 × 13¾ × 2¼ in.)

Colour range: black, brown

Made from weatherproof PVC material, these portfolios are flexible and have an extra wide gusset, ideal for carrying awkwardly sized and shaped items. There is an interior pocket and the corners are protected with brass fittings. The flap is held by a lock fastening.

'A' SIZE EASEL PRESENTATION PORTFOLIOS

Sizes: 510 × 485 × 40mm (20¼ × 19 × 1½ in.); 380 × 360 × 40mm (14¾ × 14 × 1½ in.)

Colour range: black, brown, burgundy, sand

Presentation of ideas or finished work to a group of people is sometimes made easier by having a vertical or sloping display, rather than laying a portfolio flat on a table. These cases look like ordinary portfolios containing plastic sleeves but open out into a completely free-standing angled easel display unit. Alternatively, the case can be laid flat for page-by-page presentation. Sleeves hang suspended from a ring binder in transit and are also supported by flanges to prevent wear and tear on the welded holes. The case is fully stiffened, weatherproof and supplied with brassed corners and an internal pocket for additional storage. The square format allows both landscape and portrait material to be viewed without a change of position.

DL CASES

Sizes: 890 × 630 × 35mm (35 × 25 × 1⅜ in.); 640 × 470 × 35mm (25½ × 18½ × 1⅜ in.); 460 × 340 × 35mm (18 × 13½ × 1⅜ in.); 700 × 530 × 35mm (27½ × 20¾ × 1⅜ in.)

Colour range: black, brown, burgundy, sand

A sturdy, all-purpose carrying case for everyday use. It has a rigid construction for the protection of artwork and similar items during transit, and incorporates brassed corners and rubber feet on the base. The case opens like a book and all sizes – except the largest, which has one – are fitted with two internal pockets.

ARTSTORE CARRYING CASES

Sizes: 2000 × 850 × 40mm (73¼ × 33¼ × 1½ in.); 1125 × 820 × 40mm (45 × 32¼ × 1½ in.); 880 × 610 × 40mm (34½ × 24 × 1½ in.); 635 × 455 × 40mm (25 × 18 × 1½ in.); 440 × 370 × 40mm (17¼ × 14½ × 1½in.); 320 × 250 × 50mm (12½ × 10 × 2 in.)

Colour range: black, brown, burgundy, sand

As their name implies, these cases make excellent dual-purpose portfolios for both transportation and storage. They are fully stiffened for complete protection and open at the top with a forward folding flap which allows easy access to the contents when the case is either vertical or horizontal. They will easily hold up to 50 loose 'A' Range sleeves.

PRESENTATION FOLDERS

Sizes: 625 × 475 × 30mm (24½ × 18¾ × 1¼ in.); 350 × 445 × 30mm (13¾ × 17½ × 1¼ in.); 480 × 445 × 30mm (19 × 17½ × 1¼ in.); 320 × 260 × 30mm (12½ × 10¼ × 1¼ in.); 360 × 320 × 30mm (14⅜ × 12½ × 1¼ in.); 270 × 325 × 50mm (10½ × 12¾ × 2 in.)

Colour range: black, brown, burgundy, sand

This range of hand-stitched display binders is compatible with the 'A' Range portfolios and display sleeves. They do not have zipper fastenings and so are not as practical for general use as traditional portfolios, but they are good for prestigious presentation of artwork.

BOYT

Not available in the UK

ARTISTS' PORTFOLIO CASES

Sizes: 18 × 14 × 3 in., 22 × 17 × 3 in., 26 × 20 × 3 in., 31 × 33 × 2 in.

Colour range: all black, navy with beige trim, brown with beige trim

These zippered canvas portfolios have a wire-structured frame, waterproof backing, gussets and pockets.

PRESENTATION BINDERS

Sizes: 8½ × 11 in., 11 × 14 in., 14½ × 17 in.

Colour range: black, brown, burgundy

Nylon-covered presentation binders with ten presentation sheets each.

ZIPPER PORTFOLIOS

Sizes: 17 × 22 in., 20 × 26 in., 23 × 31 in., 25 × 31 in., 31 × 42 in.

Colour range: black only

All sizes in this convenient range of carry-alls have 2½ in. gussets and two zippers, enabling the user to open one or both sides of the case. Metal studs protect the bottom of the cases.

DALER

FOLIO CASES

Sizes: 594 × 841mm (23½ × 33 in.); 420 ×

594mm (16½ × 23½ in.); 297 × 420mm (11¾ × 16½ in.)

Colour range: black, brown

An economical but robust portfolio for carrying tools and materials. It has two zippers, a reinforced spine with protective studs and durable plastic handles on both sides.

PORTFOLIOS

Sizes: 1160 × 815mm (46 × 32 in.); 815 × 580mm (32 × 23 in.); 661 × 523mm (26 × 20½ in.); 875 × 610mm (34½ × 24 in.); 610 × 440mm (24 × 17¼ in.); 440 × 310mm (17¼ × 12¼ in.)

Colour range: maroon only

The traditional artists' portfolio, made from rigid board covered in tough maroon book cloth. It has deep capacity, gussetted retaining flaps which are fastened with tape ties. This type of folio is good for carrying and storing sketches, drawings, layouts and so on but, although remarkably durable, a PVC case is really more convenient for sustained use.

ECONOMY PORTFOLIOS

Sizes: 875 × 610mm (34½ × 24 in.); 610 × 440mm (24 × 17¼ in.); 440 × 310mm (17¼ × 12¼ in.)

These are similar to the standard range but of a lighter construction. The manilla flaps are ungussetted but have tape ties and the portfolio is provided with metal protective corners.

EXX PROJECTS

PLAX FOLIOS

Sizes: 870 × 655 × 40mm (34½ × 25¾ × 1½ in.); 687 × 480 × 40mm (27 × 19 × 1½ in.); 490 × 355 × 40mm (19½ × 14 × 1½ in.); 325 × 260 × 40mm (13 × 10¼ × 1½ in.)

Colour range: black, translucent, blue, red, yellow

Although simply constructed from lightweight polypropylene corrugated plastic, these make remarkably strong, hard-wearing cases for transporting and storing tools and materials. They open at the top, with a forward folding flap for easier access, and fasten with strong press-studs. The sturdy tubular handles are comfortable to hold and come in a choice of co-ordinating or contrasting colours. The range of colours and name tag facility provided on the spine can be exploited to develop a colour-coded indexing system for filing, especially when used in conjunction with the Plax Planchests (see below).

Overall, these make an excellent economical alternative to a PVC portfolio, especially for students.

PLAX PORTFOLIOS

Sizes: 870 × 665 × 40mm (34½ × 25¾ × 1½ in.); 687 × 480 × 40mm (27 × 19 × 1½ in.); 490 × 355 × 40mm (19½ × 14 × 1½ in.); 325 × 260 × 40mm (13 × 10¼ × 1½ in.)

Colour range: black, translucent, blue, red, yellow

These cases are of similar construction to the Folios but are reserved for presentation of design or photographic work, and have ring binders to carry documents or mounted transparencies. (They will not take standard display sleeves.) The case opens out completely flat and the top flap is full width, fastening with press-studs along the bottom edge.

PLAX PLANCHESTS

Sizes: 1090 × 736 × 365mm (43 × 29 × 14 in.); 735 × 545 × 365mm (29 × 21½ × 14 in.); 545 × 367 × 365mm (21½ × 14¹/₁₆ × 14 in.); 367 × 272 × 365mm (14¹/₁₆ × 10¾ × 14 in.)

Colour range: grey only

Modular five-shelf melamine units designed to carry Plax Folios or Portfolios. They can be combined in a variety of ways and will stack by means of double-sided rubber suckers. Alternatively, screw-in wire legs can be fitted to raise each unit to working height. The two larger sizes include a magazine rack and the large chest also has space reserved for rolled drawings. Each unit comes supplied with five Plax Folios and makes an economical and space-saving way to create an efficient storage system.

Plax Planchests, designed to hold Plax Folios or Portfolios.

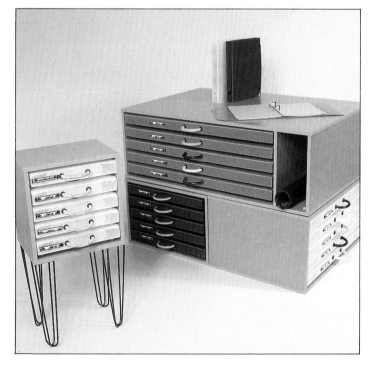

Faber-Castell display portfolio with PVC sleeves.

ECONOMY PORTFOLIOS

Sizes: 420 × 594mm (16½ × 23½ in.); 297 × 420mm (11¾ × 16½ in.)
Colour range: black only
A simple, inexpensive, general-purpose carrying case with comfortable carrying handles on both sides.

GELIOT WHITMAN

MULTI-VISION DISPLAY PORTFOLIOS

Sizes: 864 × 660mm (34 × 26 in.); 622 × 502mm (24⅞ × 19¾ in.); 508 × 400mm (20 × 15¾ in.); 324 × 267mm (12¾ × 10½ in.); 254 × 381mm (10 × 15 in.)
Colour range: black only
A rigid presentation portfolio which looks like an ordinary briefcase but opens up into a free-standing angled display unit. Transparent sleeves are held by spring-lock ring binder and can easily be flipped over during presentation. The cases are available with or without a 150mm (6 in.) deep gusseted pocket and all models are fitted with a moulded handle and leather closure straps .

GRAPHIC PRODUCTS

MONZAC PORTFOLIO

Size: 510 × 660mm (20 × 26 in.)
Colour range: black only
A folio which is very light in itself is a good choice for anyone who has to carry heavy artwork about. This case has a thin metal framework covered in waterproof nylon material with a reinforced cord webbing handle to give maximum portability and strength. A detachable shoulder strap is provided for particularly heavy loads. Three external pockets make useful and convenient storage for frequently used items and two-way zippers give easy access to the contents.

FABER-CASTELL

PROFESSIONAL PORTFOLIOS

Sizes: 594 × 841mm (23½ × 33 in.); 420 × 594mm (16½ × 23½ in.); 297 × 420mm (11¾ × 16½ in.)
Colour range: black only
Similar in robust design to the Artcare 'A' Range portfolios, these also feature a tough, waterproof covering material, brassed corner protectors, an all-round zipper and a spring-lock ring binder to carry PVC display sleeves vertically. The case will open completely flat for presentation and has two internal storage pockets. The toughened spine has a window to allow insertion of a name card. Five display sleeves are included and further supplies are available individually.

RAINBOW PORTFOLIOS

Sizes: 594 × 841mm (23½ × 33 in.); 420 × 594mm (16½ × 23½ in.); 297 × 420mm (11¾ × 16½ in.)
A range of light, durable canvas portfolios lined with PVC for extra weather protection. They have two-way zippers and internal pockets.

INSCRIBE

INSCRIBE ARTBINS

Size/Colour range: 8299 – 2 trays, 7 compartments, cobalt blue; **8399** – 2 trays, 6 compartments, terracotta; **8713** – 3 trays, 18 compartments, terracotta; **9276** – 6 drawers, 38 compartments, birch grey; **9066** – 6 swing-out trays, 27 compartments, terracotta; **8999** – 6 trays, 28 compartments, green
A sturdy storage container (based on anglers' tackle boxes) for all drawing, painting and graphic materials. The cantilever shelves conveniently unfold to reveal everything you need neatly

sorted and arranged. The case can be easily carried by means of an inset plastic handle in the lid, and is ideal for students or anyone who has to transport their tools between different venues.

REXEL NYREX

SLIMVIEW ART DISPLAY BOOKS
Sizes: A1, A2, A3, A3 square, A4, A4 square/ 8½ × 11 in., 11 × 14 in., 14 × 17 in., 18 × 21 in.
Colour range: black, fawn
Slim, rigid display books for presentation of artwork. The unique binding system allows sleeves (open on both short edges) or pockets (open on one short edge) to be changed easily and grips them firmly but does not look obtrusive. Sleeves and pockets are made from non-reflective, lightweight material and can also be used in standard portfolio ring-binding mechanisms. The 12mm (½ in.) spine has a recommended capacity of 15 pockets.

SLIMVIEW EASEL DISPLAY
Sizes: A2, A3, A3 square, A4, A4 square/8½ × 11 in., 11 × 14 in., 14 × 17 in., 18 × 21 in.
Colour range: black, fawn
Similar to Display Books and employing the same binding mechanism, these have an additional slanting easel display capability. If you lift and flip over the front cover, locating it against the clips at the back, the book forms a firm free-standing unit for displaying the pockets and sleeves inside. With a convenient slide-on carrying handle these make slim, neat folders for both transportation and presentation. The square format can be used comfortably for both landscape and portrait work without any change of position.

SIMAIR

LOCWYN MEGAFILE
An excellent, space-saving and versatile alternative to a planchest, especially for a small studio, this is a modular, vertical filing system for work in progress, proofs, films and finished artwork. A tubular metal frame holds interlocking tracks from which tough transparent folders are suspended. A range of different sized and subdivided folders are available for different needs. Hard-backed pockets, either single- or double-sided, protect unsupported materials such as films, negatives and tracings, and are ideal for presentation and display. Sling sleeves, open along both short edges, accommodate bulky items and can take up to 25 sheets of heavy artboard, while standard pockets, open along one short edge, can take up to ten sheets. The range

also includes top-loading job files and bags with resealable flaps.

The units can be made mobile by fitting castors or stacked to provide extra space. Wall tracking is available for hanging Megafiles on doors, walls, and so on.

UNO

UNO CONSUL CABINET
Size: H1435mm (56½ in.) × W 910mm (33½ in.) × D 433mm (17 in.)
A heavy-gauge steel cabinet for storing up to 750 drawings (approximately 380mm/15 in. deep) suspended from two chrome suspension bars. The cabinet has opening top and front flaps and can be locked for complete security.

WESTWOOD GRAPHICS
Not available in the USA

WEB PLAN FILES
Sizes: A0, A1
Free-standing or wall-mounted frame units for the vertical filing of plans and drawings. Materials are suspended from cross-bars using WEB self-adhesive polyester Suspension Tape which also helps to minimize damage incurred during handling. The A0 unit will hold any sheet up to a maximum width of 1260mm (48 in.) and the A1 unit any sheet up to a maximum width of 640mm (24½ in.).

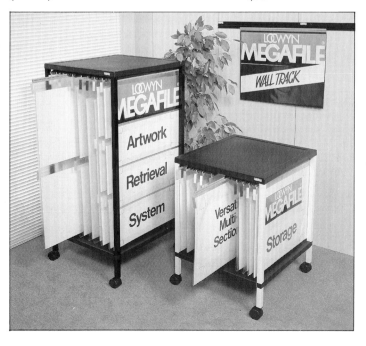

Simair Locwyn Megafile art retrieval and storage system.

BOOKLIST

The Advanced Airbrush Book, Cecil Misstear with Helen Scott Harman, Orbis Publishing, London, 1984; Van Nostrand Reinhold Co. Inc., New York, 1984.

The Airbrush Book, Seng-gye Tombs Curtis & Christopher Hunt, Orbis Publishing, London, 1980.

Airbrush: The Complete Studio Handbook, Radu Vero, Columbus Books, Bromley, 1983; Watson Guptill, New York, 1983.

Art and Illustration Techniques, Harry Borgman, Watson Guptill, New York, 1983.

The Artists Airbrush Manual, Clement Marten, David & Charles (Holdings) Ltd, Newton Abbot, 1980; David & Charles Inc., North Pomfret, VT, 1980.

The Artists Manual, Stan Smith & Prof. H. F. Ten Holt, Macdonald Educational, London, 1980; (Mayflower Books) Smith Pubs, Inc., New York, 1981.

The Coloured Pencil, Bet Borgeson, Watson Guptill, New York, 1983.

The Complete Guide to Airbrushing, Judy Martin, Thames & Hudson, London, 1983.

The Complete Guide to Illustration and Design, ed. Terence Dalley, Phaidon Press Ltd, Oxford, 1980; (Mayflower Books) Smith Pubs, Inc., New York.

The Creative Handbook, Creative Handbook Ltd, London, 1984.

The Designers Handbook, Alastair Campbell, Macdonald, London, 1983.

Do-It-Yourself Graphic Design, Consultant ed. John Laing, Ebury Press, London, 1984; Macmillan Publishing Company, New York, 1984; Facts on File, Inc., New York, 1984.

Drawing and Modelmaking, Alexander Ratensky, Watson Guptill, New York, 1983; Phaidon Press Ltd, Oxford, 1983.

Forget all the rules you ever learned about Graphic Design, Bob Gill, Watson Guptill, New York, 1983.

AIGA Graphic Design USA 5, Watson Guptill, New York, 1985; Columbus Books, Bromley, 1985.

Graphic Designers Production Handbook, Norman Sanders, David & Charles (Holdings) Ltd, Newton Abbot, 1984; Hastings House Publishers, Inc., New York, 1982.

Graphic Ideas Notebook, Jan V. White, Watson Guptill, New York, 1980.

Graphics UK, Ed. Fred Lambert, Designer Publications Ltd, London, 1983.

The Language of Layout, Bud Donahue, Spectrum Books, Englewood Cliff, N. J., 1979; Prentice Hall International Inc., Hemel Hempstead, 1979.

Layout – The Design of the Printed Page, Allen Hurlburt, Watson Guptill, New York, 1983.

Manuals of Graphic Techniques, Tom Porter and Bob Greenstreet, Astragal Books, London, 1980; Charles Scribner's Sons, New York, 1980.

Mastering Graphics, Jan V. White, Bowker Publishing Co., Epping, 1983; Bowker R.R.Co., New York, 1983.

Mechanical Color Separation Skills, Tom Cardamone, Van Nostrand Reinhold (UK) Co. Ltd, Wokingham, 1980; Van Nostrand Reinhold Co, Inc., New York, 1980.

More Studio Tips for Artists and Graphic Designers, Bill Gray, Van Nostrand Reinhold (UK) Co. Ltd, Wokingham, 1979; Van Nostrand Reinhold Co. Inc., New York, 1978.

Pasteups and Mechanicals, Jerry Demoney & Susan E. Meyer, Watson Guptill, New York, 1982.

Paste-up and Production Techniques, Rod van Uchelen, Van Nostrand Reinhold (UK) Co. Ltd, Wokingham, 1977; Van Nostrand Reinhold Co. Inc., New York, 1976.

The Pencil, Paul Calle, Watson Guptill, New York, 1983.

Production for the Graphic Designer, James Craig, Watson Guptill, New York, 1983.

Rendering with Markers, Ronald B. Kemnitzer, Watson Guptill, New York, 1983.

Rendering in Pen and Ink, Susan E. Meyer, Watson Guptill, New York, 1983.

Rendering in Pencil, Susan E. Meyer, Watson Guptill, New York, 1983.

Studio Tips for Artists and Graphic Designers, Bill Gray, Van Nostrand Reinhold (UK) Co. Ltd, Wokingham, 1976; Van Nostrand Reinhold Co. Inc., New York, 1976.

The Thames & Hudson Manual of Rendering with Pen & Ink, Robert Gill, Thames & Hudson, London, 1984.

SUPPLIERS' ADDRESSES

ALFAC

UK
Pelltech Ltd
Station Lane
Witney
Oxon OX8 6YS
Tel: (0993) 72130
Telex: 83147 VIA
or PELLTECH

USA
Refer to Canada

AUSTRALIA
ATSCO Australia Pty Ltd
Lot 27-49
Taunton Drive
Cheltenham
Victoria 3192

CANADA
Merit Distributors Inc.
1680 50th Avenue
Lachine
Quebec H8T 2V5

APOLLO

UK
Refer to USA

USA
Supplied by:
Arthur Brown & Bro. Inc.

AUSTRALIA
Refer to USA

CANADA
Refer to USA

ARTCARE

UK
Artcare UK Ltd
2 Heybridge Way
Lea Bridge Road
London E10 7NQ
Tel: (01) 558 1281
Telex: 291428

USA
Refer to UK

AUSTRALIA
Refer to UK

CANADA
Refer to UK

ARTONE

USA
Supplied by: A.I. Friedman
Inc.

AUTOTYPE INTER-NATIONAL

UK
Autotype International
Grove Road
Wantage
Oxon OX12 7BZ
Tel: (02357) 66251
Telex: 837275

USA
Autotype USA
1525 Greenleaf Avenue
Elk Grove Village
Illinois 60007
Tel: (312) 593 1955
Telex: 5101008423

AUSTRALIA
Howson Algraphy Australia
PO Box 213
Nunawading
Victoria 3131
Tel: (0532) 737475
Telex: 34077

CANADA
Refer to USA

BABS

UK
Business Aids Ltd
3 Whitby Avenue
London NW10 7SQ
Tel: (01) 965 9821

USA
Refer to UK

AUSTRALIA
Refer to UK

CANADA
Refer to UK

BADGER AIR-BRUSH COMPANY

UK
Morris & Ingram (London)
Ltd
156 Stanley Green Road
Poole
Dorset BH15 3BE
Tel: (0202) 673757
Telex: 418297

USA
Badger Air Brush Co.
9128 West Belmont Avenue
Franklin Park
Illinois 60131
Tel: (312) 678 3104

AUSTRALIA
Zimbler Pty Ltd
PO Box 2
Kew
Victoria 3101

CANADA
Hobby Industries
24 Ronson Drive
Rexdale
Ontario M9W 1B4

BELMONT

UK
Refer to USA

USA
Supplied by: A.I. Friedman
Inc.

AUSTRALIA
Refer to USA

CANADA
Refer to USA

BEROL

UK
Berol Ltd
Oldmeadow Road
Kings Lynn
Norfolk
PE30 4JR
Tel: (0553) 761221

USA
Berol Corporation
Eagle Road
Danbury
Connecticut 06810

AUSTRALIA
Refer to UK

CANADA
Berol Inc.
PO Box 310
Ville Lemoyne
Quebec J4P 3P8

BEST-TEST

UK
Hansa Technik GMBH
Postfach 620227
Oehleckerring 25
2000 Hamburg 62
Tel: (040) 531 2086

USA
Union Rubber Inc.
PO Box 1040
232 Allen Street
Trenton
N.J. 08606-1040
Tel: (609) 396 9328

AUSTRALIA
Import-Export
Management Service Inc.
2205 Royal Lane
PO Box 59309
Dallas
Texas 75229

CANADA
Demco Manufacturing Inc.
1660 Route 209
Franklin Centre
Quebec J0S 1E0

BIEFFE (BFE)

UK
BFE Unit 9
Armstrong Way
Great Western
Industrial Park
Windmill Lane
Southall
Middlesex UB2 4SD
Tel: (01) 843 9993

USA
Bieffe Di Bruno Serrarese
Spa.
PO Box 489
Padova
Italy

AUSTRALIA
Refer to Italy

CANADA
Refer to Italy

BLAIR

UK
Refer to USA

USA
Blair Art Products Inc.
8282 Boyle Parkway
PO Box 286
Twinsburg
Ohio 44087
Tel: (216) 425 2148

AUSTRALIA
Refer to USA

CANADA
Refer to USA

BLUNDELL HARLING

UK
Blundell Harling Ltd
Lynch Lane
Weymouth
Dorset DT4 9DW
Tel: (0305) 783275

USA
Refer to UK

AUSTRALIA
Staedtler
PO Box 576
Dee Why
NSW 2099

CANADA
Pico
Concord
Ontario L4K 1L3

BRAUSE

UK
Refer to USA

USA
Supplied by: Charrette
Corp.
31 Olympia Avenue
Woburn
Mass. 01888
Tel: (617) 935 6000

AUSTRALIA
Refer to USA

CANADA
Refer to USA

ARTHUR BROWN

UK
Refer to USA

USA
Arthur Brown & Bro. Inc.
2 West 46th Street
New York
NY 10036
Tel: (212) 575 5555
Telex: 220588

AUSTRALIA
Refer to USA

CANADA
Refer to USA

CARAN D'ACHE

UK
Jakar International Ltd
Hillside House 2/6
Friern Park
London N12 9BX
Tel: (01) 445 6376
Telex: 268209

USA
Caran D'Ache of
Switzerland Inc.
454 3rd Avenue
New York
NY 10016
Tel: (212) 689 3590

AUSTRALIA
Swiss-Anglo Agencies Pty Ltd
168 Waverley Road
East Malvern
3145 Victoria
Tel: 211 9908

CANADA
Dewana Trading Ltd
136 Skyway Avenue
Rexdale
Ontario M9W 4Y9
Tel: (416) 675 9260

CARDINELL

UK
Refer to USA

USA
Cardinell Products Inc.
107 Forest Street
Montclair
N.J. 07042
Tel: (201) 744 4500

AUSTRALIA
Refer to USA

CANADA
Refer to USA

CASLON

UK
Caslon Ltd
Woodbride House
30 Aylesbury Street
London EC1R 0ES
Tel: (01) 253 1432
Telex: 24744

USA
Refer to UK

AUSTRALIA
Tristania Trading Co. Pty Ltd
37 Somerset Road
Glen Iris
Victoria 3146
Tel: (03) 29 5499
Telex: INTMB AA 10104

CANADA
Refer to UK

CHARTPAK

UK
Chartpak Ltd
Station Road
Didcot
Oxon OX11 7NB
Tel: (0235) 812607
Telex: 83379

USA
Chartpack Customer
Services Dept.
One River Road
Leeds Mass. 01053

AUSTRALIA
Edward Keller
Trading Pty Ltd
493-495 Kent Street
Sydney NSW 2000

CANADA
Chartpak Inc.
1565 Britannia Road East
Unit No 17
Mississauga
Ontario L4W 2V6

CONTÉ À PARIS

UK
Conté UK Ltd
Park Farm Industrial Estate
Park Farm Road
Folkestone
Kent CT19 5EY
Tel: (0303) 43535
Telex: 966640 Conté G

USA
Refer to UK

Australia
Refer to UK

Canada
Refer to UK

DAHLE

UK
Dahle (UK) Ltd
Coburg House
2 Portland Close
Houghton Regis
Beds. LU5 5AW
Tel: (0582) 696622
Telex: 827541

USA
Dahle USA
6 Benson Road
Oxford
Connecticut 06483
Tel: (203) 264 0505
Telex: WUTCO
  7104503689

AUSTRALIA
Dahle Australia Pty Ltd
PO Box 91
Tarago Road
Bungendore
NSW 2621
Tel: (062) 38 1381

CANADA
Dahle Canada
201 Snidercroft Road
Concord
Ontario L4K 1B1
Tel: (416) 669 6322
Telex: 6964819
EFF-N-T-EE-

DALER ROWNEY

UK
Daler Rowney Ltd
12 Percy Street
London W1A 2BP
Tel: (01) 636 8241

USA
Leisure Craft
3061 Maria Street
PO Box 5528
Compton
California 90224

AUSTRALIA
Vitrex Camden
4 George Place
Artarmon
NSW 2064
Tel: 428 5044
Telex: 70132

CANADA
Weber Costello
(Canada) Ltd
6800 Rexwood Road
Mississauga
Ontario L4V 1LB
Tel: (416) 667 4970
Telex: 06968637

DESIGNER PLUS

UK
AM Admel
Brooklands Road
Weybridge
Surrey KT13 0RL
Tel: (0932) 47212

USA
Plan Hold Corp.
17421 Von Karman Ave.
Irvine
California 92714-6293
Tel: (714) 660 0400

AUSTRALIA
OCE Reprographics Ltd
89 Tulip Street
Cheltenham
Victoria 3192
Tel: (03) 584 1011

CANADA
Plan Hold Canada Inc.
354 Humberline Drive
Rexdale
Ontario M9W 553
Tel: (416) 675 1552

DE VILBISS

UK
Royal Sovereign Graphics
Britannia House
100 Drayton Park
London N5 1NA
Tel: (01) 226 4455
Telex: 267668

USA
Koh-I-Noor
Rapidograph Inc.
100 North Street
PO Box 68
Bloomsbury
N.J. 08804-0068
Tel: (800) 631 7646
Telex: 6858126 NJ

AUSTRALIA
Staedtler Pacific Pty Ltd
1 Inman Road
Dee Why
NSW 2099
Tel: 982 4555

CANADA
The Testor Corporation of
Canada Ltd
206 Milvan Drive
Weston
Ontario M9L 1Z9

DR MARTIN

UK
Winsor & Newton
Whitefriars Avenue
Wealdstone
Middlesex HA3 53H
Tel: (01) 427 4343
Telex: 927295

USA
Salis International Inc.
4093 North 28th Way
Hollywood
Florida 33020
Tel: (305) 921 6971
Telex: 441608 SALIS UI

AUSTRALIA
Vitrex Camden Pty Ltd
23 Atchison Street
St Leonards
NSW 2065

CANADA
Refer to USA

EBERHARD FABER

UK
Refer to USA

USA
Eberhard Faber Inc.
Crestwood, Box 760
Wilkes-Barre
PA 18773
Tel: (717) 474 6711

AUSTRALIA
Refer to USA

CANADA
Refer to USA

ECOBRA

UK
Technical Sales London Ltd
32-32ᴬ Lupus St.
London SW1V 3EA
Tel: (01) 834 5155

USA
Dietzgen Corp.
250 Wille Road
Des Plaines
Illinois 60018
Tel: (312) 635 5200

AUSTRALIA
Tackson's Drawing Supplies
Pty Ltd
103 Rokeby Road
Subiaco 6008
Perth
W. Australia
Tel: (09) 381 2488

CANADA
W. Carsen Co. Ltd
25 Scarsdale Road
Don Mills
Ontario
Canada M3B 3G7
Tel: (416) 449 4100

EDDING

UK
C.W. Edding (UK) Ltd
North Orbital Trading Estate
Napsbury Lane
St Albans
Herts AL1 1XQ
Tel: (0727) 34471
Telex: 295481

USA
C.W. Edding Inc.
PO Box 416
Edison
N.J. 08818
Tel: (201) 9550310
Telex: 6858029

AUSTRALIA
Excelsior Co. Supply Pty Ltd
24 South Street
Rydalmere
NSW 2116
Tel: 6384888
Telex: 23454

CANADA
Culmer
Distributors Inc.
620 Cathcart Street
Suite 400
Montreal
Quebec N3B IMI
Tel: (514) 8660646
Telex: 55608011

ELMER'S

UK
Humbrol Ltd
Marfleet
Hull
N. Humberside HU9 9NE
Tel: (0482) 701191

USA
Borden Inc. International
Dept. CP
Columbus
Ohio 43215
Tel: (614) 225 4000

AUSTRALIA
Borden Australia Pty Ltd
PO Box 57
46 Wellington Road
Granville NSW 2142
Tel: 632 3717

CANADA
The Borden Co. Ltd
250 Consumers Road
Willowdale
Ontario M2J 4V6
Tel: (416) 497 9901

ERASA/DURE

UK
Refer to USA

USA
Supplied by: A.I. Friedman
Inc.

AUSTRALIA
Refer to USA

CANADA
Refer to USA

EXX PROJECTS

UK
EXX Projects
72 Rivington Street
London EC2 4AY
Tel: (01) 739 8030
Telex: 896616

USA
Refer to UK

AUSTRALIA
Refer to UK

CANADA
Refer to UK

FABER-CASTELL

UK
A.W. Faber-Castell (UK) Ltd
Crompton Road
Stevenage
Herts SG1 2EF
Tel: (0438) 316511

USA
Faber-Castell Corp.
4 Century Drive
Parsippany
N.J. 07054
Tel: (201) 539 4111

AUSTRALIA
A.W. Faber-Castell
(Australia) Pty Ltd
PO Box 97
Guildford
NSW 2161
Tel: 632 3333

CANADA
Faber-Castell
Canada Inc.
77 Browns Line
Toronto
Ontario M8W 4X5
Tel: (416) 259 5051

FILM SALES LTD

UK
Film Sales Ltd
145 Nathan Way
Woolwich Industrial Estate
London SE28 0BE
Tel: (01) 311 2000
Telex: 896942 G4037

USA
Refer to UK

AUSRALIA
Refer to UK

CANADA
Refer to UK

A. I. FRIEDMAN

UK
Refer to USA

USA
A. I. Friedman Inc.
44 W. 18th Street
New York

NY 10011
Tel: (212) 243 9000

AUSTRALIA
Refer to USA

CANADA
Refer to USA

FRISK

UK
Frisk Products Ltd
4 Franthorn Way
Randlesdown Road
London SE6 3BT
Tel: (01) 698 3481
Telex: 8954987

USA
Frisk Products (USA) Inc.
4896 North Royal
Atlanta Drive
Suite 304
Tucker
Georgia 30084
Tel: (404) 939 9496

AUSTRALIA
Rankworth Enterprises (Pty)
Ltd
36 Clarence House
2nd Floor
Sydney
NSW 2000
Tel: 295255

CANADA
Refer to USA

GELIOT WHITMAN LTD

UK
Geliot Whitman Ltd
Herschell Road
Forest Hill
London SE23 1EQ
Tel: (01) 699 9262

USA
Refer to UK

AUSTRALIA
Refer to UK

CANADA
Refer to UK

GOODKIN

UK
Refer to USA

USA
M. P. Goodkin Inc.
140-146 Coit Street
Irvington
N.J. 07111
Tel: (201) 371 1199
Telex: 5106011054

AUSTRALIA
Refer to USA

CANADA
Refer to USA

GRAPHIC PRODUCTS

UK
Graphic Products
International Ltd

36 Manchester Street
London W1M 5PE
Tel: (01) 486 4667
Telex: 25247-21879
Attn GRD

USA
Refer to UK

AUSTRALIA
Refer to UK

CANADA
Refer to UK

GRUM-BACHER

UK
Rexel Ltd
Gatehouse Road
Aylesbury
Bucks HP19 3DT
Tel: (0296) 81421

USA
M. Grumbacher Inc.
460 West 34th Street
New York 10001
Tel: (212) 279 6400

AUSTRALIA
Fordigraph (Aust) Pty Ltd
The Corner Rachel
Close and Slough Street
Slough Park
Silverwater
NSW 2141
Tel: (02) 647 2488

CANADA
M. Grumbacher of Canada
Ltd
460 Finchdene Square
Scarborough
Ontario M1X 1C4
Tel: (416) 299 7000

HALCO

UK
Halco
Halco Works
Gresham Road
Staines
Middlesex TW18 2BS
(0784) 61332

USA
Refer to UK

AUSTRALIA
Refer to UK

CANADA
Refer to UK

J. J. HUBER

UK
J. J. Huber Ltd
Bellbrook
Uckfield
E. Sussex TN22 1QL
Tel: (0825) 61533
Telex: 957318

USA
Refer to UK

AUSTRALIA
Refer to UK

CANADA
Refer to UK

HUMBROL

UK
Humbrol Consumer
Products Ltd
Marfleet
Hull
N. Humberside HU9 5NE
Tel: (0482) 701191
Telex: 592534

USA
Monogram Models Inc.
8601 Waukgan Road
Morton Grove
Illinois 60053
Tel: (312) 966 3500

AUSTRALIA
Southern Model Supplies Pty
Ltd
63 Boothby Street
Panorama
Adelaide
S. Australia
Tel: (08) 276 7722

CANADA
Whitman Goldman Ltd
200 Sheldon Drive
Cambridge
Ontario N1R 5X2
Tel: (519) 623 3590

INGENTO

UK
Refer to USA

USA
Ideal School Supply
11000 Lavergne Avenue
Oak Lawn
Illinois 60453
Tel: (312) 425 0800

AUSTRALIA
Refer to USA

CANADA
Refer to USA

INSCRIBE

UK
Inscribe Ltd
Woolmer Industrial Estate
Bordon
Hants GU35 9QE
Tel: (04203) 5747
Telex: 858025

USA
Refer to UK

AUSTRALIA
Refer to UK

CANADA
Refer to UK

ITM

UK
ITM Ltd
15 Holder Road
Aldershot
Hants GU12 4PU
Tel: (0252) 28512
Telex: 291829 (attn ITM)

USA
International Graphic
Products Inc.
5504 Park Place
Edina
Minneapolis 55424

AUSTRALIA
Refer to UK

CANADA
Refer to USA

JAKAR

UK
Jakar International Ltd
Hillside House 2/6
Friern Park
London N12 9BX
Tel: (01) 445 6376
Telex: 268209

USA
Refer to UK

AUSTRALIA
Refer to UK

CANADA
Refer to UK

KOH-I-NOOR

UK
Koh-I-Noor Ag
Liechtensteinstrasse 155
A1091 Vienna
Austria
Tel: (0222) 341381

USA
Refer to Austria

AUSTRALIA
Refer to Austria

CANADA
Refer to Austria

KROY

UK
Kroy (Europe) Ltd
Worton Grange
Reading
Berks RG2 00Z
Tel: (0734) 861411
Telex: 849143

USA
Kroy Inc.
PO Box C-4300
14555 N. Hayden Road
Scottsdale
Arizona 85261
Tel: (602) 948 2222
Telex: 249996

AUSTRALIA
Letraset Australia Pty Ltd
13 Clearview Place
Brookvale
NSW 2100
Tel: (02) 920293

CANADA
Refer to USA

KRYLON

UK
Humbrol Ltd
Marfleet
Hull
N. Humberside HU9 9NE
Tel: (0482) 701191

USA
Borden Inc. International
Dept CP
Columbus
Ohio 43215
Tel: (614) 225 4000

AUSTRALIA
Borden Australia Pty Ltd
PO Box 57
46 Wellington Road
Granville
NSW 2142
Tel: 632 3717

CANADA
The Borden Co. Ltd
250 Consumers Road
Willowdale
Ontario M2J 4V6
Tel: (416) 497 9901

LEROY (KEUFFEL & ESSER CO)

UK
G. H. Smith Ptnrs (Sales) Ltd
28 Bere Church Road
Colchester
Essex CO2 7QH
Tel: (0206) 48221
Telex: 987801

USA
Keuffel & Esser
900 Lanidex Plaza
Parsippany
N.J. 07054
Tel: (201) 428 7018
Telex: 178134

AUSTRALIA
Jasco Pty Ltd
PO Box 135
West Ryde
NSW 2114
Tel: 807 1555

CANADA
Keuffel & Esser of Canada
Ltd
124 Milner Avenue
Scarborough
Ontario M1S 4B6
Tel: (416) 298 1750

LETRASET

UK
Letraset UK Ltd
195/203 Waterloo Road
London SE1 8XJ
Tel: (01) 928 7551

USA
Letraset USA Ltd
40 Eisenhower Drive
Paramus
N.J. 07652
Tel: (201) 845 6100

AUSTRALIA
Letraset Australia Pty Ltd
13 Clearview Place
Brookvale
NSW 2100
Tel: (02) 920 293

CANADA
Letraset Canada Ltd
555 Alden Road
Markham
Ontario L3R 3L5
Tel: (416) 495 7511

LIQUITEX

UK
H. W. Peel & Co Ltd
Norwester House
Fairway Drive

Greenford
Middx UB6 8PW
Tel: (01) 578 6861
Telex: 934265

USA
Binney & Smith Inc.
PO Box 431
1100 Church Lane
Easton
PA 18044-0431
Tel: (215) 253 6271

AUSTRALIA
Binney & Smith (Aust.) Pty
Ltd
459 Dorset Road
PO Box 296
Bayswater
Victoria 3153
Tel: (613) 7292811

CANADA
B.F.B. Sales Ltd
Unit 5
10 Falconer Drive
Mississauga
Ontario L5N 3L8
Tel: (416) 858 7888

MARVY

UK
Refer to USA

USA
Uchida of America
Corporation
1100 Stewart Avenue
Garden City
New York 11530-4813
Tel: (516) 832 9600

AUSTRALIA
Refer to USA

CANADA
Refer to USA

MECANORMA

UK
Mecanorma Ltd
10 School Road
North Acton
London NW10 6TD
Tel: (01) 961 6565
Telex: 926079

USA
Martin Instrument Co.
13450 Farmington Road
Livonia
Michigan 48150
Tel: (313) 5251990

AUSTRALIA
Refer to UK

CANADA
Refer to USA

MOTORASER (KEUFFEL & ESSER)

UK
G. H. Smith Ptnrs (Sales) Ltd
28 Bere Church Road
Colchester
Essex CO2 7QH
Tel: (0206) 48221
Telex: 987801

USA
Keuffel & Esser Inc.

900 Lanidex Plaza
Parsippany
N.J. 07054
Tel: (201) 428 7018
Telex: 178134

AUSTRALIA
Jasco Pty Ltd
PO Box 135
West Ryde
NSW 2114
Tel: 807 1555

CANADA
Keuffel & Esser of Canada
Ltd
124 Milner Avenue
Scarsborough
Ontario M1S 4B6
Tel: (416) 298 1750

NIJI (YASUTOMO & CO. LTD)

UK
Refer to USA

USA
Yasutomo & Co.
500 Howard Street
San Francisco
California 94127
Tel: (415) 981 4326
Telex: 278285

AUSTRALIA
Refer to USA

CANADA
Refer to USA

NIKKO

UK
Cannon & Wrin Ltd
68 High Street
Chislehurst
Kent BR7 5BL
Tel: (01) 467 0935
Telex: 896158

USA
Itoya of America Ltd
PO Box 2015
Santa Monica
California 90406
Tel: (213) 829 9811
Telex: 3719768 Penclus

AUSTRALIA
Australasian Merchandisers
Pty Ltd
PO Box 164
South Brisbane
Queensland 4101
Tel: (07) 844 7236
Telex: 145532 Ausmer AA

CANADA
Refer to USA

NOBO

UK
Nobo Visual Aids Ltd
Alder Close
Eastbourne
E. Sussex BN23 6QB
Tel: (0323) 641521
Telex: 877486

USA
Refer to UK

AUSTRALIA
Refer to UK

CANADA
Refer to UK

NUPASTEL

UK
Refer to USA

USA
Eberhard Faber Inc.
Crestwood, Box 760
Wilkes-Barre
PA 18773
Tel: (717) 474 6711

AUSTRALIA
Refer to USA

CANADA
Refer to USA

PAASCHE

UK
Microflame Ltd
Vinces Road
Diss
Norfolk IP22 3HQ
Tel: (0379) 4813
Telex: 97492

USA
Paasche Airbrush Co.
7440 West
Lawrence Avenue
Harwood Heights
Illinois 60656
Tel: (312) 867 9191

AUSTRALIA
Kellergraphics Ltd
493-495 Kent Street
3rd Floor
Sydney
NSW 2000
Tel: (02) 267 5388
Telex: 75484

CANADA
Richard Thompson
Thompson Group
PO Box 24006
Seattle
Washington 98124
Tel: (206) 623 9433

PEBEO

UK
Western Partners
684 Mitcham Road
Croydon
Surrey CR9 3AB
Tel: (01) 684 6171
Telex: 5194 7938

USA
Pebeo of America
PO Box 373
Williston
Vermont 05495
Tel: (802) 658 9516

AUSTRALIA
Franchebille
East Brunswick
Victoria 3057
Tel: 419 8995

CANADA
Hopper Koch Inc.
1281 Shearer Street
Montreal
Quebec H3K 3E5
Tel: (514) 933 4019

AUSTRALIA
Refer to UK

CANADA
Refer to UK

PELIKAN

UK
G. H. Smith Ptnrs (Sales) Ltd
28 Bere Church Road
Colchester
Essex CO2 7QH
Tel: (0206) 48221
Telex: 987801

USA
Pelikan Inc.
Corporate Offices
200 Beasley Drive
Franklin
Tennessee 37064-3998
Tel: (615) 790 6171

AUSTRALIA
Agents:
Jasco Pty Ltd
PO Box 135
West Ryde
NSW 2114
Tel: 807 1555

CANADA
Refer to USA

PENTEL

UK
Pentel Ltd
Unit 1
The Wyvern Estate
Beverley Way
New Malden
Surrey KT3 4PF
Tel: (01) 949 5331
Telex: 929621

USA
Pentel of America Ltd
2715 Columbia Street
Torrance
California 90503
Tel: (213) 775 1256

AUSTRALIA
Pentel Australia (Pty) Ltd
Unit 10
31 Waterloo Road
North Ryde
NSW 2113
Tel: 887 2444

CANADA
Pentel Stationary of Canada
Ltd
5900 C
No 2 Road
Richmond
British Columbia
Tel: (604) 270 1566

PILOT

UK
Pilot Pen Co Ltd
9 Bethune Road
North Acton
London NW10 6NJ
Tel: (01) 961 6661

USA
Pilot Pen Co
60 Commerce Drive
Trumbull
Connecticut 06611
Tel: (203) 377 8800

AUSTRALIA
Refer to UK

CANADA
Refer to USA

PLATIGNUM

UK
Platignum Plc
PO Box 1
Royston
Herts SG8 5XX
Tel: (0763) 44133
Telex: 81145

USA
M. Grumbacher Inc.
460 W. 34th Street
New York
NY 10001
Tel: (212) 279 6400

AUSTRALIA
Refer to UK

CANADA
Leslie Agencies Inc.
R.R.5
Orangeville
Ontario L9W 222

PORTA-SCRIBE

UK
Harkness Screen Ltd
Gate Studios
Station Road
Borehamwood
Herts WD6 1DQ
Tel: (01) 953 3611

USA
Da-Lite Screen Company
Inc.
PO Box 137
Warsaw
Indiana 46580
Tel: (219) 267 8101

AUSTRALIA
Australux
81 Beauchamp Rd
Matraville
NSW 2036
Tel: 6664802

CANADA
General Films
Halifax and 13th
Regina
Saskatchewan S4P 0T9
Tel: (306) 522 8512

PRANG

UK
Refer to USA

USA
Dixon Ticonderoga Co.
1706 Hayes Avenue
PO Box 2258
Sandusky
Ohio 44870-7258
Tel: (419) 625 9123

AUSTRALIA
Refer to USA

CANADA
Dixon Pencil Co. Ltd
531 Davis Drive
Newmarket
Ontario L3Y 2P1

PRESTO

UK
Refer to USA

USA
Columbia Cement Co. Inc.
159 Hanse Avenue
Freeport
New York 11520
Tel: (516) 623 6000

AUSTRALIA
Refer to USA

CANADA
Letraset Canada Ltd
555 Alden Road
Markham
Ontario L3R 3L5
Tel: (416) 495 7511

REMBRANDT

UK
See Frisk

USA
See Frisk

AUSTRALIA
See Frisk

CANADA
See Frisk

REXEL

UK
Rexel Ltd
Gatehouse Road
Aylesbury
Bucks HP19 3DT
Tel: (0296) 81421

USA
M. Grumbacher Inc. (Pentalic Div.)
460 West 34th Street
New York
NY 10001
Tel: (212) 279 6400

AUSTRALIA
Fordigraph (Aust.) Pty Ltd
The Corner Rachel Close
and Slough Street
Slough Park
Silverwater
NSW 2141
Tel: (02) 647 2488

CANADA
M. Grumbacher of Canada Ltd
460 Finchdene Square
Scarborough
Ontario M1X 1C4
Tel: (416) 299 7000

REXEL NYREX

UK
See Rexel

USA
See Rexel

AUSTRALIA
See Rexel

CANADA
See Rexel

ROSCOART

UK
Refer to USA

USA
Supplied by A. I. Friedman Inc.

AUSTRALIA
Refer to USA

CANADA
Refer to USA

ROTATRIM

UK
Rotatrim Ltd
35-43 Dudley Street
Luton
Beds LU2 0NP
Tel: (0582) 420441
Telex: 825966

USA
Alvin & Co. Inc.
PO Box 188
Windsor
Connecticut 06095
Tel: (203) 243 8991

AUSTRALIA
Pics Australasia (Pty) Ltd
399 George Street
Waterloo
Sydney
NSW 2017
Tel: (02) 698 2200

CANADA
Lisle Kelco Ltd
6799 Steeles Avenue
Rexdale
Ontario M9V 4R9
Tel: (416) 742 9210

ROTRING

UK
Rotring UK
Building 1
GEC Estate
East Lane
Wembley HA9 7PY
Tel: (01) 908 2577

USA
Kin Rapidograph Inc.
100 North Street
PO Box 68
Bloomsbury
N.J. 08804-0068
Tel: (201) 479 4124

AUSTRALIA
Jasco Pty Ltd
939 Victoria Road
West Ryde
New South Wales 2114
Tel: 807 1555

CANADA
Kin Canada
1815 Meyerside Drive
Units 1-3
Mississauga
Ontario L5T 1B4
Tel: (416) 671 0696

ROYAL SOVEREIGN GRAPHICS

UK
Royal Sovereign Graphics
Britannia House
100 Drayton Park
London N5 1NA
Tel: (01) 226 4455
Telex: 267668

USA
Catalogue Sales Inc.

181 N.E. Union Avenue
Portland
Oregon 97212

AUSTRALIA
Staedtler Pacific Pty Ltd
1 Inman Road
Dee Why
NSW 2099
Tel: 982 4555

CANADA
Refer to USA

SAKURA

UK
R. J. Gray
Distributor Ltd
72 High Street
London Colney
Herts AR2 1QY
Tel: (01) 612 4966
Telex: 299447

USA
Refer to UK

AUSTRALIA
Refer to UK

CANADA
Refer to UK

SCHWAN-STABILO

UK
Swan Stabilo Ltd
74 Buckingham Avenue
Slough
Berks SL1 4PA
Tel: (0753) 821941
Telex: 847829

USA
Schwan-Stabilo
USA Inc.
435 Dividend Drive
Peach Tree City
Georgia 30269
Tel: (404) 487 5512
Telex: 804219

AUSTRALIA
Jasco Pty Ltd
PO Box 135
West Ryde
NSW 2114
Tel: 807 1555

CANADA
Heinz Jordan & Co Ltd
900 Magnetic Drive
Downsview
Ontario M3J 2C4

SELLOTAPE

UK
DRG Sellotape Products
Elstree Way
Borehamwood
Herts WD6 1RU
Tel: (01) 953 1655
Telex: 261750

USA
Caltape Inc
11693 Sheldon Street
Sun Valley
California 91352
Telex: 279602

AUSTRALIA
Leather Accessories Pty
360 Eastern Valley Way

Chatswood
NSW
Telex: 22556

CANADA
DRG Sellotape
Canada
10 Esandar Drive
Toronto 352
Ontario
Telex: 0621 7618

SIMAIR

UK
Simair Graphics Equipment Ltd
16 Woodsley Road
Leeds
Yorks LS3 1DT
Tel: (0532) 448527
Telex: 55293

USA
Frisk Products (USA) Inc.
4896 North Royal
Atlanta Drive
Suite 304
Tucker
Georgia 30084
Tel: (404) 939 9496

AUSTRALIA
Rankworth Enterprises (Pty) Ltd
36 Clarence House
2nd Floor
Sydney
NSW 2000
Tel: 295255

CANADA
Refer to USA

SIMMONS

UK
Refer to USA

USA
Robert Simmons Inc.
45 W. 18th Street
New York
NY 10011
(attn. 5th Floor)
Tel: (212) 675 3136

AUSTRALIA
Refer to USA

CANADA
Refer to USA

SLIMVIEW EASEL DISPLAY

UK
See Rexel

USA
See Rexel

AUSTRALIA
See Rexel

CANADA
See Rexel

SPEEDBALL

UK
Refer to USA

USA
Hunt International Co.

230 South Broad Street
Philadelphia
PA 19102
Tel: (215) 732 7700
Telex: 7106703095

AUSTRALIA
Excelsior Supply Co.
24 South Street
Rydalmere
NSW

CANADA
Hunt Canada International
5940 Ambler Drive
Mississauga
Ontario L4W 2N3

STACOR

UK
Refer to USA

USA
Stacor Corp.
285 Emmet Street
Newark
N.J. 07114
Tel: (201) 242 6600
Telex: 132097

AUSTRALIA
Refer to USA

CANADA
British Blueprint Co.
1831 St Catherine Street
Montreal 108 Quebec
Tel: (514) 935 9919

STAEDTLER

UK
Staedtler (UK) Ltd
Pontyclun
Mid-Glamorgan CF7 8YJ
Tel: (0443) 222421

USA
J.S. Staedtler Inc.
21034 Osborne Street
PO Box 7102
Canoga Park
California 91304

AUSTRALIA
Staedtler Pacific Pty Ltd
1 Inman Road
Dee Why
NSW 2099
Tel: 982 4555

CANADA
Staedtler Mars Ltd
6 Mars Road
Rexdale
Ontario M9B 2K1

3M

UK
3M UK Plc
3M House
PO Box 1
Bracknell
Berks RG12 1JU
Tel: (0344) 426726
Telex: 849371

USA
3M Centre
St Paul
Minnesota 55144-1000
Tel: (612) 733 1110

AUSTRALIA
3M Australia Ltd

PO Box 99
950 Pacific Highway
Pimble
NSW 2073
Tel: (612) 4989333

CANADA
3M Canada Inc.
PO Box 5757
Terminal A
London
Ontario N6A 4TI
Tel: (519) 451 2500

THAYER & CHANDLER

UK
Refer to USA

USA
Thayer & Chandler Inc.
2041 W. Grand Avenue
Chicago
Illinois 60612
Tel: (312) 226 3567

AUSTRALIA
Refer to USA

CANADA
Loomis and Toles
963 Eclinton Avenue East
Toronto
Ontario M4G 4B5
Tel: (416) 423 9300

TOMBOW

UK
Tombow Pencil & Pen
GMBH
Postfach 620266
Niehler Strasse 272
5000 Koeln 60
West Germany
Tel: (0221) 763041

USA
American Tombow
5352 Sterling Center Drive
Westlake Village
CA 91361
Tel: (818) 889 3440

AUSTRALIA
Refer to USA

CANADA
Merit Distributors Inc.
1680 50th Avenue
Lachine
Quebec H8T 2V5
Tel: (514) 636 8750

UNO

UK
Western Partners
684 Mitcham Road
Croydon
Surrey CR9 3AB
Tel: (01) 684 6171
Telex: 5194 7938

USA
Refer to UK

AUSTRALIA
Geoff Penney (NSW) Pty
Ltd
PO Box W5
Warringah Mall
NSW 2100
Tel: (6129) 384555

CANADA
Refer to UK

VUGRAPH

UK
Harkness Screen Ltd
Gate Studios
Station Road
Borehamwood
Herts WD6 1DQ
Tel: (01) 953 3611

USA
Da-Lite Screen Company
Inc.
PO Box 137
Warsaw
Indiana 46580
Tel (219) 267 8101

AUSTRALIA
Australux
81 Beauchamp Road
Matraville
NSW 2036
Tel: 666 4802

CANADA
General Films
Halifax and 13th
Regina
Saskatchewan S4P 0T9
Tel: (306) 522 8512

WESTWOOD GRAPHICS

UK
Webb International Ltd
54-58 Park Royal Road
London NW10 7JF
Tel: (01) 961 5252
Telex: 21581 WEBB G

USA
Refer to UK

AUSTRALIA
Refer to UK

CANADA
Refer to UK

WINSOR AND NEWTON

UK
Winsor & Newton
Whitefriars Avenue
Wealdstone
Middlesex HA3 5RH
Tel: (01) 427 4343
Telex: 927295

USA
Winsor & Newton Inc.
555 Winsor Drive
PO Box 1519
Secaucus
New Jersey 07094-0519
Tel: (201) 864 9100

AUSTRALIA
Jasko Pty Ltd
939 Victoria Road
West Ryde
NSW 2114
Tel: 807 1555

CANADA
Anthes Universal Ltd
341 Heart Lake Road South
Brampton
Ontario L6W 3K8
Tel: (416) 451 0200

ZENITH

UK
Zenith UK Ltd
195 High Street
Egham
Surrey TW20 9ED
Tel: (0784) 34722

USA
Refer to UK

AUSTRALIA
Refer to UK

CANADA
Refer to UK

ACKNOWLEDGEMENTS

Swallow Books gratefully acknowledge the assistance given to them in the preparation of *Graphic Tools and Techniques* by the following people and organizations. We apologize to anyone we may have omitted to mention.

Stephen Hammond; Aziz Khan; National Arts and Materials Trade Association, New York; Chris Prior, Steve Tucker (C J Graphic Supplies Ltd).

Equipment:
Atlantis Paper Company, Wapping Lane, London E1; C J Graphic Supplies Ltd, 35-39 Old Street, London EC1; Owen Clark & Co. Ltd, 133 Cranbrook Road, Ilford, Essex.

Photographs:
Agfa-Gevaert 134; BFE 12,13; Dahle 23,24; EXX Projects 147; Faber-Castell 148; ITM Astrolux 135; Morris & Ingram (London) Ltd 94; Rotatrim 25; Simair Products 149.